BRITAIN AND CHINA, 1941–47

In *Britain and China, 1941–47* Aron Shai has made a detailed study of the developments which affected Britain's traditional privileged position in China in the course of the Pacific War and the period which immediately followed it. The author argues that British attempts to return to China under a new and more acceptable cloak of a friend, utilizing Britain's colonial heritage in Asia, are discernible. As a result of this unique heritage and of China being part of Britain's informal empire, Sino–British relations in the 1940s were not ordinary bilateral relations between two equal political entities, but more in the nature of an "imperial hangover."

While the Second World War accelerated the process of British imperial decline and hastened the rate of change of the objective realities, obsolete perceptions lagged behind. This was evident in Britain's general attitude towards China and was made particularly clear in the case of the restoration of British authority in Hong Kong, where an adamant stand in the face of Chinese nationalism was taken.

No other recently published study has examined Sino–British relations in the 1940s in depth or analyzed them within the broad imperial context. The author shows that Kuomintang China, immediately prior to the final Communist victory, was in the midst of becoming less a subject of imperial activity and more self-reliant and independent as an actor in the international arena. The two main political streams in China, drawing conclusions from the experience of foreign penetration of China, adopted decidedly nationalist principles. Leaders on both sides of the ideological divide became persuaded that imperialist exploitation must end forthwith. "True independence" (though defined differently) and freedom from colonial rule seemed the way forward for China. Under such circumstances it became clear not only that informal imperialism had to end, but also that the comforts of "imperial hangover" could no longer be enjoyed.

Dr Aron Shai is a Senior Lecturer in History at Tel Aviv University, Israel, and a former Senior Associate Member of St Antony's College, Oxford. His previous books are *Origins of the War in the East* and (in Hebrew) *China in International Affairs, 1840–1979*.

BRITAIN AND CHINA, 1941–47

Imperial Momentum

Aron Shai

St. Martin's Press   New York

© Aron Shai 1984
St. Martin's Press, Inc., 175 Fifth Avenue, New York, NY 10010
Printed in Hong Kong
First published in the United States of America in 1984

ISBN 0–312–09764–6

Library of Congress Cataloging in Publication Data

Shai, Aron.
  Britain and China, 1941–47.

  Bibliography: p.
  1. World War, 1939–1945—Diplomatic history.
2. Great Britain—Foreign relations—China.   3. China—
Foreign relations—Great Britain.   4. Great Britain—
Foreign relations—1936–1945.   5. Great Britain—
Foreign relations—1945–   .   I. Title.
D750.S5   1983   940.53'2   82–23030
ISBN 0–312–09764–6

In memory of my father
JOSHUA N. SHAI

Contents

Maps

Abbreviations

ABDA	American, British, Dutch and Australian Command
AVG	Air Volunteer Group
AMMISCA	American Military Mission to China
BAAG	British Army Aid Group (China)
BT	Board of Trade
CAB	Records of the Cabinet
CIGS	Chief of the Imperial General Staff (GB)
CO	Colonial Office
COS	Chiefs of Staff
CP	War Cabinet Memoranda, London
CRT	Commercial Relations and Treaties
DOT	Department of Overseas Trade
FASM	Federal Archives, Suitland, Maryland
FO	Foreign Office
FRUS	Foreign Relations of the United States
ICI	Imperial Chemical Industries
NAUS	National Archives of the United States, Washington, DC
OANHD	Operational Archives, Naval History Division, Navy Yard, Washington, DC, US Navy: Double Zero Files
Parl. Deb.	Hansard, Parliamentary Debates, House of Commons, 5th series
Pre.	Prime Minister's Office
PRO	Public Record Office, London
SAC	Supreme Allied Commander
SEAC	South East Asia Command
T	Treasury
WO	War Office

Acknowledgements

I should like to express my gratitude to all those who have helped me in conducting my research. I am indebted to the Warden and Fellows of St Antony's College, Oxford, for affording me the opportunity to pursue my research in their most congenial company during the 1978–9 academic year when I stayed at the College as the Israeli Visiting Fellow. I am also indebted to Sir Isaiah Berlin for assisting me to complete my research in England.

The Aranne School of History at Tel Aviv University has assisted me in the latter stages of my research. I am grateful to my colleagues there for their help. My friends and colleagues Stuart Cohen, Norman Rose, Avi Shlaim and David Katz carefully read the manuscript. I should like to thank them for their scholarly advice and valuable suggestions. I am also grateful to the staff of the Public Record Office, London, and to the staff of the National Archives of the United States, Washington, DC, for their kind attention. I have been very fortunate to be able to supplement the extensive archive material now available by interviews and correspondence with various individuals who were involved in the developments covered by this book. Many other institutions and individuals in England, the United States, Hong Kong and Israel extended assistance in the form of recollections, facilities for research and helpful suggestions. Although they are thanked collectively, their contributions, I must stress, are remembered individually and most gratefully.

A.S.

Jerusalem

'We reappeared in the Far East . . . and re-established ourselves for a few years in something like our former colonial majesty; but the anachronistic dream has rapidly and rightly faded.'

SIR ANDREW GILCHRIST
Bangkok Top Secret: Force 196 at War (London, 1970) p.5

'Great Britain was fighting the Second World War in order to recover the British Empire . . . Those who did the actual fighting had simpler aims. They fought to liberate the peoples of Europe from Germany and those of the Far East from Japan. That spirit dominated after the war.'

A. J. P. TAYLOR
Quoted in Wm. Roger Louis, *Imperialism at Bay* (Oxford, 1977) p. x

MAP 1   *The situation in the Pacific 1941*

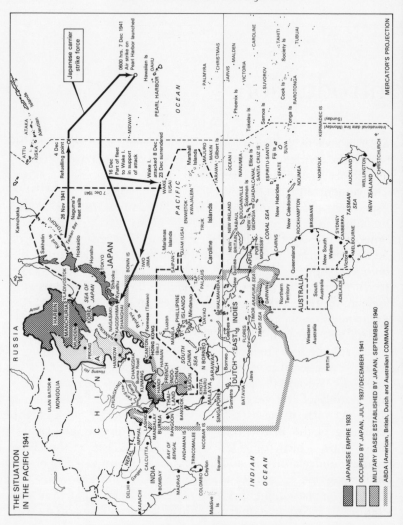

Source: P. Young, *Atlas of The Second World War* (New York, 1977).

Introduction

In 1942, exactly a century after Great Britain had managed to impose the articles of the Nanking Treaty on China as a result of her victory in the first Opium War, her economic and political achievements in China lay in ruins. Indeed, 1842 and 1942 mark respectively the beginning and the end of an era, the success and the failure of the British experience in China. Between those two signposts, many a fluctuation occurred in the mutual relations of the two countries. They ranged from extreme animosity and war, to understanding, entente and even co-operation. The story of the British presence in China, however, does not start in 1842, nor does it abruptly end in 1942. It stretches far back to Lord Macartney's China mission of 1793 and continues well into the present, albeit in an inherently different manner.

This volume seeks to look into the developments which affected Britain's traditional privileged position in China in the course of the Pacific War and the period which immediately followed it. It is thus a study of the very end of the British imperial decline in China. As such, it serves as a sequel to my former book on the beginning of the British retreat from China in the late 1930s.[1] Those years, which coincided with the first phases of the Sino–Japanese undeclared war and the gathering storm in Europe, saw the irrepairable erosion of the British position in East Asia. The policy of appeasement directed towards rising Japan and the attempts to accommodate the Japanese forces in China in no way succeeded in counteracting this process. On the contrary, they merely cost the dwindling British Empire the remaining goodwill existing in China, both among the Nationalists and the Communists.[2] The first years of the Second World War until mid-1942 witnessed the logical outcome of the previous developments and policies – the total British, indeed Western, retreat from East and South East Asia in face of the rapidly advancing Japanese.

An attempt is made here to analyse and to evaluate reactions in

1

Britain to these developments. It is proposed to uncover the more significant plans and efforts made in various official and non-official quarters to regain a foothold, mainly an economic foothold, in China once the war was over; to return there under the new, and more acceptable, cloak of a friend[3] and to utilise the colonial heritage in South East and East Asia to Britain's advantage. Indeed, it is due to this very unique heritage that it is suggested that Sino–British relations in the period under review should not be regarded as ordinary bilateral relations between two equal political entities, and that terms such as 'imperial spasm', 'imperial momentum' or 'imperial hangover' should be used. The term 'imperial hangover' is admittedly problematic. After all, a hangover is a condition directly attributable to excessive consumption of alcohol. It is questionable, therefore, whether it may be freely used to describe a political phenomenon. At the same time, however, the term ignites the imagination and makes one wonder, as Hugh Seton-Watson has already pointed out, whether indeed, 'the different types of malaise visible in societies whose rulers have recently lost an empire can be causally connected with that loss'. Loss of empire, while involving loss of economic resources and military powers at times, caused more significantly, perhaps, a 'metropolitan identity crisis'. That is, of course, when 'classical' as opposed to 'neo' imperialism is concerned. While a General Theory of Imperial Hangover can hardly be constituted, specific cases may certainly be analysed. For example, as Keith Robbins has argued, over the last decade, when the United Kingdom appeared to be on the brink of dissolution, it has been fashionable to see that supposed development as an inevitable concomitant of the loss of Empire.[4] Such a claim can, and should, be critically investigated.

Here, in this study, the term 'imperial hangover' refers not so much to the internal malaise of an ex-metropolitan society, as to developments connected with its relationship with the *subject* of imperialism, or more specifically, to China as a significant part of Britain's informal empire.[5] It thus may reinforce terms such as 'imperial spasm' or 'imperial momentum' which express attempts at restoring the unique and traditional relationship that existed between Britain and China before the war.

It must be immediately added that no attempt is made here at passing a value-judgement on either policies adhered to or policies proposed. (The impact of the foreigner on Chinese economic development lies largely outside the scope of the present volume.) This is especially so in light of the recent works published by Robert Dernberger, D. C. M. Platt and Britten Dean.[6] These have suggested that British and foreign impact under the unequal treaties system had not *ipso facto* been harmful to China. They have likewise shown the need for more research before a final verdict on this question can be reached. The academic debate on the issue is still going on. For instance, it is being asked whether the rapid development in response to Western economic demand of such traditional Chinese agricultural industries as tea and silk production proved in the long run advantageous or disadvantageous to China.

Owing among other reasons to objective difficulties and imperial rivalry, China never became a formal colony of either Britain or any other world power. Sino–British relations, as China's relations with other countries, have always been based in the strict legal sense on the equality and respect of each other's sovereignty. In London it was officially the Foreign Office through its diplomatic channels, not the Colonial Office, which dealt with affairs related to China. In reality, however, things were quite different. There was a basis for regarding China as being in a colonial situation. Extraterritorial concessions and international settlements existed in many of her most important commercial centres.[7] Also, like other parts of Asia, China had until the late 1940s been almost entirely an object rather than a subject of foreign, and particularly of British, political behaviour. It can only marginally be said to have behaved as an actor in the international arena. Economically, politically and strategically she had been far from shaping her own destiny.[8]

Not being a formal colony, a commonwealth country or an allied state, but rather an 'independent' country, China found herself *vis-à-vis* Britain in a status inferior to that of an ordinary colony.[9] As a semi- or sub-colony she was deprived of the meagre *beneficae* of colonial rule, such as British governmental investment in the fields of education, administration, health and financial assistance (as distinct from sporadic or voluntary assistance). When threatened and attacked by Japan in the 1930s, she could rely on none of the colonial powers to save her. Britain and the United States failed to defend her, just as soon afterwards, during the early phases of the Pacific War, they failed to fulfil their first, and most sacred, obligation of defending their own respective Asian

subjects from Burma to the Pacific Islands. France and the Nether-
lands followed the same inglorious path, 'One ... must understand what the government ... meant, to appreciate the almost
volcanic convulsion of this change' wrote Van Mook. 'Gone overnight was a structure that had seemed solid and trustworthy and
immovable as granite... A psychiatrist has compared it to the
sudden loss of the father image'.[10] Thus, just at the very moment
when China needed assistance, it was denied to her by Britain and
the other powers who, after a century of active presence in her
ports and rivers, were discovered as the proverbial broken reed.

No wonder, therefore, that some thirty-two years after these
events it was asserted that 'whatever the ultimate outcome of the
Pacific War, 15 February 1942 was the end of the British Empire; it
was also the end of the European colonialism in Asia'.[11] But was
this indeed the wide historical significance of the military setbacks
which Western colonial powers suffered before and after the fall
of Singapore at the hands of the Japanese? Did the British Empire
come to so abrupt an end? Can it not be argued that, despite
British loss of face and of territories in Asia, imperial ideology,
affiliations and, indeed, practical plans for the restorations of the
former position died hard; and that an 'imperial hangover' or
'imperial momentum' survived the upheavals of the war and
played a significant role at the dawn of the post-imperial period?
British post-war reoccupation of colonial South East Asia including
Hong Kong, and the subsequent reinstatement of British, French
and Dutch regimes there strengthen such a belief. Deliberations
and actions related to China illustrate that the British 'imperial
momentum' affected not only the formal colonies.

In his study of British defence policy in the Indian Ocean
region after 1947, Philip Darby has shown how the Indian
Government's 'regional shield' and the assumed responsibilities
related to it survived the independence of India.[12] The fact that
Britain had certain continuing interests and obligations in the
Indian Ocean was plain to everyone. 'British presence in the area
outlived the Indian Empire. Militarily, diplomatically, psychologi-
cally, Britain remained committed in the region'.[13] East of India
the situation prevailing during the war and immediately after it
was similar in principle, though commercial rather than defence
issues mostly preoccupied those who were engaged in day-to-day
policy-making. Here too, the problem of continuing imperial
momentum or disharmony between the rapidly evolving new

reality and the outdated conceptions characterised British policy. Here too, it can be argued that 'the end of the empire . . . was not seen as necessarily affecting British interest or commitment'.[14]

By the time Japan surrendered in 1945, a new political and economic reality had come into being all over East and South East Asia. The returning white European who had been humiliatingly defeated in the war and whose comrades-in-arms had been compelled by a rising Asian nation to participate in forced-labour projects and to be incarcerated in camps, came face to face with societies distinctly different from those he had known four years earlier.[15] It was not only during the war that that reality came about. Its roots lay far deeper.[16] Yet this process of change which was already underway was dramatically hastened in the course of Western colonial absenteeism, and of the national struggle of the Asians for survival. In China, the dynamics of change ran beyond the defeat of her most bitter enemy. Paradoxically, she was being reshaped while torn by a civil war which by 1949 determined the communists' right to the traditional Mandate of Heaven. Notwithstanding basic ideological differences between the rivals, it seems that new China, under whatever post-war regime, would have changed her relationships with the Western powers and with Britain in particular. This was a necessity in view of her ripened nationalism in its modern form, and of her pre-war and wartime experience. The Japanese defeat which was to do away with the threat from the East, opened the way for re-examination and consequently for the curbing of traditional European imperial influence in China. Even well-meant Western proposals to help and become 'friendly mentors' were by now 'a distrusted and distasteful anachronism'.[17] This attitude was only compatible with a new reality in a new world in which the United States was to become not merely the policeman but also the banker.

In the past, nationalist feelings in China had been coupled with strong anti-Western and anti-imperialist campaigns. Such was the case in 1919 when the Paris Peace Conference hurt Chinese national feelings and helped nourish the May Fourth Movement. Such was also the case in the mid-1920s when Britain was conceived as China's Number One national enemy and British establishments and subjects in China were fiercely attacked. Since the Japanese drive into Manchuria in 1931, however, the Chinese national movements, the Communist and the Nationalist, had *temporarily* altered their course of action and shifted the main target of their criticism from the British to the Japanese. This was a natural step to take at a time when Japan caused an *immediate* state of emergency and symbolised a *direct* threat to the nation. Hostility toward Britain and Western imperialism had to be restrained for a while.

There seems to be an inherent justification for linking South East Asia, which had an outright formal colonial status, with China, which had always retained a legal independence. First, experiencing Japanese rule served all the people in the occupied lands – albeit in different and contradictory ways – as a catalyst in the process of moving towards ripened nationalist consciousness.[18] By contrast, Indian nationalism, though affected by wartime events, was not directly influenced by the experience of Japanese occupation.[19] Second, from a British point of view, the issue of a physical return to areas conquered by Japan (to some extent with an eye to the future, but certainly with a concern for regaining lost prestige) was a major issue relating to South East Asian colonies and China alone. It did not exist *vis-à-vis* India or any other colony, protectorate or mandate, though internal problems in other areas too raised the question of self-rule or independence. Third, desires to re-exert and enjoy anew influences similar to those the British Empire and its subjects had retained in China prior to the outbreak of the War could by no means have been divorced from colonial plans as regards South East Asia. Strong, united and extremely nationalist post-war China was most likely to frustrate any imperial plans in the region. This was particularly true in view of both the example new China could set for her neighbour, and the extraordinary leverage any Chinese regime traditionally enjoyed in South East Asia in the form of the generally loyal overseas Chinese.

Turning to the British metropolitan society, it must be stressed that at the outset that the changes that occurred in it during the war years were most remarkable. Britain ended the Second World War, as D. C. Watt observed, 'in a state of virtual bankruptcy and with the status and commitment of a superpower'.[20] Indeed, while the war hastened the rate of change in the objective, financial, military and diplomatic realities, old legacies and obsolete perceptions were lagging behind. It was this very dichotomy which characterised Britain's attempts, pathetic at times, to carry on playing a role she had played for decades. On the whole, this was the state of affairs even after the Labour government was formed in London in July 1945, and it continued for at least two more years in various quarters within Britain, even though a consensus on specific post-war policies towards China did not exist.[21] There were two main reasons for this. First, since policies relating to the Far East were of secondary importance, the former Conservative line was automatically pursued by civil servants in the various departments for quite some time. Second, and more significantly, after their electoral victory, the leaders of the Labour Party – contrary to their practice at home – were not concerned drastically to change, let alone to abandon altogether, the colonial policy adopted by their predecessors. True, the war and post-war years 'eventually completed the transformation of the British industrial pattern and shifted its commercial orientation towards the developed high-wage economies of Europe and America'.[22] Yet at the same time it was appreciated by the Party leadership that 'in a period of crisis, when innovations are slow in lifting an economy out of the rut, a sheltered colonial market may provide a useful means of shortening the crisis and initiating a new secular boom'.[23] It is, perhaps, in this light too that one should examine Attlee's insistence on a British reoccupation of Hong Kong after the Japanese surrender, despite the initial Chinese objection and American disapproval.[24] Was he *in practice* so distant from Churchill on this question? Discussing Hong Kong with General Patrick Hurley, President Roosevelt's special representative in China, in the spring of 1945, Churchill stressed that never would Britain 'yield an inch of the territory that was under the British Flag'.[25]

Sino–British relations in an era of transformation and confusion were an early indicator of post-war relations between developed and developing states. The issues that stood between the two countries during the war and immediately after it, namely the economic, the territorial and the question of spheres of influence, represent to a great extent the classical issues of the post-war era. They will, therefore, be analysed in detail, whether they preoccupied officials or the big commercial houses represented in the 'China Association'. The Association, founded in 1889, protected and promoted the interests of British firms trading with China, its functions being akin to those of a chamber of commerce. During the period discussed here it kept in close touch with the British government and had access to the Chinese government trade authorities.

When discussing the gradual decline of the British Empire with its wide global implications, and this study is part of such a discussion, it is quite useful to pay special attention to some unique events which hastened the long historical process. These events or turning points serve as milestones in the general trend. Of course it is possible to trace back 'turning points' in the gradual erosion of the British Empire to, say, the Boer War and its aftermath, if not earlier. Yet the special case of the Second World War should certainly be viewed most attentively.

Two excellent studies have thrown new light on this issue and have thus contributed a great deal to the understanding of the British imperial decline. Wm. Roger Louis's *Imperialism at Bay: the United States and the Decolonization of the British Empire* deals with American and British wartime planning for the future of the colonial world, American anti-colonialism and expansion, and British reaction to American informal empire. Christopher Thorne's *Allies of a Kind: the United States, Britain and the War against Japan 1941–1945* concentrates on the Far East where Anglo–American rivalry and mutual suspicions emerged as the two Anglo–Saxon powers were co-operating in the defeat of Japan. Neither of these works, however, has tackled specifically the Sino–British relations nor analysed them within the wide imperial or 'imperial hangover' context. Also, though the 1945 elections in Britain and the defeat of Japan respectively marked a 'revolution' in Britain[26] and the beginning of a new era in world history, the transformation from empire to Commonwealth was far from being abrupt or clearly cut. Within the Chinese context too, the interregnum years of 1945 to 1949, during which fierce and bloody civil war took place, should neither be discarded nor ignored. Communist victory was not at all guaranteed and the probability of some sort of political continuation in China with an 'ancient regime' flavour persisted in the minds of decision-makers in East and West. The year 1945, therefore, while being an ideal ending date in some cases, might be quite misleading in others. Indeed, this is the central theme this study attempts to pursue.

I FROM PEARL HARBOR TO THE JAPANESE SURRENDER

MAP 2 *Japanese attacks December 1941–January 1942*

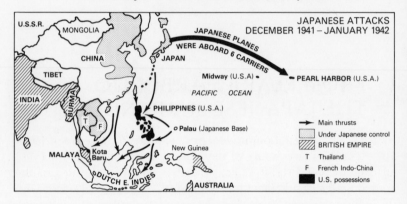

Source: B. Catchpole, *A Map History of Modern China* (Heinemann, 1976).

1 The War Breaks Out

By 9.45 a.m. (West Longitude Time) Sunday, 7 December 1941, after less than two hours of devastating bombing by a Japanese airforce of 360 aircraft at Pearl Harbor, eight battleships of the United States Pacific Fleet had been sunk or put out of order with three light cruisers, three destroyers and a number of auxiliaries; 2403 men of the United States Navy, Marine Corps, Army and civilians were killed and 1178 wounded. The Japanese had gained control of the Pacific. Coincidentally, within a few hours of the shattering attack on Pearl Harbor, on Monday, 8 December (west of the International Date Line), Japanese planned attacks were carried out on the American Philippines and on British Hong Kong and Malaya.[1] A new phase in the Second World War had started – the Pacific War.

In the course of the next six months swift Japanese operations completed Tokyo's control over a substantial part of the globe from Mandalay in north Burma to Wake Island in the mid-Pacific, from Manchuria in north China to Dutch and Portuguese Timor north of Australia, roughly twice the area of Germany, France, Britain and Italy. The distance between Tokyo and the farthest occupied area was around 6000 kilometres. The British, American, French and Dutch empires in the perimeter collapsed. In terms of East–West confrontation the disaster could only be compared to the Russian defeat in the course of the 1904–5 war with Japan. This time, however, the legend of the invincible European evaporated for good. With it disappeared the psychological 'fear barrier', as far as the Asians were concerned. No gunboat flying a European flag could again serve as an instrument of colonial policy in Asia.

For the United Kingdom the war in Asia put to the test British strategy and military capability. The results were the most calamitous in the military history of the British Empire. Disaster followed disaster. Despite its reinforcements, the colony of Hong Kong had

11

held out for barely eighteen days – a fifth of the time expected.[2] By Christmas Day it surrendered. The Japanese casualties were under 3000, while they had captured the whole of the reinforced garrison, nearly 12 000 men. The loss of the island came, symbolically perhaps, in the centenary year of its occupation.

On their part, the Chinese were both surprised and worried by the fall of Hong Kong. Surprised because what they had hitherto regarded as a strong British base should be occupied by their bitter enemy with such ease; worried because not a few of them (particularly those in senior government positions) had been using the colony as a refuge for their wives and children.[3]

Soon afterwards came the defeats in Malaya and Singapore. A Japanese force comprising *in toto* about 110 000, a small expedition for such a far reaching aim, managed to overcome the British defence strength of 88 000 who were supported by an inferior airforce. On 10 December the battleship *Prince of Wales* and the battle cruiser *Repulse*, which had sailed to Singapore eight days earlier as a deterrent naval force without any aircraft-carrier, were attacked and sunk. They had not even engaged the enemy. The escorting destroyers managed to save over 2000 men out of 2800 in the two ships' crews. From 10 December onwards the British retreat down the west, and later the east, coasts of Malaya became continuous. Within fifty four days Malaya had been conquered. The Japanese total casualties were only about 4600 whereas the British had lost about 25 000 (mainly prisoners) and a large quantity of equipment.[4] On Sunday 8 February 1942 two leading divisions of the Japanese invading force crossed the narrow channel that separates Singapore island from the mainland. Exactly a week later, on Sunday 15 February, Singapore capitulated. 'These two black Sundays ...' Liddell Hart observed 'were fatal to the imperial sway of what had been proudly called for many years "The Empire on which the sun never sets".' Singapore, the symbol of Western and particularly British domination in the Far East, collapsed. So much emphasis had been given since the First World War to the creation of a great naval base there 'that its symbolical importance had come to surpass even its strategical value'. Its easy capture was an irrecoverable blow to British prestige in Asia. No belated re-entry could efface the impression. The old threads could not be taken up as though there had been no interruption. 'The white man had lost his ascendancy with the disproof of his magic.[5] While the British snatched glory from

defeat at Dunkirk, from Singapore they got nothing but humiliation. Indeed, it was, as Churchill gloomily observed, 'the worst
disaster and largest capitulation in British history'.[6]

With their southern flank now secure, the Japanese pursued
their invasion of Burma and the Dutch East Indies. It was a two-
pronged sweep that brought them menacingly close to India on
the one hand and Australia on the other. Soon in Burma, too,
British forces found themselves on the retreat. Their ground
forces were semi-trained and insufficient in numbers and their
initial thirty seven aircraft could in no way meet the 100 Japanese
aircraft which were doubled by another air brigade after the fall
of Manila in January.

The Japanese invasion of Burma had started as early as mid-
December. On 23 and 25 December 1941 heavy air-raids were
delivered on Rangoon, which was captured and deserted on 8
March 1942.[7] With the abandonment of Rangoon most of the
British were withdrawn to India. Early in April the Japanese forces
moved up the Irrawaddy river towards Mandalay in fulfilment of
the aim of cutting and closing the Burma Road which until then
supplied China with materials she badly needed. A British force
now 60 000 strong were holding an east–west line 150 miles south
of Mandalay with the aid of Chinese forces on their eastern flank.
Yet the Japanese, who outwitted the defenders, managed to move
round them. No wonder, therefore, that in the British command it

MAP 3   *Japan invades Burma and cuts the road link with China 1942*

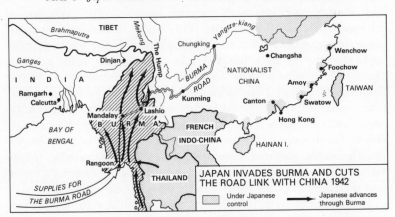

Source: B. Catchpole, *A Map History of Modern China* (Heinemann, 1976).

was now decided not to make a stand at Mandalay but to withdraw towards the India frontier. Though on the whole the retreat
was orderly, the British casualties had amounted to three times
those of the Japanese: 13 500 against 4500.[8] On May Day 1942
Japanese troops entered Mandalay. The words of Rudyard
Kipling, who died seven years before, 'Come you back, you British
soldier, come you back to Mandalay', received a totally different, if
not opposing, meaning. By June 1942 both the British and the
Chinese forces had been almost completely driven out of Burma
into India and China. The Japanese advance halted some way
short of the Indian border owing to the break of rains and
transport difficulties. Thus was created the Frontier Fringe, that
part of Burma which the Japanese failed to control.[9] The Governor of Burma, Sir Reginald Dorman-Smith, then already a month
in India, was in the process of creating the nucleus of a headquarters of what can be paradoxically perhaps termed 'a civil
colonial government-in-exile'. Britain's position in South East Asia
had collapsed with astonishing rapidity. 'It found itself pushed
back to its imperial centre in Asia, from which British power had
expanded in the nineteenth century'.[10] The Japanese completed
their capture of the western gateways to China and the Pacific. In
no time their irresistible power seemed to endanger the Indian
Ocean and the great island of Ceylon, which was considered by
the British a potential springboard for the Japanese navy from
which it could threaten Britain's troops and supply route to the
Middle East round the Cape of Good Hope, and South Africa, as
well as the sea-routes to India and Australia. The prospects of
preserving Ceylon looked poor. On 5 April a hundred Japanese
planes attacked the harbour at Colombo inflicting great damage
and repelling the air counter-attacks. Later on the same day fifty
Japanese bombers sank two British cruisers. The British
Command retreated the older battleships to East Africa, and the
faster ones to Bombay.[11] Soon, however, the Japanese fleet withdrew from the area after having inflicted heavy and humiliating
defeat on British seapower.[12] British maritime control in the
Indian Ocean and consequently British prestige in the region
suffered a devastating blow. It was on the verge of causing irrepar-
able damage to British positions in the Middle East as well.

The Japanese were rapidly reaching an old dream of establishing a Greater East Asia Co-Prosperity Sphere. They were now the
masters of a vast Asian population which found itself scattered

and disoriented after decades of white colonial rule. They likewise controlled important oil, rubber, tin and other essential resources which were critical for a long defence against counter attacks.

Britain's only consolation could be that Japan had brought the United States into the war. Although the American Pacific Fleet had been temporarily neutralised, it was hoped in London that once the Americans re-asserted themselves with their immense resources and skill, victory would eventually come. In this very development, however, lay the roots of the total dismemberment of the British Empire. An empire totally dependent on other power for its very existence could in no way last for long. The story of growing American influence in the Far East, therefore, is in a way the story of British decline there. Was Churchill right all the way when exclaiming in joy upon learning of America's entry to the war: 'England would live; Britain would live; the Commonwealth of Nations and the Empire would live'?[13]

At the initial stages of the struggle it seemed that India and Ceylon would be most significant as bases for the Powers' return to both South East Asia and China. It likewise looked natural that Britain would play a central role in the coming attempts to contain Japan and defeat her. However, developments took a different turn. In the ring formed around Japan, the area of the British responsibility was modest in size even following the establishment in October 1943 of the South East Asia Command (SEAC) headed by Admiral Lord Louis Mountbatten, the only British command in the Pacific War. Initially, SEAC included Burma, Siam, Malaya and Sumatra.[14] The American Admiral, Chester W. Nimitz, and General Douglas MacArthur took upon themselves to command the crucial Central Pacific and South-West Pacific commands respectively. Generalissimo Chiang Kai-shek was appointed the commander of the China Theatre. Within a few months, it was hoped, the four commands would manage together to tighten this ring around Japan 'to a noose'.[15] By August 1945 it became quite clear that it had been mainly American manpower, resources and technological progress that brought Japan to her knees, enabled Britain to restore her pre-war position in her former colonies in South East Asia and allowed her to entertain the idea of establishing her previous position in China. Indeed, during the four and a half years of the Sino–Japanese undeclared war from July 1937 to December 1941, British interests in China suffered immense damage.[16] Britain's material interests in that huge country were,

nevertheless, until the outbreak of the Pacific War greater than
those of any other country. Her possessions were estimated at
about one thousand million dollars as compared to about a
quarter of that amount the Americans had. Also, British interests
varied and were represented by shipping, coastal steamship lines,
banks, insurance companies, commercial firms of great variety,
cotton mills, factories, etc. Britain also maintained the greatest
number of foreign nationals living in China.[17] Indeed, since the
first British traders arrived in China, trade and commerce both
with and in China were the paramount concern at both the official
and the non-official levels. Other considerations remained always
marginal. The idea of 'uplifting', 'civilising', or 'Christianising' the
'natives' had never been a major force to the British in China as it
had been to the Americans. Nor were strategic or territorial
calculations so significant.[18]

Historically, the war against Japan and Britain's role in it served
as a crossroads to Britian's role in post-war Asia. Strong British
resistance to Japanese aggression, adamant determination not to
yield, and a successful independent military British return to areas
from which British forces had been forced to evacuate could have
revitalised British prestige and even extended the life of the
Empire albeit in a substantially different manner. On the other
hand, retreat, lack of determination to resist the Japanese, growing dependence on the United States for military and economic
assistance, and apparent inability to struggle independently on the
way back to reoccupation, could diminish the Empire's prestige
both in the formal and informal colonies. The Chinese on their
part watched closely and most carefully the Powers' contribution
to their prolonged struggle against Japan. For both the official
authorities in Chunking and the Communists in their capital
Yenan, from their respective angles of course, the war served as a
test of the Powers' intentions and willingness to assist their
nation.[19] In the 1930s both Britain and the United States had failed
to satisfy the Chinese of their unreserved support in the face of the
Japanese attacks. Now that a new phase – the war in the Pacific –
had emerged, a second test had started.

Unlike the British (who aimed at averting war with Japan and
whose limited resources while battling for national survival prevented them from providing China sufficiently)[20], and the
Russians (who, having signed the non-aggression pact with Japan
in April 1941, virtually ceased assisting China), the United States

was in a position to come to China's help. Indeed, following Dr Lauchlin Currie's mission to China in early 1941 and the passing of the Lend–Lease bill by the Congress, actual steps were taken to aid China in that hour of crisis.[21] By late spring about $150 million

MAP 4　*Main Nationalist battle areas 1941–5*

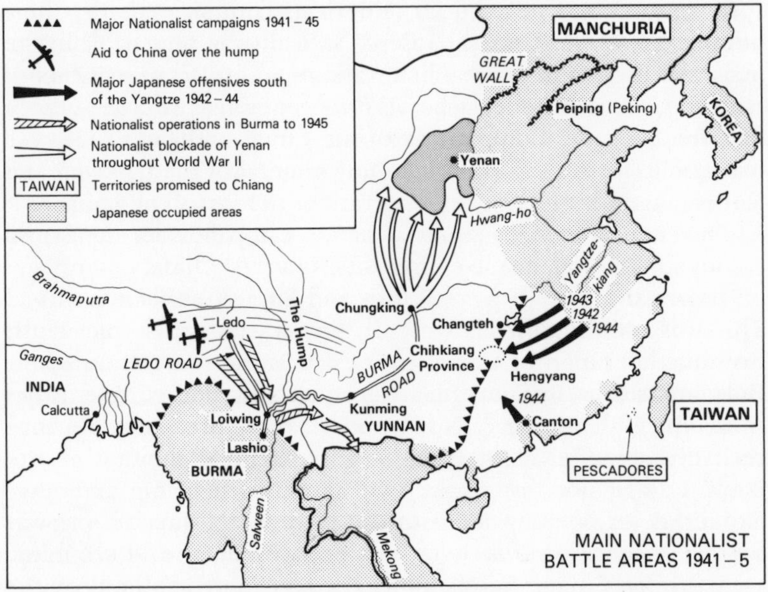

Source: B. Catchpole, *A Map History of Modern China* (Heinemann, 1976).

worth of military equipment had been allocated to China. In the summer the American Military Mission to China (AMMISCA) was created. On 9 June 1941 the first contingent of pilots and mecha-nics – the American Volunteer Group (AVG) – consisting of private recruits of crews from the military service, began their journey to China. Within a few months these men and their P-40 fighter planes would become famous as the Flying Tigers. Essen-tially this force was a mercenary force under contract, and not under either American or Chinese discipline. Their Supervisor – not commander – was Claire Chennault, a former US Army Air Force colonel.[22] In July 1942 AVG was formally reincorporated into the Army Air Force and renamed the China Air Task Force. It remained under Chennault's command but subordinated to the 10th Air Force in Delhi. Later, Chennault became a major-general and his force was called the 14th United States Air Force. By the end of the war this difficult and dangerous service was bringing more supplies into China than the Burma Road could ever carry. During the crucial years 1942–3, however, both aircraft and supplies were limited because of the demands of other theatres of war which were being given priority in the Allied planning.[23]

By early 1942, full official American commitment to China became apparent. General Joseph Stilwell was sent to China to assist the government in military affairs and to serve as Chief of Staff to Chiang Kai-shek who was then, among his other capacities, the Supreme Commander of the Chinese Theatre.[24] Stilwell was also to serve as the commanding general of the United States forces in the China Theatre of operations in Burma and India.

Once Burma fell into Japanese hands, campaigns for the British colony's liberation, just like direct assistance to China, emerged as an important issue in Sino–British and Sino–American relations. This was only natural in view of Burma's potential role in the eventual liberation of China. In the 1930s the completion of the Burma Road by Britain similarly played a significant role in her relations with China.[25] No wonder, therefore, that Burma's recovery, as a result of Chinese and British combined efforts, could be a major test of the two nations' friendship and serve Britain as an opening for a future return to China on pre-war footing once the war was over. Yet, already from the outset, things went wrong. Chiang Kai-shek proposed a council at Chungking to advise on every aspect of Allied War effort in the Far East. The Foreign Office agreed with the need for co-ordination of policy, but obviously did not wish Britain alone to be committed to an agreement with China.[26] On 22 December 1941 General Sir Archibald Wavell, formerly Commander-in-Chief in India and now the newly appointed Supreme Commander-in-Chief in the American, British, Dutch, Australian (ABDA) area, visited Chungking. Chiang outlined to him proposals for discussions about combined Allied strategy, the conduct of the war in the Pacific area and an inter-Allied war council. General Wavell politely advised that it would be better to use the time available for their meeting to settle matters of immediate concern, for example the defence of the Burma base, the disposal of the limited air force available for this purpose, Chinese assistance in the defence of Burma and the pooling of Lend–Lease material. Chiang apparently resented the way in which his attempts to discuss the wider strategy of the war were brushed aside. He was greatly disappointed and particularly hurt at what he later complained to Roosevelt was Wavell's refusal to accept Chinese proffered help. Even though Wavell denied that this had been the case, it seems plain from Wavell's reply that he was not eager for Chinese help. He remarked that, low as British prestige in China was, it would be depressed still further by an admission that Burma could not be held without Chinese aid. The Burmese too were not likely to relish the presence of ill-supplied and poorly disciplined Chinese troops in their country.[27]

Even after the signature of the Declaration of the United Nations (including China) in Washington on 1 January 1942, and the announcement that Chiang Kai-shek had accepted the Supreme Command in the China Theatre, Chiang continued to feel neglected and resentful. Indeed, whatever was the true sequence of events and their nature, Chinese sensibilities were outraged.[28] Consequent anti-British resentment in China was added to the already corroded Anglo–Chinese relations.[29] For both the Chinese and the British, Burma retained primarily a *political* significance. It was perhaps on this ground that full and sincere co-operation between the two was most difficult to achieve. For the Americans, on the other hand, Burma remained throughout the war mainly a *military* consideration. Yet they too recognised the long-term political implications that military developments there might have, for example by way of diminishing Chinese confidence in the capacity of both Britain and the United States, or by way of national disillusionment developing into serious anti-foreignism.[30] Indeed, could the Chinese retain the same respect for the two Anglo–Saxon powers after their heavy defeat and losses sustained in Asia? To the Chinese it seemed

> the height of irony that the entry of Great Britain and the United States into war against Japan – a development for which ... [they] have been hoping for several years – has not only resulted in relieving their precarious situation, but, by misadventure, has actually been followed by appearance of Japanese armed forces at China's back door and has led to the closing of China's main channel of trade and communications with the outside world.[31]

Changing Chinese attitude arose also from disappointment 'at the meagreness of military assistance' furnished to China and from a

feeling of being neglected as regards provision of military supplies in favour of Allied forces elsewhere. It was, therefore, from
this point of departure that considering China as an equal ally and
as a full partner in the common cause emerged in Washington.
China, it was felt, had to be brought into the various councils
whenever and wherever appropriate and practicable. Every consideration should be given to Chinese sensibilities in regard to the
status of China's partnership with America and the status of China
as a potential leader among the nations of East Asia. Such an
American attitude, adopted formally, not without British reservations, in the course of 1943, was to have significant repercussions
during the rest of the war years.

By January 1943 both the United States and Britain abolished
their extraterritorial rights in China,[32] and in December of the
same year the Cairo Declaration seemingly opened the door for
China's admission to the exclusive circle of the Big Powers. These
two events coincided with fierce battles that were then being
fought in the Far East, marking the turning of the tide and the
beginning of the end of the Japanese Asian empire.

The negotiations on the abolition of exterritoriality which started in 1929 had been in abeyance since 1931, the year of the
Japanese invasion of Manchuria. Throughout the 1930s the attitude of the British government remained that it had gone as far as
it could to meet the wishes of the Chinese and that the matter
must be suspended until other powers had made similar progress.
Following the outbreak of war in Europe and further exchanges
between the British and the American governments, the road had
been paved for the signing of agreements on extraterritoriality.[33]
On 11 January 1943 two bilateral treaties for the relinquishment
of extraterritorial rights and regulations of related matters were
signed in Washington (between China and the United States) and
in Chungking (between China and Britain). No extraterritorial
jurisdiction in China, no special rights to station troops there, no
privileges in the international settlements nor in the British
concession were to be enjoyed by the two powers, their representatives or their subjects.[34] Accompanying exchange of notes
abolished any rights in relation to inland navigation and cabotage
the powers had possessed. The annex to the exchange notes in the
Anglo–Chinese document included also a paragraph in which
Britain relinquished her rights to claim appointment of a British
subject as inspector-general of the Chinese Customs. Symbolically

perhaps, and in accordance with the new structure of power in the international arena, 1943 saw the replacement of Sir Frederick Maze by the first American ever in this job.[35] Britain did not relinquish her special rights in Hong Kong. The Chinese government reserved the right to raise at a later date the question of the future of the Kowloon Leased Territory, its aim being apparently to secure eventually the rendition of Hong Kong in its entirety.[36]

It is interesting to note, and undeniably relevant to the internal deliberations in Britain on the return to China after the war, that when negotiations on the relinquishment of extraterritoriality took place, China Association officials objected to what they regarded as the British government's unconditional surrender of assets. As P.H.B. Kent, a member of the general committee of the Association later put it, the British Government 'had not contributed a single penny piece to building up the assets of these areas; why, then should they give them away?'[37] The representatives of the business houses whose trade with and in China was their main line emphasised that that trade had been built upon the extraterritorial system. They were greatly disturbed by the future difficulties their respective companies would face in the post-war era.[38] Moreover, the Old China Hands feared the political equality China was likely to enjoy in the future. This, they believed, would create an environment 'very different from what it was', making it most difficult to work.[39] Even a belligerent Labour Party patriot like Emmanuel Shinwell adopted not-too-distant views. Apparently reluctant to throw the British Commonwealth of Nations overboard,[40] he expressed fears as regards the wide consequences the agreement on the abolition of extraterritorial rights might have on the British workers. Late in 1943 he referred to the subject in Parliament and emphasised the importance of British shipping activities on the coast of China to the British shipping industry. He pointed out that if they were to be relinquished 'a very severe burden will be imposed on our Mercantile Marine'. He went as far as suggesting the correction of what he considered 'a serious mistake'. It was the Conservative Richard Law, the Parliamentary Under-Secretary of State, who had to remind Shinwell that Britain could not have it both ways, 'relinquish extraterritorial rights in China and still retain them'.[41] The position taken by the representative of the Labour Party at this stage was perhaps indicative of Labour's future Hong Kong and China policies following the electoral victory of 1945. Could, indeed, commercial ties between the two countries or activities of British companies in China be resumed as in bygone days? A Foreign Office letter to 10 Downing Street immediately following the signature of the treaty on the abolition of extraterritorial rights gave the department's view. Britain's financial position after the war, it was stressed, would be 'far from strong'. There would be many claims on it apart from China, and too-high hopes should not be given to Britain's future export position.[42]

Legally speaking, the treaties ushered in a new era in Sino–foreign relations. The 'unequal treaty' system, established a century earlier, vanished, never to return. In reality, however, the extraterritorial areas and rights relinquished did not actually exist when given up.[43] Japan had taken and occupied the coastal provinces of China and in a series of humilating measures had deprived the British, as well as other Allied nationals, of any privileges they had acquired and practised in the past. Moreover, on 1 January 1943 they announced to the puppet Chinese govern-ment of Nanking their own surrender of extraterritorial privi-leges. The abolition of extraterritorial rights seemed therefore a gesture forced upon the powers by objective events beyond their control, rather than a wilful act; a mere *de jure* recognition of a reality existing *de facto*. It could tacitly serve the powers' interests in a bid to paralyse Japan's manoeuvres, then widely advertised, aimed at demonstrating a readiness to fight for the complete equality of the yellow race.

In essence, the abolition treaty deprived the British Empire for good of all its territorial bases in China. Any future contacts between the Empire and China were to lack (except in the case of Hong Kong) the territorial element. Sino–British relations were to be conducted from then onwards on an entirely new basis unknown since the mid-nineteenth century. The Chinese by no means regarded the new development as an act of grace taken by their war time allies. Rather, it seemed to them as a new stage achieved in fulfilment of one of Sun Yat-sen's chief aims.

The Cairo Conference and the Cairo Declaration must also be examined in light of the new wartime reality and the Anglo–American tension which characterised their alliance in the Far East. Before meeting Stalin in Teheran to discuss Mediterranean and European strategy, Roosevelt and Churchill conferred with Chiang Kai-shek in Cairo. Deliberations on the formulation of military operations in the China theatre took place.[44] Churchill, however, was almost totally excluded from these talks, which were to redraw the political map of the Far East.[45] The Cairo Declaration of 1 December 1943 (made after the Teheran Conference) was aimed at boosting Chinese morale at China's seventh year of war against Japan. It stated that the Allies would demand Japan's unconditional surrender as well as her with-drawal from her overseas empire. Manchuria, Formosa and the Pescadores Islands were to be returned to China. China was thus to regain not only territories lost to her enemy since the Manchurian incident of 1931, but also areas Japan had taken as result of the Sino–Japanese war of 1894–5. As far as world opinion was concerned, China was to become one of the Big Powers with heavy, yet respectable, international burdens.

A close analysis of the hasty preparation leading to the declara-tion and the somewhat surprising deliberations preceding it reveal, however, that the Cairo achievement was 'a clear cut piece of propaganda'.[46] On the British side, Sir Alexander Cadogan, the Permanent Under-Secretary of State at the Foreign Office and his colleagues objected to the naming of Manchuria and other terri-tories as having been stolen from China.[47] Their feeling was not incompatible with Churchill's view expressed earlier in a minute to Cadogan that China was not after all a world power equal to Britain, the United States or Russia.[48] 'That China is one of the world's four Great Powers is an absolute farce' Churchill would reiterate less than a year later.[49] Attlee, too, would say years later that 'it was absurd . . . to have China as a permanent member of the Security Council [of the United Nations]'. He refused to regard her as a Great Power and considered the American official view on the issue a fallacy.[50] Indeed, Churchill could not accept the idea that Britain and China were mentioned in the same breath. Equality between the two countries and their peoples were, as far as he was concerned, simply unthinkable. 'I told the President' he would write years later,

> how much I felt American opinion over-estimated the contribu-tion which China could make to the general war. . . I said I would of course always be helpful and polite to the Chinese, whom I admired and liked as a race and pitied for their endless misgovernment, but that he must not expect me to adopt what I felt was a wholly unreal standard of values.[51]

Churchill's upbringing, basic beliefs and aspiration resisted any suggestion that China should bulk as large as Great Britain in the mind of anyone.

In Cairo, a minor incident illustrates his views. Meeting Madame Chiang Kai-shek, Churchill urged her to visit England and learn more about it, as it was a very old country. Madame Chiang Kai-shek, apparently hurt by Churchill's attitude towards the Chinese aspirations, reminded the Prime Minister that it was he who had to visit China – her motherland – which was an even older country.[52] Despite repeated British diplomatic efforts, the Generalissimo's influential wife refused to visit Britain. Regardless of the real reason for adopting that stand, her anti-British prejudices never even stood the chance of disappearing. Racial prejudice, lack of knowledge and even unwillingness to know China and the Chinese also characterised Churill's opinions and policies relating to the biggest country in the world.[53] It could be termed 'cultural aggression' or 'cultural imperialism'.[54]

Relating the proceedings of the Cairo Conference, Churchill did not mention the incident with Madame Chiang Kai-shek. 'What we have apprehended from Chiang Kai-shek's presence', he recalled,

> now in fact occurred. The talks of the British and American Staff were sadly distracted by the Chinese story, which was lengthy, complicated and minor, . . . the President, who took an exaggerated view of the Indian–Chinese sphere, was soon closeted in long conferences with the Generalissimo. All hope of persuading Chiang and his wife to go and see the Pyramids and enjoy themselves till we returned from Teheran fell to the ground, with the result that Chinese business occupied first instead of last place at Cairo.[55]

The Chief of the Imperial General Staff, General Sir Alan Brooke, also felt in Cairo the uselessness of the discussions with the Chinese. To him, too, the order of priority imposed by the Americans at the Conference was wrong. 'We should never have started our Conference with Chiang,' he wrote after the war, 'by doing so we were putting the cart before the horse. He had nothing to contribute towards the defeat of the Germans, and for the matter of that uncommonly little towards the defeat of the Japanese'.[56] Describing the meeting with the Chinese generals, Brooke concluded 'that was a ghastly waste of time'. It was evident, he added 'that they understood nothing about strategy or higher tactics and were quite unfit to discuss these questions'.[57] As for Madame Chiang Kai-shek, he felt that she was the 'leading spirit' among the Chinese present at the conference. Yet he noted, 'I would not trust her very far'.[58]

On the American side too, the statements made in Cairo could hardly hide the real intentions regarding China's new role in the international arena. When Roosevelt learnt in Teheran of the Russian's lack of an ice-free port in the Far East, he hastened to suggest the Chinese port of Dairen as a free port under international guarantee to serve them. This was done without even consulting his Chinese colleagues.[59] This initiative undoubtedly augured the agreement reached in Yalta more than a year later. There the Soviet Union was to be guaranteed a price for entering the war against Japan at China's expense: to have a lease of Port Arthur as a naval base, and to enjoy an internationalised Dairen with 'permanent interests' safeguarded. The same spirit was to apply to Soviet interests in South Manchurian and Chinese Eastern Railways and to Outer Mongolia.[60] Roosevelt was to go even further. He was to take it upon himself to secure China's fall-into-line and acceptance of the American–Soviet scheme.[61] In Teheran, Stalin was half-hearted about the inclusion of China among the post-war 'Four Policemen'.[62] He doubted whether China would be a powerful state after the war, and in this respect his views were not too distant from Churchill's.

Thus, by 1943 the leaders of the three Big Powers were in different degrees unwilling to sincerely accept China as an equal partner. The publicised gestures were incompatible with true feelings expressed in closed circles.[63]

The Chinese government on its part were quite aware of this dichotomy. Very soon it was to understand that, despite the Cairo Declaration, China was as far as ever from attaining the status of a Great Power.[64] It was not the first time that the Chinese felt that the Western powers treated them unfairly, that despite promises to deal with them as equals and on a mutual basis, they were pushed to the back of the line. Chiang Kai-shek's book *China's Destiny*, published in 1943, was the most celebrated expression of this frustration. Containing strong nationalistic and anti-foreign sentiments, the book notably caused a great deal of concern in London. In fact, so great was the impact of the book that the

Generalissimo apparently directed his Ministry for Foreign Affairs to mildly alter the negative impression it created.[65] After all, Chiang Kai-shek was still hoping to improve relations with Britain and other powers and gain their assistance. It was against this background that Dr K. C. Wu, China's Vice-Minister for Foreign Affairs, observed in a personal and secret conversation with Berkley Gage of the British Embassy in Chungking that certain non-official translations had reached the West and caused 'unfortunate reactions'. 'The average Chinese', he stressed, 'would not become anti-foreign through reading the book.' Chiang could not help feeling proud of his achievements sometimes or refrain from talking or writing about them especially as, with the abolition of extraterritoriality, he felt he had fulfilled 'the most important injunction in Dr Sun Yat-sen's testament'.[66]

The prolonged Japanese occupation of Manchuria, north China and the coastal provinces of China increased China's feeling of self-assertiveness.[67] This, it can be argued, was a reaction to Tokyo's hopes and plans to foster the Co-prosperity Sphere in Asia, to achieve a close amalgamation of the industrious Chinese, the natural resources of South East Asia and the leadership and military power of Japan.[68] In both South East Asia and China the Japanese were caught in a difficult dilemma. Encouraging local struggle against Western colonialism by attacking foreign rule amounted in fact to a simultaneous encouragement of the anti-Japanese movements as well. No wonder, therefore, that they often tried to prevent what they considered 'premature' independent movements. However, from 1944 onwards they had to gear their organisational and propaganda facilities to the task of fostering national unity in the occupied areas. As the Allied counter-attacks gained momentum it became more and more urgent for the Japanese to win the active support of the local population wherever they were in control. If they were to hold their conquests, they had to try by various projects and promises to gain the natives' support. This reality enhanced the bargaining position of the nationalists in South East Asia.[69] The latter, even if not aiming initially at a genuine social revolution, now intensified the social slogans whenever foreign influences seemed to be responsible for either the lack of economic opportunities for the middle class or the low standard of living of the masses. The anti-foreign aspect of the new leaders' social awareness 'fitted in well with the anti-colonial element of the nationalist struggle'.[70] In any case it did not take long for the inhabitants of the occupied areas to realise that the Japanese were no better for them than their Western colonial predecessors. This was also clear in the economic sphere where the Japanese were found not to have shied away from exploitation.[71] The Japanese failed to understand that freedom from European imperialism was not enough, that each national movement was striving for a freedom of its own.[72] This was the reason why the Japanese thought that independence of the various peoples of South East Asia should be based on constructing East Asian political entities existing within the New Order and not on Western liberalism and national self-determination.[73] Japan, as Professor Ieynaga observed, did not liberate the Asian people but, rather, 'each people began to struggle to attain independence in the midst of the process of the resistance struggle against Japan. Asian people did not become independent through the power of Japan, but they attained independence in resisting Japan.'[74]

In the case of China circumstances were different from those existing in South East Asia. The pattern crystallising *vis-à-vis* the Japanese occupation was also different. Yet here, too, the Japanese presence helped the Chinese in moulding their renewed national feelings and served an important role in shaping their war-time and post-war behaviour.

2 British Perception I

Unlike the members of the China Association and the Old China Hands who had direct trade relations with China, some Foreign Office officials who helped shape Britain's Far Eastern policies were sceptical about the prospects of re-established Sino–British commercial ties. In particular they did not regard resumption of British exports to China as likely. Notwithstanding this feeling, however, what was seen as China's great industrial future and her prospective need for Britain's goods and technical assistance continued to maintain a general magic attraction on the British side. This emerged both in the report of the Parliamentary mission of 1942 to China and in notes written at the Foreign Office based thereupon.

Britain, it was stated in a Foreign Office memorandum attached to the mission's report for Churchill, would not be as able as would the Americans to spare much in the way of capital goods to China after the war.[1] She had, however, to do what she could in order to treat such exports 'as a political rather than a commercial investment'. Such a policy would ensure that China developed on broad lines of world co-operation and not on those of 'militarism and economic nationalism'. Improvements in the working conditions of Chinese labour were likewise regarded not only as in the interest of Chinese labour itself, but rather as means to avoid 'serious repercussions throughout the world from the employment of cheap labour in China'.

The Parliamentary mission to China headed by Lord Ailwyn (Conservative) toured parts of unoccupied China between 10 November and 9 December 1942. The sending of the mission, announced in Parliament on 10 September 1942, followed an alarming depression in Anglo–Chinese relations in the preceding months and a British failure to assist the Chinese in almost all the ways previously proposed.[2] Back in England the members of the mission accepted the fact that serious trade difficulties with China

were inherent in Britain's economic situation.[3] They stressed the
changes to be expected in China. 'It would be a serious mistake on
our part', they pointed out, 'if we were to assume that China will
continue to be a weak and disorganised power.' They dwelt on the
new Treasury law in China which deprived the customs – still
managed mainly by Britons – of its financial autonomy, thus
tightening Chinese, as opposed to foreign, control over it and
stressed that it had become more difficult for a foreign official to
remain in his employment. The Chinese government tended to
prefer Chinese even at a price of being defrauded of the greater
part of its revenue. Suffering the humiliation of receiving it from
the hands of an honest but alien inspectorate seemed to them to
be the worst option. The members of the mission felt that it would
become even more difficult for British traders and businessmen in
China to compete with Chinese firms. Chinese courts and laws
seemed likely to discriminate against foreigners. As for trade
with China, prospects seemed likewise quite gloomy. It was
appreciated, however, that foreign loans would be needed for the
purchasing by China of machinery required to begin China's
industrial plans. Indeed, the abolition of extraterritoriality, which
was then agreed upon in principle, though not yet signed, and the
inability to spare much in the way of capital goods for China,
seemed set to become obstacles for the re-establishment of
Britain's pre-war position in China.

In the military sphere the mission's report pointed out that
Britain could assist China by recovering Burma.[4] As far as other
military questions were concerned, the Parliamentary mission
reported that British Commando troops who had been sent to
China had to be withdrawn after a few months of exasperating
disappointment. Chinese generals had allowed the British to do
almost nothing. Whether this was due to the Chinese dislike of
foreign auxiliaries, to fear of provoking the enemy who might
advance further into China's hinterland, or rather simply to sheer
incompetence, could not at all be determined.[5] Another possible
explanation not mentioned in the report, yet one that could
perhaps explain Chinese obstructionist policy, was the personal
interest some local Chinese commanders maintained in the trade
and commerce prevailing between the two combatant parties
across the 'enemy' lines. Western involvement in typically Eastern
dealings of that kind could naturally damage the atmosphere of
local co-existence. Any serious British intervention had, therefore,

to be actively discouraged.

The report dwelt on anti-British feelings and anti-British demonstrations of which they learnt during their short visit. Britain, they insisted, had been singled out in this respect, and the criticism and hostility towards her were rather stronger than towards the United States, Germany or other European states.

The members of the Parliamentary mission stressed that most of the soldiers in China were 'badly fed and their pay, if they ever received it, is miserable'. They likewise pointed out that China was to a great extent controlled by the secret police headed by General Tai Li and that a vast system of espionage extended into every corner of unoccupied China. During their tour of China the members of the mission themselves were all the time closely spied on. When in Chungking, for example, they were often amused to watch an industrious work-party of six young coolies who were engaged in the work of road-surveying outside their house. 'They were always busily occupied in measuring the length of the road, from the corner to the garage to the top of the terrace, a total distance of about thirty yards. They had between them one long tape measure which they unrolled, rolled up and unrolled again.'

Interestingly enough, yet quite typically, the British Parliamentary mission, as other British organs in China, paid only little attention to the Chinese Communists. 'We do not think that the Communists could attain power without a long and bloody civil war', stated the members of the mission. They predicted that Chiang Kai-shek would find himself after the war in a strong enough position, and would come to terms with the Communists, allowing them to continue with the administration of the provinces they occupied, thus achieving 'unity without bloodshed'.

A great deal of the report was naturally devoted to Sino–British relations once the war ended, and to the prospects of revitalising the trade between the two countries. Again, doubts were expressed as to whether, in view of the abolition of extraterritoriality, business would be able to continue as in the pre-war era. British traders, said the report, did not think it likely that British firms which kept honest accounts and paid their taxes could compete in the future with Chinese firms 'which keep dishonest accounts and pay no taxes'. The members of the mission expressed the fear of British firms that the Chinese courts of law would discriminate against them. Echoing the hesitations of a century earlier as to whether foreign trade could at all be pursued

when regulated by the laws of the 'natives', the report underlined
the British traders' discouragement by the knowledge that 'anyone
who enters a Chinese prison is very fortunate if he ever comes out
of it alive'. This, given the abolition of extraterritoriality, was
indeed the question. In the distant past imperial commerce tended
to establish a territorial base for itself. It very rarely could accept
trade on the basis of local conceptions, regulations and laws.
Could it be revived again in a new era when no territorial or
colonial situation was likely to re-emerge? Moreover, Chinese
government seemed likely to assume a monopoly of foreign trade
after the war. Local officials, it was feared, would again behave as
they saw fit, leaving the foreigner with no security. More serious
yet seemed the situation whereby the quantities of tea, silk, wood-
oil, tungsten, antimony, and other such commodities which China
could export in peace time, would not be at all sufficient to pay for
the foreign machinery that China was likely to need to begin her
industrial plans. The only way was for China to have foreign loans.
As loans on economic grounds were very unlikely, on account of
China's war time inflation and unstable conditions, political loans
were the only alternative. These loans were to be guaranteed by
the governments of highly industrialised countries who could
export the machinery China would require.

What were the chances of a British political loan to China?
Deliberations over this question, while taken with a view to
helping China, were, it must be emphasised, part of a war time
thinking about re-establishing Britain's pre-war position in China.
In December 1941 Chiang Kai-shek had asked for a loan of
£100 million from England and $500 million from the United
States, on the grounds that he wanted to give a psychological
stimulus to his people, and restore their faith in their own
country.[6] Subsequently the British Treasury expressed its willingness to grant £50 million on condition that it should be spent in
the sterling area on some purpose connected with the war. The
Chinese government and particularly Dr H. H. Kung, the Minister
of Finance, had made a grievance of this, contrasting American
generosity (allowing them to use part of their loan to provide for
the security of an internal loan which they wished to raise for the
purpose of checking inflation) with British meanness. They
expected friendly nations to aid their post-war industrial progress
and not to treat such aid as a business transaction.[7] Now, in 1942,
in view of the fact that the loan negotiations had not yet been

completed, the issue was raised again.

The members of the Parliamentary mission expected British external trade in the post-war era to be determined by government policy and governed by international trading agreements. Since former foreign investments would most likely be exhausted, and as Britain would doubtless need to import a great deal of consumer goods in order to maintain the standard of living of the British people, it seemed that a great part of Britain's foreign trade would need to consist of the exchange of goods for goods, and not of the export of capital whose return was to be deferred until the distant future. Britain, it seemed, would have to be obliged to seek trade with those countries who would be able to supply her immediate necessities.

Likewise, it was well appreciated that the rebuilding of Britain, the improving of housing and a variety of development projects would require a very large production of capital goods for domestic use. Consequently, it was realised that only a small proportion of British capital goods, in comparison with the pre-war period, could be exported. After all, China was not on top of the priority list. The Empire, sadly underdeveloped, was regarded as entitled to the first claim on any capital that Britain would be able to spare and export.

Though the picture drawn by the members of the Parliamentary mission to China was rather gloomy as far as possible future British assistance to China was concerned, it was felt that China's condition was 'certainly not more unfavourable than the condition of Russia appeared to be at the time of Brest-Litovsk, and for several years afterwards'.[8] The belief in China's ability was immense. China, it seemed, could overcome the post-war difficulties and go through a substantial and impressive reconstruction. 'Provincialism, local disaffection, the ambition of individual war lords, or the opposition of political minorities will not be able to impede ... the purpose of the ruling party.' Moreover, the refusal of foreign capital and skilled technical assistance seemed at the most to create a delay but not to frustrate altogether the ultimate transformation of China into a great industrial power. Indeed, the refusal of Britain and other industrialised countries to help China would isolate her economically and 'would foster the growth of anti-foreign hatred and of extreme nationalism'. In light of the Chinese high regard for the quality of British goods and the value of British experience, they were likely to be eager to accept any capital exports that Britain would be able to spare. 'It would be prudent to regard such exports as a political rather than a commercial investment.'

Again, the great, almost legendary, Chinese market seemed to strike the members of the mission. 'The potential wealth of China is enormous', they stressed. Whether this wealth and the power that would accompany it was used 'to promote prosperity and peace, or whether it is used for militarism and national selfishness, will greatly depend on the sympathy and consideration with which China is treated by the older industrial nations'. Japan's attack on China was regarded as having 'temporarily retarded' the progress of China. Yet it stimulated the patriotism of her people and their readiness to submit to a central authority.

Since the first British traders arrived in China, trade and commerce was the reigning concern in both the official and non-official levels. Other motives and factors remained always marginal and in the background. In the 1930s and the 1940s, whenever the actual economic achievements were examined in light of expectations and the result was the predictable disappointment, there emerged an expressed hope for promising prospects in the future.[9] Indeed, so common was this practice that by late 1944 a Board of Trade memorandum claimed in anguish that the old sceptical saying that 'China is the greatest potential market in the world, and always has been' was perhaps more justified then than ever before.[10] Though difficult to calculate exactly, the volume of British pre-war exports to China including goods passing through Hong Kong seems not to have exceeded the 2 per cent mark of overall British exports.[11] A table quoting the leading countries' percentage shares of China's import trade in 1940 shows the United Kingdom as ranking third after Japan (22.81 per cent) and the United States (21.30 per cent), with only 3.99 percent.[12] A similar table relating to China's export trade shows the United Kingdom as ranking second after the United States (28.63 per cent) with only 9.96 per cent. The United Kingdom's imports into China fell progressively from 11.68 per cent in 1937 to the above mentioned level. The position with regard to exports from China to the United Kingdom was different. In 1940 it was higher by 0.38 per cent than in 1937. As far as trade in China was concerned, British ships carried almost 42 per cent of the total tonnage of foreign coastal and inland shipping.[13] In relative terms, investments were not very high. Could it again be expected, amid the turbulent war years, that the 'good old days' and the hope they carried would return?

A memorandum on China prepared in August 1942 at the Department of Overseas Trade of the Board of Trade with particular reference to reconstruction and development, manifested a great concern over the new national atmosphere likely to prevail in China after the war and its likely influence on British participation in China's national life.[14] 'Events and attitudes of the United Kingdom during the recent past, such as the temporary closing of the Burma Road and the policy of appeasement towards the Japanese with, at best, its negative harmful effect upon the Chinese', it was stressed, 'did much to impair that [friendly] feeling' between the two countries. British prestige in China was estimated to have sunk considerably owing to the recent military developments. It was recalled that already in 1940, after having made an extensive tour of China, Sir Stafford Cripps had felt that the prestige of Britain had fallen to a low ebb. He had likewise observed that 'if matters continue as at present, there will be nothing upon which Great Britain will be able to rely for getting any special position, or perhaps any position at all, in the reconstruction of China'. Indeed, in the time that lapsed between Cripps's observations and the comments made at the Department of Overseas Trade, Britain's position in China had further worsened. The Soviet Union and the United States were becoming preeminently the countries upon which the Chinese seemed to hope to rely in the future. This was likely to create a new situation for British interests in China at a time of her reconstruction and to threaten the existence of Britain's valuable export market.

Officials at the Department foresaw China's difficulties regarding transport, finance and credits. They appreciated that the participation by foreign countries in China's reconstruction would depend upon the degree to which each country would be ready to help China in respect of these difficulties. Analysing various economic aspects such as trade, industry, imports and exports, the Department's conclusion was quite clear. Both military and economic aid to China, generous in scale, was essential in order to restore 'good feeling' between the two nations. Assistance and participation in various economic undertakings in China should be made in a spirit of 'co-operation and not exploitation'. The new nationalistic and egalitarian feeling prevailing in China should be recognised and conformed with. Britain's tactics for regaining a position in China ought to be based on technological aid as well as trying to impress upon the Chinese Britain's desire to assist in promoting the future welfare and development of China.

Within the official realm, the Treasury played a different, if not an opposing, role. When the Chinese government found out that the greater part of the 1941 Arms Credit mentioned above and promised by Britain could not be used within the strict original limitations, they asked that the balance would be made available for post-war reconstruction. Theoretically this could have fallen within the lines advocated by the Department of Overseas Trade. The Treasury, however, refused the Chinese request without even consulting the Department or anyone else at the Board of Trade.[15] This, of course, could have resulted in turning China towards the United States whose loan to China was largely free from restrictions as regards the use of funds. Both the Secretary of the Department of Overseas Trade, H. Johnstone, and Sir Frederick Leith-Ross, Chief Economic Adviser to His Majesty's Government, strongly opposed this 'banker's treatment' of China by the Treasury. Nevertheless, both S. D. Waley of the Treasury and Sir Otto Niemeyer of the Bank of England adhered to the view that resources would be very limited after the war and were, therefore, to be used according to a strict security as to where they would be most profitable financially. They believed that China was not likely to be a rewarding region since she would encounter political disturbances, civil war and perhaps even a general break up. Sir Otto Niemeyer had good reason for being so sceptical. In September 1941 he had gone to China at the request of the British government and attempted to advise the Chinese government as to the proper measures against inflationary tendencies in time of war. In his report, submitted in December, he expressed his opinion that there was little chance of improvement during the war. Ministers and officials were incompetent to deal with problems of administrative reform. Internal forces were out of control and foreign help such as the export credits and stabilisation loans provided at the end of 1940, or the grants in 1941 under Lend–Lease, were stop gaps unrelated to a general scheme accompanied by proposals for reform.[16] In the course of 1942 Niemeyer's stand as regards aid to China was by far harder and more demanding than his colleagues' at the Treasury.[17]

The Board of Trade officials were far from accepting Waley's and Niemeyer's pessimistic observation, especially in view of the fact that the Americans had formed a different judgement and were acting towards China in a more liberal and helpful manner. The Treasury's defeatist view, it was held at the Board of Trade, ignored the fact that China was an ally and needed assistance. The Foreign Office's support of the Treasury's stand was likewise regarded as surprising. Was it not quite strongly advocating the surrender of extraterritorial privileges in order to forestall a further deterioration in Sino–British relations? Why, therefore, the supine acceptance of a line so potentially dangerous to these relations?[18] Was not what remained of the large British commercial investments in China in danger?[19] This departmental disagreement on the specific issue of the loan to China was finally resolved at the ministerial level two years later.[20]

Meanwhile discussions among the various official quarters on British interests in China and on plans to be made in light of these interests continued. The proceedings of a meeting held at the Foreign Office on 6 October 1942 and chaired by H. Johnstone, the Secretary of the Department of Overseas Trade, for example, reveal some of the more basic thoughts on the issue as existing at that early date.[21] At the opening of the meeting Johnstone stressed that 'whatever we did now to help China would undoubtedly have a lasting effect'. He pointed out that the meeting had been called to consider Britain's present economic policy towards China as well as the post-war policy. It was desirable, he thought, to consider what could be done to improve Britain's position in China.

In the course of the discussion, China's requirements were reviewed in light of Britain's capability to assist her. Likewise, the possibility of giving technical assistance to China was debated. Yet, generally speaking, the difficulties both on account of Britain's economic and strategic hardships and American activity in supplying and assisting China were stressed as obstacles in the way of more dominant British role. Nevertheless, it was agreed that the Foreign Office should again approach the Air Ministry to make approximately twenty-five civil aircraft available for a British-operated air-route between China and India. As for technical assistance there was general agreement that it could not usefully be afforded. As concrete steps to help China did not emerge in the course of the meeting the Chairman had to remind his colleagues that 'we ought not to wait for the end of the war before starting to make enquiries about the possible demand'. In his view it seemed an excellent idea if Britain could have, 'say, a five or 10 year programme for China', and it seemed to him not unreasonable to start immediately on the investigation of the Chinese demand and on the finance that would be required. While A. S. Gilbert of the Board of Trade accepted this view, Sir Otto Niemeyer of the Bank of England again maintained a different view. He felt that 'it would be fatal to our prestige to allow the Chinese to think now that we were going to be able to do a great deal for them at the end of the war'. Aware of Britain's prospective financial diffi-culties, he doubted Britain's ability to lend substantially. He there-fore warned against misleading the Chinese. In his view, if British trade in China was to survive, the most vital need was to get away from the 'Treaty Port regime', with the special privileges for foreigners, which Chinese nationalist feeling so strongly resented. He emphasised the importance of inducing Chinese to visit and study in the United Kingdom and to improve Britain's information service in China. Sir Frederick Leith-Ross, Chief Economic Adviser to His Majesty's Government, on his part felt that if Britain was to obtain a share in the Chinese market after the war, credits were essential. It seemed to him to be a question of whether Britain was prepared to take risks. He referred to the need for credits for railway development and to the importance of the railway's demand for stores and equipment which in the past had been supplied by the United Kingdom. He insisted that, unless the railway system was rebuilt, there would be serious loss to Britain's export trade. 'If we did not provide the necessary loans', he went on, 'the USA would, and so secure the railways' trade.' Ashley Clarke of the Foreign Office maintained that, as an agricultural country, China might well recover rapidly; Sir Otto Niemeyer remained sceptical. He doubted Chinese ability to pay for her needs after the war in view of the great rise in internal prices and the difficulty she would have in making the necessary adjustments. Moreover, it seemed to him that it would take some time before China again began to receive remittances from Chinese emigrants. These had previously represented a valuable item in her balance of payments. S. D. Waley of the Treasury felt that it would be very difficult to revise the terms of Britain's £50 million loan to China and make it available for post-war reconstruction. The objections to undertaking any post-war commitments at that early stage seemed to him very great. It was, likewise, quite impossible to forecast how far Britain would be able to give long-term credits in the future. Against this expressed scepticism, Gilbert of the Board of Trade again voiced his concern about the position in which the United Kingdom would find itself at the end of the war if nothing was done beforehand. He felt that it would then be too late to save more than a fraction of British trade against American competition.

At this early stage, when significant deliberations on the question of Britain's return to China in a capacity similar to the one she had held in the pre-war period took place, clear shades of opinion on the issue were discernible. Both Sir Otto Niemeyer and S. D. Waley, representing the financial consideration, were sceptical about post-war Sino–British economic ties and consequently of Britain's likelihood of re-establishing her former role in China. This view was contrasted by the representatives of the Board of Trade, A. S. Gilbert, and H. Johnstone. About a month after the above mentioned meeting, on 16 November 1942, Keynes in the Treasury had a chance of expressing his views on the question.[22] 'How, in the event of our sending exports to China on a large scale', he asked, 'are we to get paid for them'? One, he argued, had to act on the assumption that for some little time to come Britain would have no significant amount of overseas credits available for anything but the shortest term credits. Yet it seemed possible that, due to American assistance or a pool of foreign exchange available to China, China would be able to pay for her imports. He advised Lord McGowan of Imperial Chemical Industries Limited (ICI) to proceed with his plans for large-scale exports to China on the hypothesis that China would have from one source or another sufficient foreign currency to pay for it.

Indeed, within a year of the outbreak of the Pacific War, serious deliberations were made in official quarters on the question of the re-establishment of Britain's position in China. While a spectrum of diversified opinions was expressed on the matter, it cannot be denied that the issue preoccupied the decision-makers in London as well as the Old China Hands, who were greatly troubled at the prospect that the government would not give the British commercial firms active in the China market the traditional backing they had been so used to receiving.

Allied military activities both in the China and the South East Asia theatres were of great economic and political importance. And contemporaries were well aware of this fact. By May 1942, with the British withdrawal from Burma into India, the Japanese had achieved 'the planned limit of their expansion' in South East Asia.[23] They now changed over to the defensive and sought to consolidate their military achievements. Politically they embarked on a course to win the colonised people away from their former European masters.

Naturally, the British, the Americans, the French and the Dutch, immediately upon their defeat in Asia, started to plan their come-back and the restitution of their lost colonies. These feelings were strong and understandable in view of the abrupt Japanese seizure of power and the deep humiliation suffered. Indeed, MacArthur's words upon leaving the Philippines, 'I shall come back', echoed throughout the period in Asia.

It is important to pause here and to give a thought to the basic terms used by both contemporaries and historians on the question of re-establishing the 'legitimate regimes' in South East Asia, or the 'liberation' of the Asians from the Japanese. These terms seem to have completely confused the main issue. Firstly, there exists the primary questions: Can colonial regimes be regarded as legitimate? How had legitimacy been acquired, and how could it all be dropped? It seems that once the colonial governments withdrew in face of external force, their legitimacy evaporated with them. After all, was not the *raison d'être* of the Western regimes over the colonialised territories and their inhabitants the original Western success in conquering these territories? Was it not the mere ability to hold, defend and govern the countries and their inhabitants that mattered the most? Once all these basic factors disappeared, and the Europeans had been inherited force-fully by another power, was it indeed appropriate to regard the old colonial power, now in exile, as legitimate? Indeed, was not the term 'colonial-government-in-exile' a contradiction in terms? Historical analogies may make the issue even more perplexing. Would it have made any sense had the Spanish established a colonial Philippines government-in-exile after 1898? Similarly, a second thought should be given to the term 'liberation' used in this context. Can it at all be asserted that the British, for example, were striving to liberate Burma, where a strong indigenous national movement supported the Japanese (for a while, at least) as saviours, and regarded them as their main hope in their national struggle for independence?

Upon being wiped out from almost all of the territory of Burma, the British made plans for a come-back. They hoped that by the

next dry season in November 1942 these plans would materialise.
None of these plans, however, proved feasible mainly because of
logistic difficulties. The only operation attempted, the very limited
Arakan offensive, resulted in a disastrous failure and had to be
postponed.[24] The crucial areas logistically for launching a campaign to regain Burma were Assam and Bengal in India. These
regions, however, had never been regarded or planned as military
base area. Airfields, depots, roads, railways and pipelines – all had
to be built, ports enlarged and the whole area reorganised for any
serious operation to be carried out.[25]

Another problem was the need to fully co-operate with the
Chinese, whose troops withdrew from Burma in face of the
rapidly advancing Japanese to both Assam in India and the border
province of Yunnan in China. Campaigns in Burma, as already
stressed, in addition to being significant for their wide political
repercussions, their relation to the question of colonial return
and the obvious relevance to the victory over Japan, featured as
crucial in moulding Sino–British relations.

The Chinese plan of October 1942 was for a converging
advance on occupied Burma by fifteen Chinese divisions from
Yunnan and three from Assam, together with some ten British or
Indian divisions. The role of the latter, as Liddell Hart pointed out,
was not only to invade northern Burma but to launch a seaborne
attack on Rangoon. Wavell, who had reorganised the Indian
Command (in February 1942 he had resigned as Supreme Commander ABDA Command and returned to India), agreed to the
Chinese plan in principle. He was dubious, however, whether
essential air forces to dominate the sky over Burma and a fleet to
control the Indian Ocean and cover the Rangoon attack were at
all obtainable in view of what the Allies considered as more
urgent assignments elsewhere. Indeed, as a Chinese retrospective
version put it, 'The Asiatic front was the step-child of Allied
policy.'[26] Chiang Kai-shek regarded the Allies' hesitation as quib-
bles and as signs that the British were not going to make a serious
effort. He consequently abandoned his part in the operation at the
end of 1942.[27] This was one more incident in a series of Sino–
British clashes over military affairs, clashes that were to have their
weighty effect on Britain's post-war position in China.

Wavell, on his part, decided – as mentioned above – to carry out
a limited offensive to recover the Arkam coastal region. The 14th
Indian Division started to advance in December 1942 but moved

so slowly that the commander of the Japanese 15th Army, General Iida, was able to send reinforcements there and halt the British advance by the end of January 1943. By May, when the monsoon season was due, it was clear that the British forces – the 14th Indian Division having been replaced by the 26th Division – would be in no position to launch their offensive again for quite some time. They were back on the line they had held the previous autumn.

In the northern end of Burma the situation was a little more encouraging for the British. There, Orde Wingate had organised the 'Long Range Penetration Group', trained to operate in the Burmese jungle and strike at the Japanese communications as well as against the Japanese outposts. On 14 February 1943 Wingate's troops –the Chindits – crossed the Chindwin River, moved eastward and attacked Japanese outposts, cut railway lines, blew up bridges and created ambushes on the road. In mid-March Wingate's columns crossed the Irrawaddy, a hundred miles east of the Chindwin. Although within a month the military thrust was over, and the Chindits were back in India after severe losses, the constant threat to Japanese positions in northern Burma remained an important factor in that front for quite some time.

The next dry season of 1943–44 was intended to be, according to the Casablanca Conference of January 1943, a seaborne assault on Rangoon – 'Operation Anakim' – following British and Chinese offensives in the north of Burma and the capture of key points on the coast. As Liddell Hart observed, those aims meant that air superiority had to be gained, and a strong naval force assembled. Likewise, other logistical and administrative problems directly related to such a complex operation had to be solved. Since by the spring of 1943 it was realised by Wavell, Churchill and the Chiefs of Staff that the requirement for 'Operation Anakim' could not be met, a new idea to replace the former soon emerged, a move against Sumatra code-named 'Culverin'. Within a short while, however, this too was abandoned for the same reason as 'Operation Anakim', and also due to American insistence that the land routes to supply China would speedily be reopened.[28]

Stilwell's appointment as commanding general of the United States forces in the China theatre of operations in Burma and China was to some extent an insult to the Chinese. It assumed, as Stilwell's political adviser in China, John P. Davies insisted, that 'in

spite of the unbroken series of American disasters from Pearl
Harbor and the Philippines to the Java sea, an American ex-
military attaché knew better how to fight the Japanese than any
general in the Chinese army'.[29] Chiang Kai-shek was frustrated,
since he was playing the last violin in the Allied orchestra. His
clash with Wavell over the question of operations in Burma was a
mere prelude to his clash with the American administration and
particularly with Stilwell. No direct voice was given to him regarding the allotment of material as it became available. The British
and the Americans began to repossess the accumulation of Lend–
Lease supplies which had been assigned to China but could not be
sent there because of the loss of Rangoon.[30] Though he received a
great deal of sympathy from Roosevelt and saw eye to eye with
Chennault, he felt Stilwell's and Marshall's opposition strongly.
While Chennault believed that by air-power it would be possible
to break the Japanese resistance, the latter two generals leaned
much more towards ground-campaigns, to which Chiang Kai-shek
objected.

But if initially the main rivalry seemed to be between the
Chinese on the one hand, and the British and the Americans on
the other, and if later the 'air *vs* ground' controversy was the most
predominant, by the third Washington Conference (Trident) of
May 1943, the Anglo–American controversy became most
dominant. Churchill, differing from the Americans on campaigns
in Burma, insisted that they tended to over-estimate the Chinese
power. For him, as an unsympathetic observer stressed, 'war was
an art. It was making do with scant resources, manoeuvre, wile,
using others, and biding his time.[31] Aware of the political advantages to be gained by certain peripheral operations, (that is, in
colonial South East Asia) Churchill did not mind bypassing Burma.
This, he believed, was going to fall into British hands in the case of
Allied victory anyway. He much rather preferred British forces to
rush to Sumatra or to any other military objectives that were
closer to Singapore. After all, it was there more than in other
places in the east that British lost honour could be found. Like
MacArthur in the case of the American Philippines, Churchill was
obsessed with the idea of returning as quickly as possible to the
colonies that had so cruelly been seized from British hands. He
was not after all planning to preside over the dissolution of the
British Empire. On the contrary he was full of ambition to do his
utmost to retain and strengthen it. It was only through war and

courage that Britain could regain her lost prestige. The impression of the humiliation inflicted upon the white man in general and the British in particular could be weakened only by a victory that would overshadow the disaster of 15 February 1942. American and Chinese involvement in Burma as well as in other South East Asian territories, for decades under British suzerainty, could only damage Britain's prospects for post-war position there. Years later, writing about the question of military operations in Burma, Churchill observed that he intensely disliked the prospect of a large-scale campaign in northern Burma. 'One could not choose a worse place for fighting the Japanese', he stressed. Building a road from Ledo to China, he strongly maintained, was an immense task unlikely to be finished until the need for it had passed. Even if it were done in time to replenish the Chinese armies while they were still engaged, it would make little difference to their fighting capacity. As for the need to strengthen American air-bases in China, Churchill felt that this would diminish as Allied advances in the Pacific and from Australia gained the airfields of the anti-Japanese forces closer to Japan.[32] For the British, Churchill believed, the south of Burma with its port of Rangoon was far more valuable than the north. 'I wished. . .', he stressed,

> to contain the Japanese in Burma, and break into or through the great arc of islands forming the outer fringe of the Dutch East Indies. Our whole British Indian Imperial front would thus advance across the Bay of Bengal into close contact with the enemy, by using amphibious power at every stage.[33]

Indeed, there was a divergence of opinion here between the British and the Americans.

The Americans, whether supplying air-or ground-operations, regarded the British as somehow indecent in their calculations and hesitations. While they were fighting a war and shedding blood, the British were spending time in circuitous routes with thoughts of saving casualties or gaining some political advantage from the military manoeuvres. In a memorandum dated 17 September 1943 Davies dwelt on what he appreciated to be a British policy directed at conservation of manpower, repossession, and possible expansion of empire, 'preventing China from developing into a major power'.[34] He thus recommended to his government to avoid involving itself in the reconquest of British, Dutch and French colonies.

A month later he reported a conversation he had had with two British propaganda officials, Mr John Galvin, the British Political Warfare Executive Head at New Delhi, and Mr Stanley Smith, the head of the British Ministry of Information Office at Chungking. In the course of that conversation he stressed some of his feelings towards the British in Asia. When American troops fought their way into Burma and Malaya and marched out again and those areas reverted to British colonial status, he claimed 'we are going to be exposed to the risk of public demands in the United States as to why our boys had to die to repossess British colonies for Great Britain'.[35] Discussing some Asiatic issues in the post-war era he remarked that these pointed up how deeply his country was embroiled in 'power politics' because of her commitment to recreate Britain as a first-class power. 'But', he added,

> Britain can be a first-class power only as it has its empire to exploit. Imperial rule and interests means [sic] association with other peoples on a basis of subjugation, exploitation, privilege and force. It means a constant struggle between the urge to revolt and the compulsion to suppress. It means a turning by the colonial peoples to any nation or group of nations which can promise them a change, nations to whom the colonial peoples would not turn were it not for their servitude.

He further complained that the United States had chosen to bring

> a third-class island kingdom back to its anachronistic position as a first class empire. We are rejecting the opportunity to move boldly forward with historical tide. We were helpless to make any other decision. The naivete of the American public regarding international affairs, their attachment to a static conception of the American way of life and the neo-imperialistic conditions of many of our businessmen meant that we had no other choice.

In a note of warning, he concluded:

> Having now made our choice, we must recognise that while we have purchased security and, possibly, world stability for a generation or more, we have probably also committed our-

selves to a tremendous future war between revolution and counter-revolution, the lines of which are now being drawn.[36]

George R. Merrell, Secretary-in-Charge in the Office of the Personal Representative of the President of the United States in New Delhi, added that there was almost complete unanimity among British officials in New Delhi that post-war Anglo–American collaboration was essential, yet they viewed British fighting in Asia as having 'the primary purpose of re-establishing and extending British imperialist interests'.[37] Distrust of the Chinese and fear of a strong and united post-war China were, he stressed, characteristic of British officialdom in India. Merrell pointed out that the Mission considered Davies's appraisement of the consequences that may be expected to flow from American apparent policy of supporting British aims in Asia to be sound.

It matters little whether this is our actual policy or whether by our silence we allow that conclusion to be drawn by Asiatics. The result is the same, namely, a growing conviction among the people of this part of the world that American policy is at one with the British in desiring the restoration and extension of 'Whiteocracy' in Asia. The long-range consequence of such a conviction will, it would seem, be an alignment of the coloured races against the whites as their only hope of freedom and progress.[38]

By the autumn of 1943 the essential role of China in the defeat of Japan had been questioned. The initial American naval success in the Pacific on the one hand, and the deadlock in opening up the routes to China on the other, brought about serious contemplations about an approach to Japan from the Pacific rather than from China. The initial grand strategy of defeating Japan, based on China's role as the anvil upon which the hammers of American power in the Pacific would smash the Japanese armies, was consequently abandoned. The creation of the South East Asia Command under Lord Louis Mountbatten, decided upon at the Quebec Conference of July 1943, was to a great extent done after the crucial hours in Burma were over.

Under these circumstances Anglo–American rivalry in the Far East grew fiercer. American officials both in Washington and China went on suspecting Britain's imperialist intentions and

objected to the 'political' war she fought at a time when the United
States was doing 'a soldier's job' with no ulterior motives. As both
Christopher Thorne and Roger Louis have shown, the issues were
complex and the arguments far from clearly cut. The British and
the Europeans could not understand; 'Why should the question of
dependent peoples be restricted to the European overseas
empires? Why should trusteeship not apply to the Indian tribes of
North America? Or for that matter to the dependent peoples
within Russia.'[39] The strained coalition was the objective result of
new circumstances that neither party could control. 'On the part
of Britain . . . there was the need to readjust to a status which by
the end of 1944 was a decidely junior one, and to a degree of
dependence on the USA'.[40] For the United States there was the
'question of how to balance her desire to make her strength tell,
against the importance of maintaining a satisfactory level of inter-
Allied trust and co-operation'.[41]

From a British point of view, the United States was a potential
threat to the empire, formal and informal. She could destroy in no
time any hope of restoring a position in those Asian lands from
which British authority had been expelled. Roosevelt's anti-
colonial sentiments were a source of anxiety and discomfort. After
all, the future of the British colonies, such as Hong Kong, and the
future of Britain's position in China, depended on the American
war effort against Japan. Would the United States try to extinguish
British traditional influence in the Far East in order to expand her
own?

Over and above the theoretical anti-colonial aspects which
preoccupied Roosevelt and so many Americans there existed,
until the abandonment of the idea by the autumn of 1943, the
pragmatic consideration related directly to the war. China had
formed a serious occupational and maintenance commitment for
Japan. By August 1943 this amounted to approximately twenty
per cent of the Japanese ground forces. As China's strength
increased, the Combined Staff planners hoped she might well
contain more Japanese troops. It was well appreciated that even if
a proportion of the Japanese forces contained by China would be
released, and became available for operations against American
forces, American problems in other theatres would be much more
difficult.[42] Moreover, military bases, particularly air bases from
which to attack Japan and her communications, seemed most
essential. The co-operation of the Chinese army and population,

too, was regarded as very important. Abandoning China, there-fore, was out of the question.

The American view on the spot, based on this assessment, was well expressed by Davies. In December 1943, repeating his feeling of three months earlier, he claimed in a memorandum entitled *The China and South East Asia Theatres: Some Political Considerations,* that 'in so far as we participate in SEAC operations, we become involved in politically explosive colonial problems of the British, Dutch, and possibly French. In so doing, we compromise ourselves not only with the colonial peoples of Asia, but also the free people of Asia, *including the Chinese*'.[43] He went on to explain that domesti-cally the American government lay itself open to public criticism ('why should American boys die to recreate the colonial empires of the British and their Dutch and French satellites?'). He likewise predicted that more Anglo–American misunderstanding and friction were likely to arise out of American participation in SEAC than out of any other theatre. He believed that in co-operation with SEAC the United States needed to retake North Burma immediately and so reopen a land route to China. 'But', he added,

> after the recapture of North Burma there comes a parting of the ways. The British will wish to throw their main weight southward for the repossession of colonial empire. Our main interest in Asia will lie to the East, from whence we can strike directly and in co-ordination with other American offensives at the centre of Japan's new Empire.[44]

In view of these prevailing feelings it is not at all surprising that there emerged the suggestion to end the traditional paternal, or even patronising, attitude towards China. The term 'Open Door' which had dominated American policies towards China since the turn of the century had to be dropped as the war approached its end. For decades it had been attractive to the United States as an aid to American business, and to the Chinese as a means of preventing or forestalling her reduction to colonial status.[45] It implied political and perhaps military support of China against further imperialist encroachments. Yet, now that the idea of treat-ing China as a great power had emerged, it was time to remove certain discriminations with respect to her, and to do away with the term 'Open Door' which, despite everything, always connoted 'a loose sort of dependent status for China with respect to the United States'.[46] 'Let us use', wrote Coppock of the Office of International Trade Policy 'words (a) which do not demean the Chinese, (b) which do not put us in the position of paternalists, and (c) which do not play into the hands of nations having different ideas as to China's future.' It was greatly hoped that by this way much could be done to convince the Pacific and Asiatic people that

> American power in the Pacific does not mean simply another imperialism to rival the British, Japanese or Russian. They should see us as liberators, not as another wave of enslavers. If we need or desire these peoples as allies, it is the liberation, not the imperialist, approach that will win them.[47]

American involvement in the war and her enormous financial and military commitments brought up the idea, expressed among others by Senator Connally, chairman of the Senate Foreign Relations Committee, that the American government had 'not only the right but the duty' to insist that the British government would make such concessions to the Indian people as would bring about an 'immediate and satisfactory solution to the Indian situation'.[48] It was felt that otherwise the Americans would be responsible for the needless sacrifice of hundreds of thousands of American soldiers and incalculable wealth in trying to save a part of the British Empire in which Americans as a whole had not the slightest interest. Senator George agreed with Senator Connally and stated that he was 'profoundly troubled' over the disposition of the Department of State to follow the British lead in the Indian crisis rather than to assert America's unquestioned right to assume the leadership herself. These views were accepted by other members of the Committee and were passed to the Secretary of State.[49]

In short, from Washington it seemed that the British failure in Burma and Britain's general order of priorities had a 'catastrophic' effect on China and the Chinese. In view of the loss of Burma and particularly Lashio (that is, the loss of the land routes to China) the British no longer intended to fight.[50] Wallace Murray, Adviser on Political Relations in the State Department, brought to Cordell Hull, the Secretary of State, and to Sumner Welles, his Under-Secretary, the opinion of Colonel Johnson and Colonel Harrington that in the campaign over Burma 'the British made no serious attempt to save Burma', that 'the British had determined long before the Japanese attack on Burma started, to lose Burma to the Japanese rather than to make concessions to the Burmese or to be indebted to the Chinese for retaining it'.[51] It was likewise alleged that the Chinese were allowed by the British to send in troops only when their offer of assistance could no longer be refused. Once the Chinese arrived, no effort to support them was forthcoming. The British preferred to lose Burma because of their belief that it would be either recaptured for them by the Americans, or returned to them at the peace conference once the war was won. They would then be committed to neither the Burmese nor the Chinese with regard to its future form of government.

MAP 5　*The US counter-offensive in the Pacific*

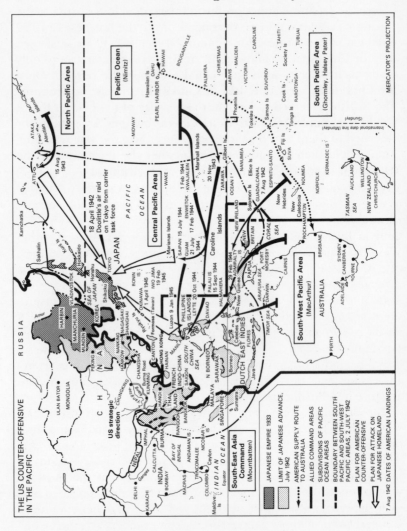

Source: P. Young, *Atlas of The Second World War* (New York, 1977).

3 The War and the Changing Chinese Views

The Japanese tide of conquest in South East Asia in the first half of 1942 was followed by an ebb in the Pacific later on. Having failed to extend their control to the American and British bases in the Hawaiian Islands and Australia, they were now on the defensive. Only in Burma did they pursue offensive operations against the Western Allies with the hope of frustrating a British counter-offensive from India. Indeed, it was here that the season's campaign ran a very different course from the Allies' expectations. It formed, as Liddell Hart observed, 'a depressing contrast to the now rapid Allied advance in the Pacific, especially the central Pacific'.[1] The main feature of the war in Burma was another Japanese offensive – the only one in the war that saw the Japanese cross the Indian frontier. This operation, though eventually un-successful, had the strategic effect of postponing the British advance into Burma until 1945.

The British on their part had been planning an offensive that would clear the Japanese invaders out of northern Burma and open the road to China. In preparation for the campaign the Allies had agreed among themselves that the reoccupation of northern Burma would be the primary objective as the shortest way to renew direct touch with China and resume supplies to her over the Burma Road.[2] The main part of the army strength under General Gifford, Mountbatten's Army commander, was the newly formed Fourteenth Army of which General Slim was given com-mand. It was this large increase of Allied strength that spurred the Japanese to embark on 'a fresh and preventive offensive' into Southern Assam in India.[3] Wingate's first Chindit raid had con-vinced the Japanese that the Chindwin River was not a secure defensive shield. If they could foil an Allied offensive in the dry season of 1944 by occupying the Imphal plain and by controlling

51

the mountain passes from Assam, they could postpone the Allied offensive and prevent the enemy forces from threatening the Japanese gains achieved in Burma. As it happened, however, the defence of Imphal and Kohima, both thirty miles inside India, caused the Japanese to exhaust their strength.

The repulse of the Japanese offensive in the spring of 1944 was a severe setback for Japan. It was not, however, crushing enough to break their very hold on Burma. As Liddell Hart put it, everything now depended on whether the British success could be followed up effectively.[4] The task that Mountbatten was set by the combined Chiefs of Staff directive of 3 June 1944 was to broaden the air-link to China and exploit the development of a land-route. Now the conquest of Burma was expected. The two main plans considered were 'Capital', an overland thrust to recapture north-central Burma, and 'Dracula', an amphibious operation to take southern Burma, which depended on outside supplies. In these circumstances General Slim and the Americans preferred the overland plan. Notwithstanding the improvement of land communications and inland water transport, the dependence of Slim's Fourteenth Army on air supply remained. That in turn depended on adequate aid from American cargo aircraft.

The second half of 1944, therefore, became primarily devoted to such developments, and to reorganisation in commands. In mid-October, when the monsoon rains ceased and the ground dried, Slim began the advance on the central front. The Japanese High Command on their part, facing the greater and near-approaching menace of the American seaborne advance to the Philippines, and being exhausted by their own protracted Imphal offensive, could spare no reinforcements for the Burma Area Army.

While the British Offensive in the central front was developing, operations in the two subsidiary areas of Arakan and northern Burma reached a successful conclusion. In the latter front Stilwell's forces, mostly Chinese, had made little progress during the spring in their effort to advance through Myitkyina against the northern flank of the Burma Road. In December, however, Stilwell had already been replaced by Wedemeyer and General Sultan, another fresh American Commander, took over the Northern Combat Area Command. The Japanese forces were forced to retreat south-westward, toward Mandalay. By mid-January 1945 this west-central stretch of the Burma Road was clear of the Japanese. By April the whole of it from Mandalay to China was again open.

From that moment onwards, the Japanese found themselves in a perilous situation in various places in Northern Burma. From 20 March, when Mandalay had been recaptured, the Japanese forces started to retreat southward. Central Burma was now in British hands and the way to Rangoon was open. The Japanese lost a third of their already depleted strength. They likewise lost a crucial amount of equipment as they had to retreat eastward by a long and circuitous route. On 1 May 1945, after an impressive advance of the British ground forces southward towards Rangoon, 'Operation Dracula' was launched – with a parachute landing at the mouth of the Rangoon River and amphibious landings on both banks. By 6 May the British reconquest of Burma was virtually complete.[5] Now there were still some 60 000 Japanese in General Slim's wake, west of the Salween river. It was important to prevent them escaping eastward into Thailand as well as to stop them causing fresh trouble in the area that had been overrun in Slim's drive to Rangoon.[6] Thus a force was sent back to hold the crossing of the Sittang and another one was despatched to meet the troops that were pushing down the Irrawaddy. During May, attempts by the remains of the Japanese 28th Army from Arakan to cross the Irrawaddy eastwards were almost totally frustrated.

The organisation of the war was becoming increasingly relevant to Sino–British relations. The Chinese, sensitive to British plans and moves, were often critical of the way British forces conducted the struggle against Japan. At times they were even suspicious, as were some prominent Americans involved in Asian affairs, as to whether there was behind the British manoeuvres a genuine intention to see Japan surrender, or whether the mere re-establishment of British influence and authority in the region was sought. These doubts were by no means unrelated to ideas on post-war political and economic relations between the two countries. Signs of weakness on Britain's part, friction with British generals and a corresponding esteem from the Americans could mean increasing chances of success for the latter in post-war China at the expense of Britain. Daily contacts on military matters that the British and Chinese maintained served an important channel through which ideas, opinions, evaluations, images, and concepts flowed from one end to the other. They were thus created and moulded. SEAC, therefore, apart from serving an obvious military function, played an important role in the wider context of Sino–British relations.

As already noted, the idea of appointing an overall or supreme commander for South East Asia by Britain, independent of the government of India and its chief commander, emerged a year after the collapse of the Empire in the East. Both Amery and Churchill were the chief advocates of such a step and it was the first who suggested Lord Louis Mountbatten for the job.[7] The combined Chiefs of Staff were to exercise a general jurisdiction over strategy in South East Asia and to be responsible for allocating resources between that theatre and China. The British Chiefs of Staff, for their part, were to oversee 'all matters pertaining to operations' and to be responsible for communications between the Combined Chiefs and the Supreme Commander. This complex structure was, not surprisingly perhaps, a source of friction between the representatives of the two Anglo–Saxon powers. Joseph Stilwell, Mountbatten's American Deputy Supreme Commander, was also answerable, as noted above, to Chiang Kai-shek whose chief of staff he was at the time. He was also the direct commander of five Chinese divisions operating in Burma and the commander of all the American forces of the China–Burma–India theatre. Thus, the 'insuperable obstacle', as he was regarded by the British at the South East Command,[8] provided a link between that Command and the China Command as well as between these two and the Americans.

Indo-China was excluded from the boundaries of the new command. It remained in the China Theatre. Thus, here, as in Burma, operational issues necessitated Sino–British co-operation, and friction between the two partners emerged.[9]

Twice in early 1942 Generalissimo Chiang Kai-shek and his influential wife made trips to Burma. On both occasions they miraculously escaped unhurt from Japanese air raids. On their second visit, when at Maymyo, the summer capital of Burma, for conferences, Japanese bombers arrived without warning. The city was without air-raid shelters or dugouts and the Generalissimo and his wife were forced to stand in the open while the Japanese fliers emptied their bomb loads. One bomb landed only fifty yards from them. It turned out to be a dud.[10] According to a British embassy report the couple saw with their own eyes burning Mandalay as British soldiers were escaping from it. This vision of the fall of the British bastion remainded for a long time alive with them.[11] From Burma, Chiang added a friend's insult to an enemy's injury by cabling Roosevelt that never in his life had he seen such unpreparedness and degradation.[12] It was from this low ebb of British prestige that fierce criticism against British war efforts emerged in China.

Thus, the report of the 1942 Parliamentary mission to China, mentioned previously, stressed that anti-British feelings in the area of Chengtu, for example, were heightened by the stationing there of RAF personnel after the British defeat in Burma.[13] British residents in general, and the RAF in particular, were treated with a good deal of hostility by the local population. A certain change to the better and to more respect for British arms was noticed after the British victories in North Africa. Chinese optimism grew also after the naval battles in the Solomons and the Russian advance north of Stalingrad. But these mild fluctuations could not alter the basic atmosphere of the strongly critical Chinese view of the British. As late as March 1944 the British Consulate-General in Kewilin reported that the local press grew more critical of the British forces' failure to launch a major offensive in Burma.[14] The Allied forces on the India–Burma frontier under Mountbatten were accused of not having fulfilled their duties of tying down the enemy in that part of the world. Suspicions and ill-feelings towards British motives grew stronger, especially as comparisons between Britain's war efforts and the Americans' were made. The launching of the American offensives in both the Central and South-Western Pacific were regarded as an example that the British had had at hand yet failed to follow. A similar report on Chinese resentment toward the British was sent to Washington by the American Consul-General at Kunming. Summarising a few editorials from the Chinese press of October 1944, the Consul-General observed that the Chinese were bitter at having received only 2 per cent of American Lend–Lease supplies while Britain and the Soviet Union were receiving 70 and 28 per cent respectively.[15] Admiral Mountbatten, observed one local paper, had been 'behind the screen for more than a year but has not yet made an appearance'. Concern was also expressed over the Allied failure to carry out a landing on the China coast.[16]

It was also from this negative point of departure towards Britain that the Chinese under the leadership of Chiang Kai-shek and his Koumintang were to reassert themselves immediately following the Japanese surrender. The demand, as the Generalissimo put it later, for 'national independence' arose from the very feeling that the powers in general, and Britain in particular, were basically unreliable. Coupled with this demand came more specific desiderata for a genuine territorial integrity, for political freedom for Manchuria and for the return to China of Taiwan and the Pescadores.[17]

As the war progressed mutual accusations grew fiercer. The Chinese were disposed to disregard the part played by British–Indian forces in the operations of 1944–5 which led to the opening of the Burma Road. At home they continued with their practice of not co-operating with British troops sent to China.[18] Chiang Kai-shek, thinking now very little of British fighting capacity and unwilling to accept the argument that war in Europe and Africa must have priority over the war in Asia, expected Britain merely to open up and guard the lines of communication in Burma through which the Americans could pour supplies into China.[19] The British on their part, though appreciative of the difficulties China encountered regarding military equipment, vehicles, aircraft, fuel, artillery and various non-military supplies, not to mention the financial problems caused by maintaining a large inefficient army, were critical of the way the Chinese operated.[20] Sir Horace Seymour, the British Ambassador to China, fiercely attacked what he read as Chinese reluctance to fight the Japanese in Burma except in so far as they could hope to restore communications to China.[21] Mountbatten, appreciating that Chinese goodwill must be gained, recommended, however, impressing upon the Chinese that the British government was very conscious of the contribution they had made to operations in Burma.[22] Notwithstanding this, however, within a few months, when the Chinese expressed their desire to withdraw from their commitments in Burma and return to China, the Supreme Commander had to warn them of the consequences of their action. He emphasised that General Sultan, the Commander of the newly formed India Burma Theatre, would not be in a position to guarantee the security of the Burma Road and the maintenance of supplies by the land route.[23]

The Chinese political influence in Burma and South East Asia, strengthened during the course of the military operations, was strongly objected to by the British during the war and immediately after the Allied victory. Mountbatten, as the Supreme Allied

Commander, maintained, for example, that the China Overseas Association ('based somewhat on the pre-1939 German model') which took a proprietary interest in Chinese communities, could work and be active only if confined to the welfare and prosperity of the Chinese communities. Political motives and activities during the military administration of Burma were decidedly objection-able. The Chinese government's desire to reopen its consulates in Burma, which were shut during the Japanese occupation, similarly aroused suspicions. British military administration adhered to the policy that it looked after all the residents of Burma irrespective of nationality. Chinese residents who remained in Burma were therefore protected and no outside body was to intervene in their defence.[24]

Another important issue standing between China and Britain was Chiang Kai-shek's involvement in the India question.[25] In late January 1942 the Generalissimo took the initiative of suggesting that he would pay short unofficial visits to Burma and India. In Burma he wanted to discuss with the Governor and the Commander-in-Chief the military situation, in India he planned to get in touch with the Viceroy and to see Gandhi and Nehru in order to impress on them the need to co-operate fully in the common cause and to support the war effort. After some delibera-tions, Foreign Office officials decided in principle to welcome the visit subject to the approval of the government of India. There remained, however, the question of Chiang's meeting with 'private individuals' such as Gandhi and Nehru. A day before Chiang left Chungking, on 3 February 1942, Churchill sent him a personal message that a visit to the two, except by arrangement with the Viceroy, would make a bad impression in Britain and throughout the Empire. Obviously he was anxious to avoid the possibility of anything that might appear to be an intervention on the part of the Chinese leader in matters affecting the relations between the government of India on the one hand, and Gandhi and Nehru on the other. Churchill was greatly worried by Chiang Kai-shek's visit to New Delhi. He foresaw what he called a 'pan-Asian malaise' spreading 'through all the bazaars of India',[26] and watched carefully the diplomatic deliberations concerning the tour. The fact that Chiang was building up a picture in India of Chinese vigour and efficiency compared with British defeats and incompetence infuriated him. Through the Secretary of State for India he instructed the Viceroy that Chiang Kai-shek had no right to intervene between the 'Government of the King–Emperor and any of the King's subjects'. 'It would be disastrous', he added, 'if you put yourself in a position where we had Gandhi and Nehru on the one side and the Viceroy of India on the other, with Chiang Kai-shek arbitrating between the two.[27] Attlee, too, commented on the subject. Noticing the connection between Chinese and Indian realties, he observed that Britain's accepting Chinese aid in her war against the Axis powers and her drive 'to a belated recognition of China as an equal and of Chinese as fellow fighters for civilisation against barbarism, made the Indian ask why he too cannot be master in his own home'.[28] Foreign Office officials, on the other hand, regarding Chiang's intention to use his personal influence and call for support of the war effort in India as desirable, considered the Prime Minister's attitude towards the visit inexpedient. After all, events in the Far East (especially the fall of Singapore) were at a critical stage. Was not Chiang Kai-shek the only man who could keep China in the war if the Japanese occupied Burma? It therefore seemed much better to accept the disadvantage of a visit to Gandhi than to cause offence by refusing to allow it. Eventually the two leaders met at Calcutta on the Generalissimo's way back home.

Departing from his Indian hosts, Chiang called upon Britain to give India her 'real political power' with all due speed.[29] Immediately upon returning to Chungking, on 24 February, he urged Roosevelt to join him in his campaign against Britain's India policy. He stressed that he had been shocked by the military and political situation prevailing in India. Roosevelt, taking up the issue, contacted the British government and subsequently received a message from Churchill. The latter updated the President on the discussions then being conducted in London and in New Delhi preparing the Cripps mission. He likewise explained the wide background to the Indian situation and the difficulties Britain face there. He dwelt particularly on the complexities emerging out of the Hindu–Moslem rivalry, the great proportion of Moslems in the India Forces, and the fact that the Indian congress enjoined only a fractional support of the total Indian population. Taking any step that would alienate the Moslems was therefore out of the question.

There is no need to dwell here on the explanations given by the British government on the Indian situation nor its projected plans, such as a declaration of Dominion status for India after the war.

As far as Sino–British relations were concerned, the cardinal point remained Chiang Kai-shek's developing pan-Asiatic and pro-Indian stands and his conviction that the responsibility for a settlement not having been reached in India lay entirely with the British. Chiang refused to appreciate the seriousness of the Hindu–Moslem problem. He stuck to the notion that the Congress represented the desires of the Indian people and was in essence comparable to China's Kuomintang. The arrest of Gandhi and Nehru in August 1942 and the civil disobedience crisis further strengthened his decided views on India. Echoing his view, the Chinese press embarked on a virulent campaign against Britain's Indian policy.[30] Chiang, on his part, warned Sir Horace Seymour, the British ambassador to China, that the Indian leaders might go over to the Japanese side if they felt they could not count upon sympathy from the United Nations.

Chiang's diplomatic moves, amounting as far as the British government felt to a sheer intervention in Indian affairs, brought about a reaction from London. Both Churchill and the Viceroy of India reminded the Chinese leader of Britain's non-interference in China's domestic affairs.[31] In a long personal message to the Generalissimo, Churchill detailed the Indian situation. Indeed, the British statesman believed that if, in the future, as a result of the constitutional process to which Britain was committed, British troops were withdrawn from India, the Moslem warriors would soon dominate the Hindu parliamentarians. Gandhi could not set up Hindu ascendacy over all India unless he had at his disposal a Japanese army to hold down the Moslems and the other non-Hindu elements and the Indian states. The Japanese on their part would not provide an army unless they had free passage through India to join up with the Germans. The wisest rule for allies, Churchill maintained, was not to interfere in each other's internal affairs. It was in light of this maxim that his government never interfered in the Kuomintang–Communist differences. He expressed his hope that the Generalissimo would not allow himself to be drawn into political correspondence with the Indian Congress nor with individuals who were trying to paralyse the war effort of the government of India. His views of the global situation, which he briefly elaborated, were that he foresaw a heavier task for China and an increase in the importance of the defence of India. At the same time he was persevering with plans for an offensive against Japanese lines of communications along the Burma Road and other roads between Siam, Malaya and China. He reminded the Generalissimo that he had asked Wavell to meet him in Cairo to discuss these plans and expressed his hope that before many months Britain could do something to relieve the pressure upon the Chinese people.

Following this message, Chiang paid little further attention to the Indian question. Henceforth it took a lower place in the list of grievances and obstacles standing between Britain and China. His wife, Madame Chiang Kai-shek, on the other hand, went on criticising British action with regard to the Congress leaders during her long stay in the United States (November 1942–July 1943).[32]

The Chinese criticism of Britain for refusing to grant India political freedom was perhaps understandable in view of the developments in the region: the conclusion of the Thai–Japanese alliance in late 1942, the occupation of Indo-China by the Japanese forces in collusion with the Vichy government of France, and the fall of Burma. These developments left India as China's only opening outside. Indian friendship was therefore becoming increasingly vital to China. The idea that the Asiatic people might band together after the war and create a pan-Asiatic movement to include not only China and India, but also Japan, naturally caused serious concern in Britain as well as in Australia.[33]

It is no doubt in light of Chiang Kai-shek's somewhat brief and actively expressed interest in the aspiration of the pan-Asiatic and particularly his support of the Congress in India that his 1943 books, *China's Destiny*, described as 'the political bible of the Kuomintang',[34] and *Chinese Economic Theory,* should be seen. It is also in this light that the attempt in mid-1944 to revive an 'Opium Day' to commemorate the first Anglo–Chinese war is to be examined.[35] Following this trend, the Chinese government deprived the Chinese Customs Administration, run by foreigners, of its financial autonomy, causing only a small proportion of the tax from reaching its treasury. There were also strong hints that after the war China was determined to get back, under her full sovereign control, Tibet and Hong Kong. China's movement towards self-assertion, though by no means homogeneous or without its twists and fluctuations, was becoming increasingly noticeable in the economic sphere. The abolition of exterritoriality was only the first step. Others were to follow soon. Here various spokesmen – official and unofficial – on China's post-war economy made it quite clear, and the corporation or company law (promulgated on 12 April 1946) proved that China was moving along a totally new road. Governmental control of the economy (in exchange control, for example) was to be increased. Concessions for specific projects would not exist, imports were to be regulated, and foreign loans were to be accepted on a more rational and planned basis.[36]

At the same time that anti-British attitude was being formed and crystallised, doubts as to the gloomy prospects of remaining alone without external investments and assistance began to creep in to the minds of the Chinese financial and political elite. Having gained their national ambition and political responsiblity resulting from the abolition of exterritoriality, they were now becoming somewhat fearful as to the repercussions the new situation might have on China's commercial, industrial and financial relationships with foreign countries. Re-establishing confidence in China's political and economic system seemed now most essential. It was against this background that, in December 1943, Hsi Yu-lin, a member of the Peoples Political Council in China and a former member of the Shanghai Municipal Council, came to England to examine the attitude of firms that had formerly been engaged in trade there.[37] Attempting to calm down apprehensions prevailing then in England, he stressed that, in the future, majority control of joint Chinese–foreign enterprises might be held just as in former days, by foreign interests, and enterprises entirely owned by foreigners. The Chinese government, he emphasised, would have to rely for a limited period of years on foreign, especially British, shipping. On the whole, he underlined his government's desire for a complete reciprocity between the two countries.

At the same time Hsi made it quite clear that, in the future, British engaged in trade in China would be subject to Chinese laws, and firms established in China would be required to register and give some evidence to their aims and objects. Likewise, he stated that exchange control would be in the future assumed by the government and that the old idea of concessions for a specific project would not exist, as it was a thing of the past. Summing up, Hsi said that post-war arrangements should be conducted mainly with Britain, who had long experience of Chinese trade and its tradition, whose goods were dependable and whose traders had a tenacity the Americans lacked.

This somewhat confused notion of strong national self-reassertion, coupled with an expressed hope for economic relationships on a new basis with the former 'imperialists' was also apparent in other cases.[38] In a talk given by Dr T. T. Chang, the director of the foreign trade department of the Central Planning Board, in Chungking in October 1944, a few more illuminating observations on this subject were made.[39] Chang stressed that the volume of trade between China and abroad in the post-war era would depend on the extent of China's need for foreign products and on her ability to pay for them. Within the decade following the war, China, in order to exist as a nation and to raise her standard of living, would have to be industrialised speedily. This in turn would mean that she would require a great deal of ships, docks, trucks, cars, air-transport fuels, etc. She would also require machines of all kinds for her light and heavy industry, as well as various kinds of instruments for her developing hospitals, schools and laboratories. While some of these requirements China would be able to produce herself, she would have to import a great many. As for consumer goods like textiles, foodstuffs, paper and cars, attempts would be made to regulate their importation for the purpose of conserving exchange resources for more urgently needed commodities. Yet, despite this projected protectionist policy, the volume of imported goods would still be large. China's increased production would automatically raise both her purchasing power and the standard of living of the masses. Her ability to pay would depend on her exports (loans and credits being substantially deferred payments plus interest). While in the past China exported agricultural and animal products, she would be able in the future, as her industry progressed, to export also industrial products. In the first decade to follow the war, however, China's unfavourable balance of trade would most likely continue. This was expected in view of the fact that during the war the United States had cultivated the tung-trees and increased the production of tung-oil, a development that would seriously affect Chinese sales. Likewise, it was feared that the export of oil would be greatly damaged by the introduction of the new nylon products. Dr Chang reminded his listeners that in the past the Chinese government had not only participated in the export–import trade, but had also monopolised the purchase and sales abroad of certain export products. This was practised as a direct result of China's creditors' demand that they be paid with delivery of certain products such as tea, tung, oil, bristles, and minerals like tungsten. So long as loans and credits would be obtained that way, the

Chinese government would continue to purchase or even monopolise the purchase of certain products for shipment abroad. There would be no justification for this practice should the whole loans-and-credits system change.

Similar views were expressed in a study published in Chungking, the wartime capital of China, in 1945, by yet another Chinese economist who based them on T. V. Soong's financial and economic experience in China as well as on Western data. In his *China and Foreign Capital,* W. Y. Lin underlined emerging Chinese economic ideas regarding trade and investment relations with the 'imperialist' powers. These ideas, undoubtedly influenced by the Sino–Japanese war, reflected the general political mood prevailing in China. Lin insisted that China should only borrow from abroad for capital development of a type likely to improve her balance of international payments in the future.[40] Any attempts to bring in foreign capital without at the same time taking steps to better equip the productive capacity of China and to provide the loan services out of such increased productive efforts, would entail a heavy burden on the national budget and on the international equilibrium. Moreover, productive employment of foreign capital would not in itself ensure its most economic or effective utilisation unless closely and completely co-ordinated with a definite and detailed plan of economic reconstruction. If foreign capital in the immediate post-war period was likely to be scarce, the available amount should be put to the best possible use, bringing into national consideration the needs of the various industries and regions. In view of the necessity of repayment and servicing of foreign loans and the difficult problems of transfer connected therewith, all foreign loans should be strictly confined to essential purchases and expenditures abroad. All the cost of domestic materials and labour procurable within China should not be defrayed out of the proceeds of foreign loans. Care should be taken to ascertain the nature of the needs and the relative extent to which foreign loans and domestic currency were respectively required. Lin warned that, in the past, in order to ensure China's capacity to pay specific revenues like the customs and salt or railways, receipts had been assigned as hypothecation for foreign loans, leading to an infringement upon China's sovereign rights in the matter of financial and railway administration. All future borrowing should be secured against the general credit of China. Shortage of long-term foreign capital, in face of China's pressing needs, lay open to the danger of substituting short-term money for long-term capital development purposes. China, stressed Lin, 'should be cautious and resolute enough *to refuse* to accept short-term money for purposes for which it is not properly applicable.'[41] However, inflow of foreign capital should not be handicapped, by legislation or any limitation of profits or restriction upon their remittance abroad. Past experience had shown that when prospects of business were good, the profits of foreign enterprises were reinvested in China for the purpose of expansion. Thus, foreign investments, given all the reservations, were far from being regarded as 'imperial evil' which should be done away with outright. Rather, the disadvantages of foreign financial intervention should be avoided with a view of extracting from it the useful and profitable.

Indeed, as Robert F. Dernberger illustrated in his assessment of the foreigner's role in China's economic development, Chinese foreign economic relations were far from a clear-cut case up to 1949.[42] In the latter phase of the Second World War, as in the immediate post-war period, Chinese economists essentially wanted to see the general scheme of Chinese–foreign relations continue without unnecessary political and military strings attached – strings that had in the past inflicted national humiliation on China and caused her considerable economic damage. Given the existence of 'a high-level equilibrium trap' in the Chinese economy, the foreigner was expected to continue to serve as an agent to start the Chinese economy on the road to modernisation. The Chinese were to enjoy, as in previous periods, gains from trade and gross transfer of foreign productive capital and technology. This practice, considered most desirable though with negative impact on the Chinese economy on the margin, was to be continued with an attempt to minimise the negative effects.

According to another Western academic, A. G. Donnithorne, the system of exterritoriality (the foreign settlements and concessions in the treaty ports) was a form of foreign economic intervention. It helped the modern part of China's economic life survive comparatively unscathed by the many upheavals that China had witnessed since the mid-nineteenth century.[43] The Kuomintang's policy of national exclusiveness seemed aimed at pushing out the remaining Sino–foreign companies, even to the detriment of China's economy. The communists, in a less arbitrary way, would later on follow the same course.[44] It must therefore be remembered that in the sphere of industry the direct results of the long war against Japan were the destruction, dispersal and decline of foreign interests. Japan, through its very aggression and presence in China, assisted the elevation of the latter to a higher stage of both political and economic self-assertiveness. The Japanese, in the course of their presence in China, often scattered among their own industries the machinery that belonged to British plants.

After the war, the proportion of China's industry owned by foreigners lessened greatly. This was a natural result of the war events since 1937. Before the war, for example, out of the total of 1 300 000 tons of shipping engaged in China's inland and coastal navigation, some 720 000 tons were foreign-owned (mostly British). After the war the Chinese government, left with only 60 000 tons, was free from her former treaty obligations to allow foreign shipping in the country's domestic trade, and promptly banned it. This was done despite the fact that it was detrimental to industry and trade, especially in such lines as tung-oil and egg exports for which foreign shipping provided special storage facilities.[45]

As in quite a few British colonies during the Second World War, in China too the internal trend of development was intensified. A strong line of self-sufficiency became imperative and local industries were given full encouragement and developed. Similarly, emphasis was given to growing more varied food-stuffs.[46] This Chinese approach to self-sufficiency was part of China's new self-image. The powers, especially Britain, found it hard to absorb. As E. Luard has already pointed out, while Britain had been ready to concede much to the nationalism of colonial peoples, she found the nationalism of China – a sovereign nation – puzzling.[47] Nevertheless, China, having advanced towards more respectability and equality at home through the abolition of exterritoriality, for example, was now hoping that her international role would also drastically change – that she would gain her deserved seat in the Big Powers Club. Chiang Kai-shek and other Chinese leaders maintained that collaboration between the Big Powers, including China, was essential for the maintenance of permanent world peace and for the promotion of economic recognition.[48] Yet, in the war years, the Chinese were not clear as to the specific arrangements they preferred. They merely clung to a general concept of an international organisation in which China would play her part. They did not object to international security bases constructed on Chinese soil. However, as already mentioned, immediately after the Cairo Conference (under specific instructions from Chiang Kai-shek) officials were starting to press the British that China would have to recover Hong Kong and secure a 'political rapprochement' with Tibet, namely a new arrangement which would give the central government a tighter hold of Lhasa.[49] These ambitions, as China's intentions *vis-à-vis* Britain's South East Asian territories, greatly worried the decision-makers in London. Would overseas Chinese in, say, Malaya carry on being 'good citizens' as in pre-war days? Or would their natural affection for their mother country in its ultra-nationalistic mood disrupt the colonial order? After all, during the war, overseas Chinese were very much on the defensive and the only overt expression of their resistance to the Japanese conqueror was made by the communist guerrillas in the Malaya jungle. On the other hand, however, these guerrillas were intent not so much on fighting the Japanese oppressor 'as on preserving their strength for the struggle with European "imperialism", if, and when, the Europeans were able to resume control of their colonies as protectorates'.[50]

Commenting on the Koumintang's intentions with regard to the Nanyang (overseas) Chinese, G. F. Hudson of the Foreign Office Research Department stressed the danger of Chinese influence in South East Asia. 'I should expect the Chinese to carry out just as much of [their programme] as they are allowed to get away with.' Of special interest, he thought, was the danger that the Chinese government would assert the claim to diplomatic protection of all the overseas Chinese on the basis of *ius sanguinis,* thus including even the Chinese settlements that had been established outside China for several generations.[51]

A Dutch view on the same question was expressed by the Netherland's ambassador to China. He believed that the Chinese, particularly since the appointment of Chang Tao-fan as minister of overseas Chinese, were preparing an active campaign for the economic and political penetration of both British and Dutch colonial territories in South East Asia. According to him they intended to assert their claims to economic freedom and privileges which would give them practically an exterritorial position. He suggested, therefore, that both the British and Dutch governments take timely steps to forestall the Chinese schemes, such as complete prohibition of political activities of every kind in these territories.[52]

Two works published in the war capital of China, Chungking, in 1945, dwelt on these issues from a different perspective. They emphasised the great danger that lay in the emerging conflicts of interests between Britain and China in the south as well as between Russia and China in the north. British imperialists in the Far East during the post-war era, stressed the first study, 'may persist in considering Southeast Asia as their sphere of interest. They not only mean to hold their own, but to protect the Dutch and even the Portuguese interests in the region as well.'[53] The second study, in a somewhat more optimistic tone, stressed the conviction that contributions made by the Chinese, and those that would be made in the future, for the development and prosperity of South East Asian countries, added to China's contribution in fighting the Japanese, would cause the allies of China to change their colonial policies. They would abolish discrimination against the Chinese and would provide means for assuring them that no such discriminations would be included in the legislative bodies throughout South East Asia.[54]

The year 1945 was to be an important juncture for the overseas Chinese. The Koumintang was to attempt to reimpose its control over the whole of China, including territories held by the communists. This posed a most precarious and delicate dilemma for the overseas Chinese: should they side with the Koumintang, or, rather, should they oppose it and transfer their allegiance to the strengthening communists? Their views regarding the rising nationalism in South East Asia were, at best, confused. They could no longer rely on the British metropolitan power to protect them. Nor could they serve for long, as in past decades, as middlemen between the British authorities and the native population. As an unpopular minority they could on the whole expect very little from participating wholeheartedly in the local nationalist movements. On the eve of the Japanese surrender, therefore, issues relating to the overseas Chinese were a few more question marks in the wide texture of Anglo–Chinese relations.

The British election results of July 1945 did not alter the basic post-war dilemmas in the Far East. Indeed, Chungking accepted the news from London most favourably. From China's war capital it seemed likely that the new power structure in London would produce a progress in Sino–British relations and a solution to the Indian deadlock with which, as stressed earlier, the Chinese government was increasingly concerned.[55] The *Ta Kung Pao,* while regretting the loss of Churchill's talents, expected a more enlightened and liberal line, particularly in colonial policies. The paper hoped for 'a happy solution of such questions as Hong Kong'. The communist *Hsiu Hua Jih Pao* more outspokenly castigated 'monopolistic capitalists' and 'appeasers' who had had so much to say in the past.[56]

4   British Perception II

The departmental disagreement in London over the question of a loan to China[1] was to some extent solved at the ministerial level by October 1944. It was then decided that the limitation originally imposed on the British loan to China would remain explicit in the £50 million loan which was finally completed.[2] Two specific possibilities of helping China remained in view of this decision and the run-away inflation which hit that country in the course of the war (purchasing power of the Chinese currency in 1943 was one two-hundred-and-twenty-eighth of the 1937 level).[3] The first was that should an international bank be established to extend substantial loans to China, British enterprise might then be encouraged to put substantial efforts in the Chinese market. The second (should the first possibility not materialise) was to supply China against cash or normal short-term commercial credit. This might indeed come as a shock to the Chinese and therefore might not help establish goodwill between China and Britain. Yet, at least, the difficult financial situation in Britain would not worsen on account of bad debts.

The basic difference of opinion between the Board of Trade and the Treasury went on into 1945. Twice the Chancellor of the Exchequer, Sir John Anderson, minuted on the China question, arguing that there was no case for long-term credits to her on political grounds.[4] Another Treasury official regarded China as a 'bad bet', stressing that she was low on the list of countries to which credits should be given on either political or economic grounds. He was not at all worried lest American export credits would go to China.[5] The War Cabinet Far Eastern Economic Sub-Committee (FEESC), whose members were senior civil servants of the various departments (for example, Norman Young of the Treasury and J. C. Sterndale-Bennett of the Foreign Office), chaired by R. G. C. Somervell of the Board of Trade, commenting on certain aspects of British commercial policy in China, however, was closer in its views to the opinions maintained by the Board of Trade.[6] It stressed the need to recover, as much as possible, Britain's previous position of influence in China, and on the assumption that trade with China would be mainly on cash or commercial credit terms, it argued that the possibility of granting credits not justifiable on purely economic grounds should not be excluded. Indeed, in the initial stage, supply of both capital and consumption goods would be strictly limited, yet with the view of keeping a footing in the China trade it was important to explore the fields of technical advice and training. The commercial treaty with China and an exchange of views with the Americans aimed at mutual understanding in this regard should be expedited. The centuries-old hope concerning the vast Chinese market was not absent from the Sub-Committee's note. 'It is obvious that a very slight *per capita* increase in the productivity and purchasing power of China's vast population', it was stressed, 'could mean a very large increase in her imports.' It was in the light of this hope and the prospects of restoring Britain's pre-war economic position in China, despite the awareness of American future competition, that background files on China were prepared at the Board of Trade to be ready on demand. They included statistics on business investments, capital investments, property rights in China, etc.[7] Between November 1944 and July 1945 both the War Cabinet Far Eastern Committee, chaired by G. H. Hall, Parliamentary Under-Secretary of State, Foreign Office, and its Economic Sub-Committee produced voluminous material uniquely devoted to the evaluation of the prospects of restoration of the British position in the Far East in general and in China in particular. These efforts and the calibre of the officials who participated in the meetings prove, it seems, the importance given to the whole issue of British economic plans as regards China. A few examples illustrating these efforts follow.

On 25 November 1944, E. A. Armstrong, Secretary of the Far Eastern Committee, circulated a despatch to the members, sent by Sir Horace Seymour, the British Ambassador in Chungking, to the Foreign Office, on British post-war commercial relations in China.[8] Seymour assumed that whether China emerged from the war as a unified state or whether centrifugal tendencies proved too strong for a central government, 'trade on a valuable scale will still be possible'. The experience of the previous thirty years showed, in his opinion, that trade with and in a disunited China was 'perfectly feasible'. The Ambassador maintained that the abolition of exterritoriality found the Chinese 'unprepared to put anything in the place of the old system'. He warned, however, of two obstacles that might make British trade with and in China difficult: nationalistic legislation and American competition. He therefore urged the Foreign Office to study 'in good time' British post-war commercial relations with China and be prepared for a period of intensive competitive trading in the China market.

The question of American competition in China in the post-war period emerged in another paper prepared two days later by Sir Humphrey Prideaux-Brune, Adviser on China at the Foreign Office. It was studied by the members of the Far Eastern Committee.[9] British policy in China, wrote Prideaux-Brune, became associated in the Chinese mind with imperialism and unequal treaties. American influence, on the other hand (felt principally in the educational and philanthropic fields), produced an abundant harvest of goodwill. He maintained, however, that as far as China was concerned 'the rehabilitation of established British interests seems to be the first thing to consider'. Having regard to the immense complexities and difficulties to be faced in the post-war era it was justifiable to hope that there would be, to some degree, a combination of British and American influence in the economic field in China.

A memorandum prepared at the Foreign Office three weeks after the first two papers was also considered by the Far Eastern Committee.[10] It advocated that British policy in China should follow the practice adopted for South America, that is a general fostering of the market through the maintenance and develop-ment of contacts and customers, by means of commercial visitors, goodwill, advertising and the supply of available commodities. The Department of Overseas Trade of the Board of Trade, on the other hand, were inclined to take the view that definite plans should be worked out for British post-war trade with China, pending the liberation of which no one should be allowed to go out to China and lay plans which might run counter to the decision eventually reached. Thus, as a result of correspondence with Seymour, it was decided to encourage British commercial firms to send representatives to China 'not with a view to their doing any immediate business, but simply to enable them to look round'. Here, it was held at the Foreign Office, there existed no necessity to obtain the prior concurrence of the American authorities before permitting a British firm to accept an engagement as consultant to the Chinese government in regard to post-war development. Save in so far as the continued receipt of Lend–Lease supplies may impose certain restrictions on British export freedom, His Majesty's Government had a free hand, though it was obviously desirable in the interests of friendly relations to continue to keep the Americans informed of developments.[11]

Dr Joseph Needham, head of the British Council's Cultural Scientific Office in China until spring 1945, held the view that Britain should concentrate on sending exports in less controversial fields, such as agriculture and medicine. And, indeed, during the crucial war years there existed within and without the official scene the activities of organisations such as the United Aid to China Fund, headed by Lady Isobel Cripps. The objects of the Fund were to create a sympathetic understanding of new China's accomplishments, problems and difficulties, and to give the Chinese people a token of British friendship in the form of moral and financial support. By 1944 almost one and a quarter million pounds sterling had been raised to the relief of China.[12] Catch-phrases, such as 'stand by China, her fight is our fight' and 'first against aggression, thank China', were often used in meetings and publications of the British United Aid to China.

Those few people in Britain who were aware of, and supported, the left in Chinese politics, created the China Campaign Committee. In their publications they enthusiastically wrote of the great Chinese communist experience in north China. Here Michael Lindsay, son of the Master of Balliol, contributed a great deal. Another aspect of informal and somewhat modest aid to China was Dr Joseph Needham's own activities in the scientific and cultural fields. He went to China on behalf of the British Council in 1942, worked with Chinese universities, and reported back to Britain on conditions there, for example the appalling medical conditions existing among Koumintang units. Aid was also supplied by the British Red Cross and the Friends Ambulance Unit.[13] The Federation of British Industries on its part introduced a scheme under which student-apprenticeships were provided for a number of young Chinese in firms and industries in the United Kingdom. Thus it was hoped the Chinese would be acquainted with British products and would achieve familiarity with British methods. This in turn would lead to orders for British goods and services on the students' return to China as future technicians, industrialists and administrators.[14]

The most interesting documents prepared by the War Cabinet Far Eastern Economic Sub-Committee in the course of the last days of 1944 reveal a wider scope of British interests in China, that is via Hong Kong and India.[15] Hong Kong, as a territory adjacent to China, stated the first document, had the 'preponderating economic interests in China of the British Colonial territories in the Far East'. These were: (1) the re-establishment of Hong Kong as the main trade channel between south China and the rest of the world, and the general resumption of trade between the colony itself and China with minimum restrictions; (2) The re-establishment of the through railway to Canton and Hankow, of shipping to Canton, to other coastal ports and to up-river ports and of satisfactory air communication with China; (3) The establishment of a sound relation between Hong Kong and Chinese currency and the continued tolerance of the cirulation of Hong Kong currency in China; (4) the re-establishment of Hong Kong banking branches in China; (5) the control of Chinese immigration into Hong Kong; (6) the control of remittances from Hong Kong to China for as long as required by the needs of exchange control within the sterling area. Both Malaya and British Borneo had also, according to the document, limited economic interests in China. Both shared Hong Kong's interest in the two last points mentioned, that is control of Chinese immigration and the control of remittances from the colonial territories of China.

As for India, trade relations between India and China, stated the second document, were governed by the treaty of 28 December 1928 between the United Kingdom and China relating to the Chinese Customs Tariff and other issues which applied in India. It provided for most favoured nation treatment for Indian goods imported into China. The treaty was of unlimited duration, yet by article 8 of the exterritoriality treaty of 1943, India, like the United Kingdom, agreed to enter into negotiations for the conclusion of a comprehensive modern treaty of friendship, commerce, navigation and consular rights. The Committee's paper stated that before the war India almost invariably enjoyed a favourable balance of trade with China. In the early years of the war the balance of trade in India's favour improved due to a revival of exports of cotton to China. Later, however, trade between the two countries had practically ceased. The hope of resuming trade between British India and China lay at the base of this document and the deliberations in the committee.

An important Board of Trade memorandum prepared for the Far Eastern Economic Sub-Committee on 9 January 1945 dwelt on British commercial policy in China and the hopes and prospects of restoring British pre-war enterprise there.[16] It stressed that the Chinese government was thinking of a wholesale development and modernisation of the country 'on a scale which represents a gigantic task'. If it was to be undertaken on a large scale and carried out energetically it could only be financed by extensive long-term credits from outside. On the basis of what China had to export, however, it was difficult to see how or when those credits could be repaid. While the Americans could be ready to cast their bread upon the waters for this purpose, Britain (according to the Board of Trade) could not compete with them as it did not seem to be able to extend any significant long-term credits to China. Thus British plans had to be based on the assumption that Britain's trade with China would have to be mainly on cash or commercial-credit terms. Also, at the initial post-war stages at least, the possibilities of supply to China, both of capital and consumer goods, would be strictly limited. At the same time, however, it would almost certainly be a mistake 'to wash our hands of the Chinese market'. Such a policy 'would antagonise the Chinese and might add to the difficulties of resuscitating our pre-war enterprises in China'. There was no reason, claimed the writer of the memorandum, 'why we should not do what we can to help [the Chinese] raise their standard of living by plans more commensurate with the circumstances of their economy'. By way of conclusion the memorandum stated, among other points, that 'we should not be deterred from doing what we can to keep a footing in the China trade'.

Similar conclusions were reached by the Sub-Committee more than a month later. 'It is of great political importance', the report of the Sub-Committee stressed, 'that we should recover as much as possible of our previous position of influence in China.' It was likewise concluded that 'the possibility of granting credits [to China] not justifiable on purely economic grounds should not be excluded'.[17] No specific figures were, however, suggested, nor was there any attempt to compare future British investments in China with those that would be made elsewhere overseas. The recommendations made by the Sub-Committee were soon endorsed by the main committee. The members of that committee stressed in their conclusion that the report adopted dealt neither with the restoration of British pre-war enterprise in China, nor with British shipping interests there, nor with the special British colonial interests, of which those of Hong Kong were the most important. Rather, they accepted the fact that it was mainly British commercial relations with China, not in China, that could now be discussed and restored. After consultation with the joint secretaries of the Armistice and Post War Committee, and with the secretary of the War Cabinet as to the procedure by which recommendations of the Far Eastern Committee should receive consideration at the ministerial level, the Committee members decided to refer their recommendations to the Armistice and Post War Committee.[18] It was only after the elections (before the results were announced) that the matter again received attention. Indeed, at a time when problems concerning coal, housing and manpower preoccupied almost every meeting of the Cabinet, the situation in China surely could not receive earlier attention.

Technical assistance to China by way of sending British experts there was considered in a Ministry of Production memorandum prepared in early 1945. The document summed up the desirable measures to be taken by the government.[19]

(a) The provision of technical experts to advise the Chinese in the development of their industrial resources in the prosecution of the war against Japan should be encouraged so long as this does not interfere with British present production arrangements.

(b) In order to assist British export trade with China after the war, any experts desired by the Chinese for help in the post-war problems should be provided if and when they can be spared 'and the view should increasingly be taken that they can be spared'.

(c) The Department of Overseas Trade and the British Council should be invited to work together closely in the matter.

A very extreme and bleak view of the post-war situation in China, not accepted on the whole by the main stream in British decision-making circles,[20] was that expressed by a secret research group functioning in India under the auspices of Sir Olaf Caroe, Secretary of the External Affairs Department of the Government of India. The group consisted of a few European officials who met informally from time to time with the object of analysing various problems that seemed likely to confront India in the post-war period. The papers the group produced were not considered official but, rather, 'independent'. Though unique and unrepresentative when expressed in condensed and exaggerated form, some of the group's ideas on China could be found in minutes and reports on various departmental and interdepartmental meetings. As such, therefore, the opinions advocated by the group do give an interesting insight into thoughts existing at the time not only in semi-official but also official circles. In a paper entitled 'Modern China's Asiatic Empire', Chinese 'imperialism', 'irredentist claims and policies', and attempts to control Chinese nationals abroad, were discussed as dangers to British Asiatic interests.[21] Sun Yat-sen's *San Min Chu I* and Chiang Kai-shek's *China's Destiny* were regarded as the theoretical basis – 'the bible' – of nationalistic China, reminiscent of what the paper called the Geopolitik of Germany, and the neo-Shintoism of Japan. While Sun's principles were a plea for Chinese nationalism dominating ultimately the rest of Asia, Chiang's ideas merely progressed on those 'racial theories and imperialist claims'. China's population, geography and lack of natural resources within the borders of China proper were factors that would press outwards. The danger-spots at the post-war period were likely to be, according to the group's paper, Burma, Siam, French Indo-China and other South East Asian countries. In these places China would most likely make use of the overseas Chinese. In the past, it was argued, Chinese expansionism manifested itself in Manchuria and in the South Seas. The coming of the Chinese colonists had always been at the expense of the native population. Economically the group's researchers envisaged an emergence after the war of a 'Nanking–Washington Axis' which would encourage China's expansion in South East Asia. Such an expansion might give a blow to Britain and her commercial interests in the region. Should a hostile communist party survive and the Soviet Union increase her activities in the Far East, this scenario seemed to the writers of the paper even more real. The paper called for a united front created by the British Commonwealth aimed at staving off all Chinese and American schemes which would have the appearance of 'altruism and internationalism'. Close co-operation between the 'Indian Ocean Commonwealth countries and the Southeast Asia Powers' would preserve the integrity of South East Asia, which would ultimately mean the integrity of Australia and India.

While in the last phases of the war officials realised how complex the situation was *vis-à-vis* China, and were well aware of the difficulties into which Britain was likely to run after it ended, members of the former British commercial community in China did not seem to be quite appreciative of the new situation. It was in light of this insensitivity, perhaps, that in 1944 one Old China Hand suggested to the British Ambassador in Chungking that certain Shanghai businessmen should be given temporary army rank and attached as liaison officers to the Allied troops when they entered Shanghai.[22] This, it was asserted, would be a proper way to ensure that British properties in the city would be handed back to their British owners at once and delays similar to those incurred in 1927, during the Northern Expedition, would not happen again. Hall-Patch, who participated in a meeting held at the Foreign Office to discuss the question of the rehabilitation of British interests in China, expressed also the fear that members of British firms might go to China 'in a wrong frame of mind', expecting too much help from the British government and 'ill prepared to face the asperities of the new era'.[23] He strongly suggested warning British merchants, in order to enable them 'to adapt themselves to the changed conditions arising from the abolition of exterritoriality'. It was not surprising, therefore, that a representative of the China Association was informed by the Foreign Office that there was going to be a 'clear cut between the past and the future, and that henceforth HMG would treat China as a sovereign state'.[24]

Indeed, the China Association, through its Chairman, W. B. Kennett, its Vice Chairman, G. W. Swire, and its Acting Secretary, M. Mason, constantly urged officials at the Foreign Office to make arrangements as soon as possible for the rehabilitation of Shanghai upon its recapture from the Japanese.

They wished to see on the British government's side the same enthusiasm for the return to China as shown by their respective member-companies. The John Swire group, for example, prepared in the course of the war new gates to their dry dock at Shanghai once they learned from American reconnaissance air photographs that the former had been damaged.[25]

The letters written and the comments made were indicative of this pressure-group's unawareness of the existence of a new process leading to a totally new reality, both at home and abroad, a reality in which even the firmest position and the best will in London were unlikely to alter objective developments.[26]

Appraising the prospects of post-war opportunities for Britain in China, Victor Farmer, in a private talk to Chatham House, distinguished between two schools of thought existing within China in regard to foreign aid.[27] The point he did not make was that often these two schools dwelt in the same Chinese political group or ministry simultaneously. The one school was suspicious, maintaining that China had been grossly exploited in the past and should, therefore, impose heavy restraint upon foreign enterprise. Appreciating that foreign aid was nevertheless essential for China, this school tended to hold that despite restrictive regulations the foreigner would rush to invest in China. The other school believed that 'if you want a paying guest, you must make him comfortable'.

Assessing post-war developments in China, Farmer believed that they fell under four main headings: agriculture, communications, and light and heavy industries. China being based on agriculture, her industries would have to be based in the future on raw materials and agriculture. The bulk of her exports would likewise be agricultural for many years. Once her communications system was developed, the way would be open for the development of her light and, later, heavy industry. Britain's assistance to China on her road to industrialisation would not ultimately tend to throw British workers out of employment. It would take China from fifty to one hundred years to reach industrialisation, and relative standards of production, both in quantity and quality, of pre-war Britain or the United States. In the meantime China would require steadily increasing quantities of consumable goods. Moreover, since Britain herself was advancing, she would find in the future new fields of export to China. Politically, no danger seemed immanent in this scenario. 'You cannot, in a short space of time, change the inherent character of a nation, and the Chinese are not essentially aggressive like, say, the Japanese.' Risks, would have to be taken, advocated Farmer, as the China market was so important to Britain. Again, the great illusion of the Chinese market and the almost legendary hope for the 'real' opening-up of China seems to have played a significant role in the deliberations on post-war China. Reality, as already indicated, was much more inglorious.

Views expressed in a somewhat old-fashioned style by Sir George Moss, a veteran of the consular service in China, and a member of the General Committee of the China Association, represented, nevertheless, the beliefs of some younger and less-outspoken officials. These views proved how deeply rooted was the distorted British version of 'la rêve Chinois'. Sir George strongly asserted that it would be 'most unwise even to entertain the idea of giving up Hong Kong'.[28] The retention of the colony, he thought, would undoubtedly render Britain much more open to immediate attack and to serious friction with China in the post-war period. Yet the risk had to be faced. 'The Faith that under God the British Commonwealth of Nations is the greatest Power on Earth for Good', he stressed, '. . . is the faith which British Imperial Statesmen charged with guidance of our Destinies are bound to spread and uphold not only in the Empire but in the World.' This faith, he thought, had to be firmly held and retained, not only by the British, but also by all their friends and allies; and particularly by the Americans and the Chinese. That faith could not be affirmed by surrender. 'If we discard Hong Kong, would that strengthen our resolution to hold Singapore, Ceylon and Aden or Malta or Gibraltar in face of pressure? Or the West Indies?' He did not believe in what he called appeasing the Chinese by the rendi-tion of Hong Kong. That colony was not, after all, the only area under British rule where the Chinese were nourishing nationalis-tic political ambitions. What would happen to Malaya, to Burma, to the South Seas and Tibet? 'Our prestige', he wrote, 'has suffered greatly in Asia; it must be restored.' Britain could not withdraw from Hong Kong, as this would imply a corresponding diminution of her interests in China and a reorientation of her strategic dispo-sitions. Britain's main interest was to establish 'the new post-war World Order'. She had to concentrate on strengthening the Empire and maintaining its commitment. The Chinese, like other allies, had the duty to see that they too would be 'strong and dependable supporters of our new superstructure'. He had no doubt that China would be convinced that she must accept Britain's position on Hong Kong if it were explained against the historical background, that is that British sea-power had sheltered China from dangerous aggressions in the past. The Chinese would then value 'our friendship and make real sacrifices to maintain it'. Thus in 1944 a British 'domino theory' was developed in order to justify imperial views and values.

A similar anachronistic assessment was made at the Foreign Office when in March 1945 an attempt was made to define British

long-term interests in China.[29] Trade, security, influence, and
international peace and good order were quoted as Britain's aims
in China. It was thus stated that 'the restoration of our position in
China will have an important bearing on our general influence in
the Far East'. In view of the too-strong American position in
China, it was likewise pressed that a more active and less luke-
warm attitude towards China's cause was desirable. Thus D. C.
Watt was right in arguing that 'as the war in the Far East turned
towards its end, British policy-makers grappled again with the
question of how to re-establish British influence in China'.[30]
However, less precise is his statement, based on a minute written
by G. F. Hudson of the Foreign Office Research Department, that
'during the war years Britain's planners in the Foreign Office
accepted that Britain's predominating position in China was a
thing of the past'.[31] Indeed, British planners were well aware of
Britain's declining prestige in China. Nevertheless, hopes and
plans to re-establish Britain's pre-war position in China persisted.[32]
This was so, despite the anxiety that the ascendancy of the United
States in building up China's war effort would project itself into
the post-war period.[33]

As for Watt's statement that 'all that Britain could provide for
the military occupation of Japan was a single brigade group, and
that had to be withdrawn later',[34] this should be seen in light of
the following fact. Prior to Japan's surrender, Lord Mountbatten's
political adviser at the Supreme Allied Command in South East
Asia, Mr (later Sir) Esler Denning, stressed the need to regain
British prestige both in South East Asia and China.[35] 'Ocular
evidence of the defeat of the hitherto all-powerful Japanese in any
given area is likely to have more effect than hearsay evidence that
British troops have taken part in an attack upon Japan proper.'
Though it was difficult to restore the British position in the
Japanese empire, Manchuria and north China after the war,
establishing and maintaining Britain's influence in the area south
of the Tropic of Cancer seemed to him significant. This would 'not
only protect those interests which are vital to us, but also offer our
best contribution to Empire solidarity and world security'. An
efficient operation to reoccupy territories evacuated after
Japanese capitulation was also stressed in the headquarters of
SACSEA (Joint Planning Staff). Achieving this goal 'with a good
show of force' was considered more significant than reaching all
areas speedily.[36] The Singapore–Malaya area seemed pre-eminent

as an area that Britain should reoccupy. 'If we are to recover our lost prestige there, it is essential that we should make the maximum display of armed force. Without this, the foundation of our whole future position in the Far East would suffer.' As for Hong Kong, it was stressed that there, too, 'a good show of force is equally desirable'; the need to arrive there before any other occupying force was also emphasised.

On their part, Foreign Office officials and other decision-makers in London were well aware of Britain's new image in Chinese government circles. They appreciated that the Chinese who witnessed or even heard of the humiliation inflicted by Japanese troops upon British subjects and soldiers in, say, Tientsin in 1939 or Singapore in 1942, were not likely to forget it.[37] Ironically, therefore, exactly a century since the first 'unequal treaty' signed in Nanking, Sir Horace Seymour, the British ambassador to China, was merely hoping, almost as his eighteenth- and nineteenth-century colleagues had done before him, that China would bring herself to accord to foreigners 'equitable treatment' such as could be expected from the government of any friendly country.[38] This indeed could seem necessary in the light of Board of Trade officials' view that the course of the war, with its reverses for the Western nations, had imbued the Chinese with a 'feeling of superiority'.[39]

The wheel had turned a full circle. With the benefit of hindsight it can be argued that this new situation became more distinct as time passed and the communists ascended to power. Yet, in the war, and the immediate post-war period, an attempt was made to use the 'equitable treatment' once achieved as a basis from which to launch a return to China, albeit with new clothing more suitable to the new era and without the previous wide territorial bases. This was so despite the fact that a full consensus on imperial restoration never existed. Nor was there a crystallised and agreed-upon pattern for a British comeback.

After £50 million had been made available by the British to the Chinese for war purposes under the Financial Aid Agreement of 2 May 1944, the Chinese government, as already mentioned, complained about the difficulty of spending the new British credit under the terms of the agreement.[40] These difficulties emerged from two factors: (a) the agreement reached at the Casablanca Conference to the effect that war supplies to China should be primarily an American responsibility, while Britain accepted the main responsibility in respect of war supplies to Turkey, and (b) the fact that the British Empire was, on balance, *vis-à-vis* the United States, an importer of war supplies. Both created a situation in which, in practice, the Americans had first choice of everything that was to be supplied by Britain to China. Moreover, the air-lift arrangements over the 'Hump' were under Sino–American control and only a very small quota of space was allocated for the cartage of British goods from India. One result of this had been the accumulation of a substantial stockpile in India of British goods intended for China. By the end of June 1945 less than £2 million worth of British goods had been supplied to China in total under the 1939, 1941 and 1944 credits.[41]

In view of this state of affairs, Sir Horace Seymour, the British ambassador, urged from Chungking that the Chinese should be given tangible evidence of British interest and support.[42] 'We should try to ensure that China gets British goods as soon as possible so as to keep the door ajar for future British commercial development in China', he wrote. Though Seymour's message represented on the whole a line advocated earlier on by the Far Eastern Committee and its Economic Sub-Committee, it gave, when reaching the Board of Trade almost three months later, a boost to a re-examination of the issue in the Board. On 17 May 1945, L. M. Skevington wrote to J. R. Willis of the Commercial Relations and Treaties Department of the Board of Trade that the Treasury was holding different if not opposing views to those adopted by the Foreign Office and the Board of Trade. 'Do we in fact wish to find a way by which China may obtain British goods under the 1944 credit?' The Treasury's answer to that, he reminded his colleagues, was an emphatic 'no'. 'The Foreign Office and ourselves have been increasingly restless and uneasy about this ruling', he added. However, the Foreign Office and the Board of Trade were far from thinking alike. According to Skevington, the Foreign Office officials were concerned with the strategic and political implications of a passive British policy in China without being totally aware of 'the gravity of our post-war balance of payments situation'. Moreover, the Foreign Office were pursing an ideal of Anglo–American co-operation in China which, Skevington admitted, seemed to him personally 'chimerical'. *Vis-à-vis* the Foreign Office, stressed Skevington, 'We are wholly of the Treasury's way of thinking. We have, however, ventured to suggest that a rigidly 'exclusionist' policy in respect of the credit may be very short-sighted, and in particular we have on occasion pleaded for a more sympathetic attitude towards Chinese requests.' These requests were a British extension of assistance as regards expenditure on such essential services as railways and public utilities (including telephone systems), where British types were already in favour in China and where, according to Skeving-ton and others in the Board of Trade, 'to withdraw from the market would probably mean sacrificing all chance of ever getting back into it'.[42] The Board of Trade also desired to come towards the Chinese demands for projects such as an aero-engine plant which, if met from Britain, 'could very largely be met from surplus machinery on hand at the end of the war'. If such British machin-ery could be got into China it should, the argument ran, open the way for a useful cash export trade at least in spares, maintenance replacements and all the intangibles that go therewith. It was thus concluded by Skevington that Britain had to do its utmost and give more sympathetic consideration to Chinese applications.

J. R. Willis, J. R. C. Helmore of the China desk in the Board of Trade, and Lord Farmer from the Department of Overseas Trade, concurred with Skevington's view. In his minute, Helmore explained explicitly that he was prepared to defend the proposi-tion that whereas Britain gave credits to Russia when it suited her within a limit, it was reasonable to extend credits to China with a certain limit as well.[43]

Yet, again, Sir David Waley from the Treasury ruled out the possibility of granting China or other countries credits not justified on economic grounds, 'in spite of the political desirability of recovering as much as possible our previous influence in China'. Waley and his colleagues at the Treasury felt that 'a consistent line of policy' had to be pursued and that nothing should be done as regards China that could prejudice the attitude that had to be adopted towards other countries. The answer to Seymour's recommendations, therefore, had to be a 'flat negative'.[44] They maintained that 'it would be better to rule the possibility out entirely from any discussion'. No policy beyond the normal prac-tice of the Export Credit Guarantee Department in regard to credit could be adopted – for example three to five years for any new capital equipment, which the government could decide that it ought to supply in order not to lose the special position in China that certain British products had successfully built up for them-selves. This too had to be limited. As for surplus, no objection existed to selling on extended credit if that was the best that could be done. After all, £10 million on ten years' credit is better than £100 000 cash for scrap. The Treasury minute, likewise, admitted that there was also the consideration that the use of British patterns ought to be given every possible encouragement for the sake of repeat orders. But China had to take her place in the list with other possible buyers, and it was to be a matter for careful consideration where her place in that list ought to be. Financial aid for general post-war industrial development in China could not come from Britain 'for some years to come'.

Characteristic perhaps of the strong views maintained by the Treasury officials was Norman E. Young's statement to T.K. Tseng, the representative of the Chinese Ministry of Finance in London in the summer of 1944: 'In the immediate future China would be relatively much better off than we should be.' He claimed that on merits Britain should be asking [China] for a loan, and not vice versa.[45] The somewhat negative attitude towards China eventually prevailed. On 24 July 1945, the Overseas Reconstruction Committee discussed in the Chancellor of the Exchequer's presence the report of the Far Eastern Committee of February.[46] While preserving almost intact the conclusions of the Far Eastern Committee, the members of the Overseas Reconstruction Committee decided to alter entirely the second recommendation relating to the granting of credits to China. 'There can be no question in present circumstances of granting political credits to China', it was stressed. 'Trade will therefore have to be based mainly on cash or commercial credits.' Thus the hard line constantly advocated by the Treasury gained the upper hand.

Notwithstanding the strong hesitations prevailing in London *vis-à-vis* the China plans, and Britain's deepening financial difficulties, for example, in extending credits, the last months of the war saw increasing American suspicions as regards Britain's intentions in China. Americans serving in Asia, as Esler Denning, Mountbatten's political adviser observed, looked at the British territories that intervened between India and Japan as an 'insuperable barrier' to real Anglo–American co-operation. They regarded American participation in the recapture of Burma as tolerable only because it stood a chances of reopening the road to China.[47] In the case of Malaya, they helped the crystallisation of a policy that saw no reason to contribute Lend–Lease material to the British, as any such assistance would mean supporting

British imperialism. The unsympathetic American attitude towards Britain in Asia was attributed by the British at SEAC to Washington's desire to score with the Asians, particularly with the Chinese.

General Patrick J. Hurley, Roosevelt's special representative in China, and General Albert C. Wedemeyer, Commander of the American forces in the China theatre, were perhaps the most outspoken in expressing their suspicions of British intentions. The latter said to Denning in February 1945 that as far as he could tell Britain did not really want a unified China.[48] The former, on his part, argued that Britain was opposed to the total destruction of Japan as a military force. Indeed, he admitted, the British Empire was 'necessary for the security and well-being of the United States'. Yet why was Britain flying some 75 tons of stores a month into China on Lend–Lease aircraft?[49] Was not Britain sending this material 'for some highly nefarious purpose?' He made it quite clear that American assistance should not be made available 'for the recovery of British colonial territory which violated the funda-mental principle on which the very existence of the United States rested, namely that the governed should have the choice of those who governed them'. But 'in nearing Burma and Malaya we are clearing important sources of supplies such as rice and rubber', minuted J. C. Sterndale-Bennett, the head of the Far Eastern Department in the Foreign Office, in despair. 'By capturing Singa-pore, moreover, we should open up a supply route into the China Sea which would be of some importance.' The Americans had used British territories, particularly India and Burma, and their considerable resources, to further their efforts in China, he reminded his colleagues, unnecessarily perhaps.

> In any case do the Americans think that no attempt should be made to liberate these colonial territories from Japan or that, when liberated, they will be in a state to look after themselves? I suppose it is too much to hope that the Americans will come to realise that our attitude towards our Colonies is one of responsibility and not of privilege.[50]

Hurley's distrust of the British was perhaps embedded in his character by his Irish ancestry, as Russell D. Buhite claims,[51] yet quite a few Americans involved at the time in Asian affairs reached similar conclusions. The British, Buhite argued, had 'assumed the lead in a clandestine attempt with the French and Dutch to promote reacquisition of their colonial possessions in Asia at the expense of the combined war effort against Japan'. They had used American Lend–Lease material towards their imperialist end. In so doing they attempted to defeat America's international policies to build her own power and pre-war influence.[52]

President Roosevelt, well aware of the views held by Wede-meyer and Hurley, asked specifically to be informed of the activities of the old colonial powers in South East Asia. These, just as some inactions within the military sphere, strengthened his already existing anti-colonial sentiments. Thus, Churchill's negative stand on the issue of possible deployment of large armies in Burma served as a good example of fertile soil for the tension between the two allies. Churchill hated the idea of 'thrashing around the jungle'.[53] He much rather preferred to bypass Burma in favour of an operation against Sumatra, which would hopefully be a great strategic blow to be struck in 1944. Yet, when it became known that the main Japanese fleet had reached Singapore, the Sumatra idea was dropped. These seemingly British political considerations nourished American indictments. British politi-cians, often at loggerheads with the military, believed for reasons of prestige that Burma and Malaya must be recaptured before the war ended. The Chiefs of Staff, however, considered that British forces should base their efforts in Australia and join the Ameri-cans in their sweep across the Pacific.[54] As for South East Asia, the more they thought of the long land advance through Burma, the less they liked it and the more they saw the advantage of an amphibious operation against Rangoon. However, this in turn caused friction with the Americans who still wanted the China Road open as soon as possible.[55]

The British, as already shown, held their own grievances against the Americans. 'We should be realistic enough to realise that American tendency is in the direction of playing a lone hand to the exclusion of Great Britain', minuted Esler Denning.[56]

It was in the light of this rivalry that intensive attempts were made in London to keep in step with American diplomatic initia-tives _vis-à-vis_ China. In both the British and the American treaties with China on the relinquishment of exterritorial rights, there was, as already indicated, an article stating that the signatories would enter into negotiations for the conclusion of a comprehensive treaty of 'friendship, commerce, navigation and consular rights' within six months after the end of the hostilities.[57] When it was learnt in London that Sino–American negotiations on the projected commercial treaty were progressing, immediate steps were taken at the Treasury and the Board of Trade to follow suit.[58] Indeed, unlike the situation prevailing in the 1930s, now it was the United States who were marching first in the Far East, Britain lagging some distance behind.

On 21 December 1944, J. R. Willis, of the Board of Trade, wrote to J. C. Sterndale-Bennett that the American moves towards the conclusion of commercial treaty with China revived the Board's anxiety over the danger that Britain may not have been keeping fully in step with the United States.[59] As far as he could see, the danger that Britain would find that the Americans had gone ahead without consulting London, and had possibly given way on some points where the interests of the two countries were similar, seemed real. He consequently pressed the Far Eastern Department to find out the lines on which the Americans were negotiating with the Chinese. Willis's anxieties were not groundless. The Americans were indeed doing their utmost to dissociate themselves from the British. The State Department, for example, insisted that in the field of propaganda and psychological warfare in the Pacific and in the South East Asia theatres American action must be independent, in order to avoid creating confusion in the minds of the people of the area with regard to the American and the British policies. It rejected the idea of making a motion picture of the war in Asia for world-wide distribution under joint Anglo–American auspices, as the political implication of such a production seemed to its officials most undesirable.[60] John Davies, a Foreign Service Officer attached to the staff of Lieutenant-General Joseph Stilwell, commenting on this question, stressed that depicting the British as wholeheartedly striving with the United States forces to open across north Burma a supply-line to China might be effective British propaganda. It was simply nothing but 'distorted history'. The Chinese audiences, he added, would be the first to recognise it as such. They would ask why the American government should be so naive as voluntarily to associate itself with, and produce, 'such a British apologia'.[61] According to Davies, not only the Chinese but most Asians considered the British policy in Asia to be more concerned with the re-establishment of colonial imperialism than

with the defeat of Japan. They regarded South East Asia Command less as a truly Allied command than as an instrument of
British policy. 'This estimate, despite fervent British protestation to
the contrary we know to be not without basis in fact. It may well
turn out to be the accepted historical evaluation.' This apparently
was the view of Joseph Stilwell as well. Roosevelt, on his part,
clearly stated, more or less on the same lines, that American
troops in India were there solely for the purpose of defeating
Japan. In so doing he attempted to counteract the widely held
impression in the Far East that Allied troops were waging a war
of imperialism.[62]

On 12 January 1945, a memorandum for President Roosevelt,
for possible use in discussion with Churchill and Stalin, was prepared in the Department of State. Entitled 'An Outline of Long-
Range Objectives and Policies of the United States with Respect to
China',[63] the paper stressed the need for China to be a principal
factor in the Far East. This, it was argued, was a fundamental
requirement for peace and security in that area. American policy
was accordingly to be directed towards three objectives: the political, the economic, and the cultural. By the first it was meant that a
strong, stable and united China, with a government representative of the wishes of the Chinese people, was most desirable. By
the second, the economic objective, it was hoped that future years
would see the development of an integrated and well-balanced
Chinese economy and a fuller flow of trade between China and
other countries (hopefully, of course, the United States). In the
cultural sphere it was expected that cultural and scientific co-
operation with China, as a basis for common understanding and
progress, would flourish.

Throughout the war years the American government supported Chiang Kai-shek. At the same time it hoped for co-operation with the Soviet Union and Britain. Towards achieving this
goal, claimed a State Department memorandum, 'we aim to
promote friendship and mutual trust in Sino–Soviet and Sino–
British relations'.[64] Where specific territorial or other issues existed, it was recommended that the government would assist in
finding 'amicable remedial arrangements'. Among the likely issues
of friction there were mentioned the restoration of Hong Kong to
China, and the 'adjustment of China's claims to outlying territories
such as Tibet and Outer Mongolia, with the concerned Soviet or
British interests, as well as the aspirations of the native peoples of

such territories for local autonomy'.

The line adopted by Roosevelt at the Yalta Conference, which was to determine the world's new post-war equilibrium, seems to have been influenced very little, if at all, by the papers prepared in Washington. There is no need to dwell here on the emergence of the Yalta System, nor on its effect on the Cold War in Asia.[65] It would, however, be useful to recall that the foundations for the decisions reached at Yalta, so far as the terms for the Soviet Union's entry into the war against Japan were concerned, had in fact been laid by Roosevelt in Teheran more than a year earlier. It was there that the President hastened to offer Stalin the Chinese port of Dairen as a free port under international guarantee to serve the Russians. It was there too that, as in bygone days, interests so crucial to the Chinese were lightly offered by a foreign power without the Chinese authorities being consulted. In Yalta, where China was not represented, in addition to Soviet–American understanding on Dairen, the Soviet Union, it was agreed, would receive a lease of Port Arthur. In the articles relating to these two ports, Stalin added at the very last minute, and Roosevelt accepted, the clause that the pre-eminent interests of the Soviet Union would be safeguarded. Henceforth the United States was also held responsible for what the Soviet Union managed to exact. Other articles determined that the Soviet Union would be guaranteed the retrocession of the Kurile Islands and South Sakhalin in the event of its entry into the Pacific War. A joint Sino–Soviet management would be established for the railways in Manchuria. As for Outer Mongolia, the United States and Britain promised to recognise its autonomy, thus separating it from China proper. The agreements concerning Outer Mongolia and Manchuria, it was agreed, would require the concurrence of the Chinese government which President Roosevelt promised to obtain.[66]

Similar to the case in Europe and in the Middle East, in the Asian–Pacific region, too, the Yalta Conference explicitly or implicitly defined the dispositions and limits of the respective spheres of influence of the Big Three, leaving China aside. Indeed, as has already been suggested, 'the Yalta agreements more or less corresponded to the realities of power politics towards the end of the war, to perceptions of these realities by the three leading nations, and to their visions of a new world order'.[67] These, rather than promises to China, therefore, seem to have been the determining factors. 'China as a *power* was no longer as relevant to

American policy as bilateral co-operation between the United States and the Soviet Union, both in the war against Japan and in building a durable structure of peace after the latter's defeat.'[68] Sacrificing part of Chinese sovereignty, as well as traditional American principles in the Far East seems to have been a price Roosevelt was willing to pay in order to deal with Russia as a main power and obtain its entry into the war against Japan.[69] In retrospect, the role of the Soviet Union in the Pacific War remained but secondary, to say the least. The Russians' attack on Manchuria on 8 August, at night, two days after Hiroshima had been bombed and a few hours before the second atomic bomb was to be dropped on Nagasaki on 9 August in the morning, could hardly be claimed to have contributed to the Japanese surrender. The Russian campaign merely helped Moscow 'to get her foot into the Far Eastern door before peace shut it'.[70]

Although Churchill was to a great extent kept in the background when discussions on the Far East took place, it must be remembered that he accepted the policy agreed on by Stalin and Roosevelt concerning China, and signed the agreement without demur, against, it must be added, Eden's advice.[71] From Churchill's point of view, emerging from his personal minute of 23 October 1944, no harm could be caused to British interests in the Far East should the Soviet Union be given a warm-water base in the Northern Pacific.[72] A Russian fleet 'vastly inferior to that of either the United States or Great Britain' having access to the sea worried him very little. 'Would not the Russian ships and commerce be hostages to the stronger Naval Powers?' he insisted. He whole-heartedly believed that it would be 'absolutely necessary' to offer Russia 'war objectives in the Far East'. No injury in his view could emerge should the Soviet Union receive 'all effective rights at Port Arthur'. Having the colony of Hong Kong in mind he insisted that 'any claim by Russia for indemnity at the expense of China, would be favourable to our resolve of Hong Kong'.

Since nothing was done in the conference to alter Britain's status in colonial regions, nor indeed to threaten her interests in Europe, there seemed to be no reason for Churchill to believe that he should object to the agreement. The trusteeship principle adopted at the conference specifically included the existing mandates and colonies from its application, thereby ensuring the continued presence, at least theoretically, of European colonialism in Asia.[73] In any case he was not faced here with any difficult dilemma. His views on the restoration of Russia's position in the Far East were decidedly compatible with the American wish, which he was not going to oppose. Churchill's strongly held opinion on the issue rendered the professional officials' views on this problem (with obvious local Far Eastern features) almost irrelevant.

Britain's position in Yalta further jeopardised China's relations with her. The conference underlined America's growing influence in the Far East. At the Foreign Office great concern was therefore expressed behind the scenes that 'the Americans are today virtually monopolising China'.[74] This development, it was observed, had been gradual and dated back to the period before Pearl Harbor. The fact that the United States claimed strategic responsibility for the Pacific theatre, which included China, gave her a great advantage over Britain. The Americans were directly assisting the Chinese in raw materials and munition. General Chennault's American Volunteer Group (the Flying Tigers) was helping the Chinese Air Force, while General Wedemeyer was engaged in building up a Chinese fighting force. Other Americans were trying to organise war production and transport and were engaged in constructing the Ledo Road and the oil pipe enterprises. China had thus become 'an exclusively American field of political, strategic and economic influence'. This, it was argued in the Foreign Office, was to have a far-reaching effect not confined to the prosecution of the war.

Indeed, the comparison of the United States' achievements with Britain's meagre economic and financial assistance to China since 1942 rendered the latter 'insignificant' and put Britain very much behind-hand. Britain's difficulties and preoccupation elsewhere was, of course, the main reason why she had furnished an unimpressive amount of supplies and services to Chinese troops in India (valued at merely just over £6 million), and why her additional assistance in the form of supplies shipped mainly from Australia just exceeded the £3 million mark. Indeed, £50 million more was made available for war purposes under the Financial Aid Agreement of 2 May 1944, and a Lend–Lease agreement for the supply of any arms, munitions and military equipment that Britain would be able to make was also signed on the same date. Yet, as already mentioned, owing to transport difficulties many of the supplies shipped out of the above credits remained in India, and only little use of the funds under the Financial Aid Agreement had been practicable. This state of affairs had made Britain's role in China that of 'a passive spectator'.[75] This uncomplimentary role became even more apparent in view of the part played by the Americans in pursuing single-handed their endeavour to promote a strong and united China through their mediation attempts between the Koumintang government and the Chinese communists. The war, therefore, hastened the decline of the British influence in China as it elevated the position the United States enjoyed there. Regaining a position similar to the one Britain had retained in the pre-war years became gradually an impossible task.

II FROM THE JAPANESE SURRENDER TO THE HOOPER MEMORANDUM

MAP 6   *1945: World War II ends*

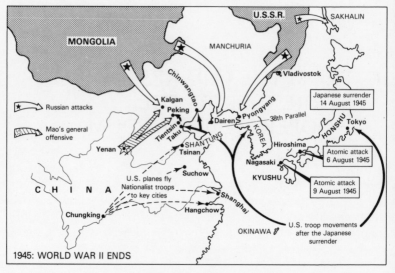

Source: B. Catchpole, *A Map History of Modern China* (Heinemann, 1976).

5   The War Ends

On 16 August 1945 Churchill telegraphed Generalissimo Chiang Kai-shek and congratulated him on the victory over Japan. He stressed the debt the world owed China for the 'tenacious and prolonged resistance' of her armies and paid a tribute to Chiang's 'inspiring leadership and steadfast adherence to the cause of freedom and democracy'. The British statesman, now out of office, expressed the hope that the two peoples would continue 'to march side by side as fellow builders of peace'.[1]

The surrender of Japan, no doubt, was a major turning-point in world affairs. The Second World War was over and a new era, the 'post-war era', had begun. Old hopes and plans had to be adapted to a totally new reality. In the respective histories of Britain and China a page was turned. Britain was no longer under Churchill's inspiring Conservative leadership. A new Labour government under Clement Attlee had inherited the burden in London. It had to lead a Britain virtually bankrupt, yet one that still retained something of the old status and commitment of a super power.[2] China, largely under the Koumintang, was heading toward a continued civil struggle to determine what regime deserved the 'Mandate of Heaven'.

Notwithstanding these drastic developments, Britain's basic pattern of attitude towards China remained almost unchanged. Only a few within both the official and the non-official quarters reached the realisation that the world that had produced and maintained Britain's privileged position in China was in existence no longer. Late in August 1945, G. V. Kitson of the Far Eastern Department of the Foreign Office asserted in a short memorandum that

British interests in the International Settlement at Shanghai, in particular, exceeded in scope and value those of any other foreign nation and it is therefore perhaps our duty to take the initiative in trying to ensure that these former international areas pass to Chinese administrative control *in such a manner that British rights and interests are adequately safeguarded.*[3]

Indeed, the transfer to the Chinese government of the administration and control of the diplomatic quarter in Peking, the International Settlements at Shanghai and Amoy and the British Concessions at Tientsin and Canton, in accordance with the treaty for the relinquishment of exterritorial rights in China of 1943, could only be carried out, according to some British officials, if made in harmony with British interests. The old game had to be continued. Within the non-official quarters it was the China Association that strongly adhered to the view that Britain's financial and commerical activities in China should be pursued as in bygone days. The Association took all the steps it could afford towards the re-establishing of British trade with and in China in accordance with the interests of its member-companies. It is perhaps in this light that a meeting held at the Board of Trade in December 1945 should be seen. On that date officials from various departments thoroughly discussed American competition in China and the reviving of Sino–British trade.[4] The hope of regaining the economic foothold lost during the war emerged as the common denominator of all the participants.

In China, on the other hand, the last months of 1945 saw parallel steps taken with the view of legislating a new company law aimed at subjecting foreigners to the Chinese legal system. These steps naturally caused great anxiety among the China Association members, merchants and all those who hoped to see Britain's former position in China re-established. The idea that foreigners would become subject to Chinese legal entity *per se,* irrespective of the national composition of the directorate or the shareholders, was difficult for those circles to grasp. Yet the China national system, being 'unequal treaty' conscious, and much inspired by the ideas of Sun Yat-sen and those expressed in Chiang Kai-shek's *China's Destiny,*[5] was adamant to recover the lost sovereign rights from malevolent foreign exploitation.

It was against this background that the Association of the British Chamber of Commerce, and Messrs John Swire & Sons, to mention only two bodies, mobilised all their political power and pressed the British government to make representations to the

Chinese concerning the proposed new law.[6] Questions in this respect were asked in Parliament. There was a general feeling that the Chinese authorities acted *male fide* with regard to British properties and that they were 'out to do us down whenever they can'.[7] Reports indicated that in Hankow, Canton, Swatow, Ichang, and many other places, official orders to return possessions or permit access to British owners were frequently ignored by illegal occupants, who were generally units of the Chinese armed forces.[8] There was a general feeling of defeatism among Britons that the Chinese, whether in Shanghai or elsewhere, would not let them re-emerge as share-brokers or in other financial key jobs.[9]

Moreover, the Americans seemed to be a most serious obstacle in the way of British companies and individuals in China. They spared 'lavish expenditure' which, as the *Manchester Guardian* observed, stood in contrast to the British capabilities. Thus American big business utilised their advantage 'to further their scheme of economic exploitation'.[10] The Chinese, it was argued by British commercial quarters, were hearing far too much of Britain being a debtor nation and were thus not the slightest concerned about the sacrifices Britain had made in order to win the war. The Chinese tended to believe that China had the greatest share in winning the war. They stressed the great American contribution towards the victory. Being interested in trade and credits Britain could no longer afford to extend, the Chinese were now inclined more than ever before to order machinery and various supplies from the United States. The hurried appointments of British consuls in all the major Chinese ports, with the hope of securing British shipping interest,[11] could not in the slightest way change the new atmosphere, based on the well-known fact that Britain's economy was crippled and that since January 1946 any further items the Chinese wanted had to be cash purchases.[12]

The Chinese company law, promulgated eventually on 12 April 1946, served as a further proof, if an additional one was needed, of China's embarkation on a new national course. Dr Sun Fo, Sun Yat-sen's son and the president of the Legislative Yuan, explained that the law was created to meet the needs of a new China in which exterritoriality did not exist.[13] As far as foreign interests were concerned, the basic principles behind the new legislation were that the Chinese government was to be regarded as an ordinary shareholder in the running of any company formed by the government and foreign or private Chinese interests, and that there should be no outside intervention by foreigners similar to that existing in the past. At the same time it was stressed that no limitation was imposed on the proportion of foreign to Chinese capital in any Sino–foreign company. In personnel too no restriction was created that prevented a foreigner from assuming any post, except that of chairman of the board of directors of a company. Also, foreigners could carry on any business in China provided that this was done in accordance with the Chinese law. The foreigner was no longer exempt from paying taxes, nor did he enjoy any privileges when appearing in Chinese courts.

These measures were taken with the hope of giving the Chinese in his own homeland the rights and privileges he was entitled to and of recovering the Chinese national economy. 'Public policy dictates', emphasised Sun Fo, 'that however desirable it may be to develop China quickly, it must not be done at the expense of the Chinese people as a whole and of the sovereignty of the State.'[14] Indeed, this was a new maxim which was to rule China's relations with the rest of the world and with Britain in particular for many years to come. In this respect the Koumintang regime paved the way for what is often regarded mistakenly as a unique Chinese communist norm.

The Americans were well aware of the fact that in the crystallising new reality a change of guards between the British and themselves in China would soon occur. After all, it was due almost solely to their military might that the Japanese empire collapsed. It was their submarine forces that so skilfully managed to attack and massacre Japan's shipping – merchant ships, tankers and warships. Without those, the Japanese empire, so dependent on overseas supplies, could not survive. Oil, iron ore, bauxite, coking coal, nickel, manganese, aluminium, tin, cobalt, lead, phosphate, graphite and potash, cotton, salt and rubber were all seaborne imports.[15] Food supplies too – sugar, soya beans, large proportions of the required quantities of wheat, and even rice – all had to be brought from abroad. The war of attrition launched by America against Japan and the strangling pressure their forces exerted against the Japanese military machine, and finally, of course, the two atomic bombs, were the dominant factors that brought Japan to her knees.

Two months prior to Japan's final collapse, Joseph Grew, former American ambassador to Japan and now Acting Secretary in the State Department, commented on this issue in a letter to

Henry L. Stimson, the Secretary of War. Post-war China, Grew stressed, was most likely to look primarily to the United States for support of her position as a major power, and for assistance in the maintenance of her security and internal reconstruction. Only to a lesser extent was the National Government of China likely to look to Britain for these ends. The Chinese authorities were going to press Britain, when expedient, for the restoration of Hong Kong and for the relaxation of restrictions on overseas Chinese in British colonial areas. Britain on her part would most probably see fit to link its overall policy towards China to that of the United States. At the same time she would 'strive to restore her . . . prestige, influence and trade in China'.[16] American military quarters in the South East Asian Command also appreciated that the British desired to cling to their interests in South East Asia and in China and were hoping to use the Command to this end. They read 'considerable consternation' in the British side of the Command as the war was drawing to a quick close.[17] The mounting of an impressive operation, considered of great political importance to British prestige in the area, was not believed to be possible. Yet, according to the Americans at the Command, every effort was being made by the British in order to hasten the commencement of the operation in question despite the difficulties. This seemed crucial to the British side. Even if the war would be over by the time the operation started, native people involved could be suitably impressed by British might and the inevitability of Britain's return. If any appreciable length of time was to intervene between the end of the war and the operation in question, the British forces would appear as merely substituting their occupation for that of Japan.[18]

It is not all surprising, therefore, that Americans involved in Asian affairs felt strongly that Washington should discontinue its participation in SEAC immediately after cessation of Japanese resistance was achieved. 'All future British military operations will be motivated in large measure, if not solely, by political considerations' argued George R. Merrell from New Delhi on 25 August 1945.[19] It was in this light that the deployment of British troops in Siam and the British plans to use troops in Indo-China were viewed. The British, it was felt, were giving big priority to operations designed to enable them to show their flag in Chinese ports. Re-entering Singapore in a manner that could restore British prestige was also believed to be of great necessity to the British.

Indeed, there almost existed an American consensus on British plans and desires in post-war Asia. Already on 28 May 1945, Wedemeyer had reported to George Marshall for Joint Chiefs of Staff that neither he nor Chiang Kai-shek had a clear picture as to Mountbatten's intentions regarding British pre-occupational activities in Indo-China. Both were most suspicious of the old colonial powers. Wedemeyer wondered how he could 'watch carefully to prevent British and French political activities in the area' as instructed by the President.[20] A week earlier, Ambassador Patrick Hurley had written to the President:

> Lord Louis Mountbatten and the diplomatic, commercial and military representatives of the other nations with colonial interests in Asia are endeavouring to obtain the appointment of Lord Louis as commander under the Generalissimo of all the United Nations forces in China. Should Lord Louis or any other British Admiral or General receive this appointment in preference to an American it would constitute an overwhelming victory for the hegemony of the imperialist nations and the principles of colonial imperialism in Asia. Such an appointment would also be a distinct setback for America and democracy in Asia.[21]

Wedemeyer tended to accept Hurley's view. 'It is my conviction', he wrote on 31 May 1945, 'that Ambassador Hurley has analysed correctly current manifestations of British intentions in the Far East Area.' He maintained that a careful British campaign had been in progress, designed to condition the minds of people in Asia for British leadership. He gave specific instances to illustrate his conviction.[22] Among them he mentioned the fact that the British government had appointed Major General Hayes as General Officer commanding all British Forces in China. As far as Wedemeyer was concerned there was no question regarding the existence of a British plan to increase the scope of their operations in the Far East, 'particularly those of political and economic nature'. This, he thought, could be facilitated by extending the existing boundaries of South East Asia Command to include all British–French–Dutch colonial possessions within the military sphere of the Command. Wedemeyer regarded British intentions and plans as incompatible with American policy in China aimed at containing, diverting and destroying the maximum Japanese forces and creating at the same time 'favorable conditions for the evolution of a strong, free, united China friendly to the United States and accessible to American post-war trade and industrial development'. Wedemeyer stated quite clearly: 'indubitably the British–French–Dutch are interested in recovering their pre-war prestige, political and economic preferment throughout South East Asia, the South-Western and South Pacific areas and Hong Kong in China'. To the North he saw the Russians exploiting favourable opportunities to spread their ideologies in the North China areas where considerable collaboration could reasonably be expected from the Chinese communists.

The South East Asia Command was disbanded only at the end of November 1946 and the post of Supreme Commander disappeared with it. (Mountbatten had left Singapore six months earlier and Lt. General Sir Montague Stopford served as the Acting Supreme Commander.) For well over a year after Japan's surrender, therefore, while the relegation of civil affairs to newly appointed civilians was in progress, a wartime organisation lingered into the post-war era. All this time Mountbatten was reflecting on the form that Britain's military organisation in Southern Asia should assume. He hoped to reconstitute the structure and give it a peacetime role. The idea was that if necessary the organisation could be easily converted back to a war organisation. Although the plan was eventually not accepted by the civil and military authorities in London,[23] the continued existence of the Command, a purely British structure with its military, civil and political activities, can serve as one more example of British imperial and war hangover in the region.[24]

Naturally, this was in direct contrast to Washington's desires in the region. A war dominantly waged by American forces could be most unpopular if resulting in the mere restoration of a colonialism almost on its way out before Pearl Harbor.[25] This point had also been stated as early as 30 May 1942 by the Under-Secretary of State, Sumner Welles, when he insisted that as a result of the war the United States must assure 'the sovereign equality of the peoples the world over'. He added that American victory 'must bring in its train liberation for all peoples. The age of imperialism is ended. The right of people for freedom must be recognised'.[26]

The repeated American expressions of anti-imperialism, while not new to Britain's political leaders, were somewhat embarrassing and problematic to the members of the newly formed Labour government. Like their Conservative predecessors, they too could not accept anti-British criticism nor sharply cut slogans such as 'the age of imperialism is ended'. At the most, they were driving at a gradual implementation of emancipation. They wished to avoid chaos created out of the ruins of Tokyo's imperial adventure. Gradualness, slowness, preparation, well-organised liberation and similar phrases replaced the old-fashioned anti-imperial terms. Indeed, it was difficult even for the more progressive elements within the British Labour movement to abruptly separate themselves from their traditional imperial sentiments. While after the war the idea of world regulation by the United Nations gave birth to the idea of trusteeship that would take care of the embryonic nations in their infancy, the colonial powers – Britain under Labour included – remained adamant in their refusal to adopt such a new scheme. A politically divided Trusteeship Council with supervisory powers, they believed, would have smacked of 'a lingering aftertaste of the colonialism that was to be abolished'.[27]

It is perhaps in this light that Mountbatten's attempt, mentioned above, to prolong the roles of the South East Asia Command well into the post-war period and to extend territorially its theatre of operations should be viewed. When the war ended, the ambition of the Command's leaders to dominate Indo-China emerged as a new source of friction between the British and the Chinese. Wedemeyer, Chiang Kai-shek's military adviser and the Commander of the American forces in the China theatre, advocated the occupation of the whole of French Indo-China by Chinese forces. Being highly suspicious of British intentions in the region, he hoped to enhance, at the expense of British prestige, the waning authority of the Koumintang's government. Eventually a compromise, based on the consideration that the South East Asia Command had shipping to reach the southern part of Indo-China, had been concluded. The delimitation between the two commands was put at 16 degrees north latitude, cutting French Indo-China in half.[28]

In Malaya, conventional plans had been made to restore Britain's pre-war colonial status. The dropping of the two atomic bombs on Hiroshima and Nagasaki and Japan's subsequent unexpected surrender, however, shattered them altogether. Operation 'Zipper', South East Asia Command's planned campaign for September to retake Malaya, became all of a sudden meaningless. It therefore never could take place as an ordinary wartime operation, but rather as a hastened operation carried out *after* Japan had already been defeated. Naturally this was an orderly operation which encountered no Japanese resistance. It merely re-established British colonial rule in Malaya and could in no way enjoy the cloak of a courageous campaign aimed at liberating the natives from the Japanese yoke. Accordingly, British troops entering Malaya were never supported by local armed guerrillas.

The political effects of the campaign were different in nature from what they would have been had the British liberated the local population from Japanese domination by their own direct and independent efforts. There was perhaps another factor hinted at by T. H. Silcock and Ungku Abdul Aziz.[29] British troops, straight from a jungle campaign and newly released from the full rigours of military discipline, were hopelessly ill-prepared to resist the temptation of the new situation. Corruption, illegal commandeering of property, gun-play against unarmed civilians, and sale of arms to gangsters, 'undermined in six months a tradition that had taken a century to build'. Thus, at the very moment when 'strict incorruptibility of administration and meticulous regard for property' was most needed, it was not manifested and could not, therefore, boost British prestige. 'The army of 1945 was the victim of circumstances no less than the army of 1942. But those who understand the roots of British prestige in Malaya appreciate that it was 1945 at least as much as 1942 that undermined the confidence of the public.'[30]

In Burma too, the local population was to learn of British intentions immediately after the war ended. They had expected a full self-government with the right to independence if the people wished to secede from the Commonwealth. This expectation, as Sir Reginald Dorman-Smith, the Governor of Burma, observed later, was not realised.[31] Indeed, constitutionally as well as in every other way, the Burmese found themselves worse off than they had been before the war. Burma had to revert from an advanced administrative status under the Japanese to a most primitive form of colonial government – that of being governed by Parliament through the Governor. Yet even Sir Reginald by no means suggested giving away part of the Empire, but rather adjusting British policy to the new reality that prevailed after the war, since 'the old conception of Empire which our fathers possessed is quite out of date'. He now maintained that 'instead of force or coercion we must substitute ability to give the right leadership'. Indeed, no intention to turn over a new leaf was altogether discernible in British policy towards Burma.

As a liberal, Mountbatten represented personalities and groups who saw the light of the new reality. He understood that Burmese nationalism had emerged as a force to reckon with and believed it was important to retain the goodwill of the Burmese people. Unlike Sir Reginald Dorman-Smith, he did not think, for example, that Aung San and others who co-operated with the Japanese during the war should suffer on account of their political opinions honestly held. Only to acts committed against the criminal law or actions repugnant to humanity should there be a reaction.[32] As far as he was concerned, Britain's return to Burma meant coming as rescuers. Burmese goodwill should not have been thrown away at all costs.[33] 'It was no good fighting against the new tide of Asian Nationalism' he stressed. The right thing to do was to try and make the Nationalists Britain's friends.[34] The short-lived attempts to carry out this policy underlined the fact that Mountbatten's job was becoming increasingly more political than military.[35] After Labour came into power and he reported to Attlee, he explained to him the line to take with the liberated territories. 'I was delighted to find that I had his full backing – I had a feeling that I was going to need it'.[36] Under Churchill, he felt, he would have been fired.[37] Liberation, with all the connotations attached to it, meant a new role for Mountbatten. He was no longer a fighting commander but rather a politician who needed a great deal of imagination. Political and humanitarian problems on an unprece-dented scale faced him wherever he turned. Supplying the people of South East Asia with food and medicine and reconstructing crumbled and crumbling economies were the order of the day. The areas he controlled and was responsible for after Potsdam included, in addition to Burma, Malaya, Singapore, Siam, Sumatra, the Netherland East Indies, Indo-China (to the 16 degrees parallel) and later Borneo and Dutch New Guinea, an area in which 128 million human beings were living.

For almost two months after Japan's surrender, Sir Reginald Dorman-Smith constantly pressed for a quick return of Burma to civil government. Mountbatten on his part, however, felt that Sir Reginald and the civil authorities would not be able to take over.[38] 'We claimed to have "liberated" not to have "re-occupied" Burma', insisted Sir Reginald.[39] Placing Burma back on the road to full self-government, he thought, could not be done until after the return of the civil government. 'Please', he wrote to the Secretary of State, Burma Office, 'compare American approach to Philippines. So convinced am I that policy outlined by Mount-batten is wrong from every point of view that I would have to be asked to be relieved of my post if it were endorsed by HMG. No other course would be open to me.'[40] It took some time before Burma returned eventually to colonial civil rule, just to become soon after an independent state. The deliberations on Burma can provide an insight into the problems related to colonial momentum and to the varied opinions connected thereto.[41] So can the complex thoughts and actions related to the formation of Britain's China policy. Officials of most of the government depart-ments, as well as officers of non-official organisations, notably the China Association, retained, on the whole, views that proved beyond doubt that they were lagging behind the dramatic regional and global developments of the war years. In no way did they share American enthusiasm for building China up as a great power after the war.[42] Only on American insistence, for example, did the Churchill government agree that China should be brought in, at the outset, as one of the permanent members of the Security Council of the United Nations Organisation. As far as colonial heritage *vis-à-vis* China was concerned, here too Washington and London differed quite considerably. This was most notable as regards Hong Kong. It is this – the Hong Kong question – there-fore, that the next chapter will attempt to unfold.

6 Hong Kong

In view of imminent possibility of surrender of Japan, I am advised that American Staff has designated two American officers to accept surrender. No reference is made to the participation of China or the Generalissimo in receiving surrender. I recommend that the Generalissimo or his designated military representative be invited to be present and participate in receiving the surrender of Japan. To do otherwise after China's 8 years of war against Japan would be injurious to China's prestige in Asia.[1]

This was the decided view expressed by General Patrick Hurley, the American ambassador to China on 9 August 1945. It was compatible with the official American policy to boost the Koumintang prestige and to impress upon the Chinese people that they were an integral part of the Allies' victory over Japan. It was in accordance with this policy that Chiang Kai-shek was asked by the American Secretary of State to notify him of the designation of the officer he wished to act as his representative in the acceptance of the surrender of Japan along with the Supreme Commander for the Allied Powers, General Douglas MacArthur.[2] Chiang Kai-shek was likewise informed that MacArthur would direct the Japanese Imperial General Headquarters to have the Japanese forces in China (other than those opposing the Russians in Manchuria) surrender unconditionally to him, or to his subordinate commanders.[3]

American efforts not to hurt Chinese national feelings in any way were also discernible in Indo-China. Although no provision in the Potsdam Declaration specifically mentioned that, the Japanese were ordered to surrender in the northern part of Indo-China to Chiang Kai-shek and in the southern part to Mountbatten, all in accordance with the operational agreement reached earlier on.[4]

In view of this American attitude, and Washington's unwillingness to assist European powers regain their lost colonial prestige in Asia, it is not at all surprising that British pressure on China, aimed at an early British reoccupation of Hong Kong, caused great alarm in American quarters. The Chinese, in accordance with their traditional practice in international relations, leaked out all the relevant details of the British requests to them. Thus a copy of a British memorandum dated 6 August 1945 to the Chinese government was passed on by Dr K. C. Wu, the Acting Minister for Foreign Affairs, to Hurley.[5] In that memorandum the British government stated that among the most urgent tasks to be tackled were the reoccupation of key areas in the occupied territories, enforcement of the terms of surrender and the disarmament of the Japanese forces. The Chinese were informed that arrangements had already been made for the despatch of the necessary British forces 'to reoccupy and restore the administration of the Japanese southern armies, which is at Saigon'. Among the post-surrender tasks the memorandum mentioned the restoration of the French administration of Indo-China and the facilitation of the return of French forces and administrative officers for this purpose as soon as they were available.

The Chinese regarded the British requests as being 'not in accord with the general order of surrender', that is, the directive by President Truman to MacArthur of 15 August 1945. That directive specified that 'the Senior Japanese Commanders and all ground, sea, air and auxiliary forces within China (excluding Manchuria), Formosa and French Indo-China north of 16 degrees north latitude shall surrender to Generalissimo Chiang Kai-shek'. The question that remained unsolved, however, was what was meant by 'within China' and whether it included Hong Kong or not. The Chinese pointed out that in the areas to be surrendered to the Supreme Allied Commander, South East Asia Command, or to the Commanding General, Australian forces, Hong Kong was not at all included. They consequently understood that the Japanese forces in Hong Kong were to surrender solely to Chiang Kai-shek. The Ministry for Foreign Affairs at Chungking likewise questioned British views and plans pertaining to Indo-China. They regarded these too as in conflict with the general order of surrender. The Chinese government claimed that it respected all legitimate British interests, and was prepared to accord them every necessary protection, but at the same time a concerted plan of accepting the surrender of the Japanese forces was essential to

the restoration of peace and order in Asia. The British government was accordingly expected to make arrangements for the
acceptance of the surrender of the Japanese forces in accordance
with the general order, and refrain from landing troops in any
place in the China Theatre without getting special authority to do
so. Hong Kong, it was inferred, was *not* part of the 'legitimate
British interests' to which China was prepared to accord 'every
necessary protection'. 'The National Government of the Republic
of China', read another telegram from Chiang Kai-shek in a somewhat threatening tone, 'is now on the most friendly terms with His
Majesty's Government. But if the British Government does take
such actions in contradiction to the agreements and the co-opera-
tive spirit of the Allied Nations, it will be indeed a matter of great
misfortune to the Allies.'[6]

In general terms, this was the situation up to 17 August 1945.
The coming fortnight was pregnant with events, communications,
and tough negotiations within the triangle of China–the United
States–Britain as regards Hong Kong. Before elaborating these,
however, it is perhaps necessary to return to some earlier events
and to some basic British considerations on the issue of Hong
Kong.

As early as 1 May 1944, Sir George Moss, whose views on China
have already been mentioned, prepared detailed notes on the
future of the colony. Though his arguments were not all accepted,
or even acceptable, within the British decision-making machine,
future events – even under the Labour government – were to
prove that Moss's view enjoyed, on the whole, a wide backing. Sir
George had served at Canton in 1929 during the time of the great
friction between Canton and Hong Kong. It was this experience,
as well as what he described as 'Koumintang methods', that
emboldened him to prepare the notes and to try and interest his
colleagues in the Foreign Office in his line of argument. In the first
part of his notes, entitled *'HONGKONG will revert to its former
status of a British Crown Colony after its recapture by the Allies. No discussion admissible'*, he examined one possible course open to Britain.
This course, he stressed, was unlikely to succeed unless Britain
could assure herself that the colony 'will be recaptured by the
British alone, or by naval, military, para-military and Air Forces
predominantly British'.[7] Here, he envisaged a situation in which
the Chinese would prove hostile or even put a fifth column into
Hong Kong and, by non-co-operation, would defeat any purely

British effort to recapture it. They could also arrange for the recapture of the colony by forces predominantly Chinese and American. Another way was a loyal Chinese co-operation with their Allies in recapturing Hong Kong so as not to prejudice the remaining course of the war against Japan. In such a case they would keep up their agitation for the retrocession of the colony, but would do that 'within bounds', that is they would encourage Britain to undertake the heavy costs of rehabilitation of Hong Kong and of settling claims. When that was accomplished and post-war commercial frictions gave them the excuse, they would then proceed, by way of local strikes, incidents and boycotts to demonstrate their power within the colony. They would go on to prove the colony's dependence on its hinterland by extending the boycott to Canton, Swatow, and Kwangtung. They could even boycott British trade and efforts throughout China, playing with certain American, Russian and other foreign interests who might find it profitable. They would try to convince Britain that far from being an asset, post-war Hong Kong would be nothing but a never-ending source of trouble and that she had better retrocede it with as good a grace as possible.

The second possibility open to Britain, according to Sir George, was retroceding Hong Kong to China, but capitalising the situation by bargaining for considerably greater improvements in Britain's general and commercial position in China than otherwise obtainable. He admitted that this line had its attractions.

> The Chinese would appreciate a successful bargain more than a gift, and might be disposed to grant more liberal rights and privileges to foreigners in return, e.g. in commercial and cultural laws, representation in municipal government at the big ports, particularly SHANGHAI, the right of participation in coastal and river shipping etc.

The raising of this alternative illustrates, perhaps, the innermost thinkings of some of the decision-makers. Returning to China and acquiring privileges there as in days past seemed, at times, more attractive than the mere rendition of Hong Kong with its unclear future.

There was, however, some great disadvantage to this course, according to Moss. Should China fall prey to civil war and the communists take over, Britain might find herself having given up her last base on the China coast and back in a position 'similar to that which we occupied in 1840'. During the Treaty Port period, Moss reminded his colleagues, the hulks anchored off the Concessions and the Settlements were often the last line of retreat for foreigners in which the Navy could guard them when there was no safety ashore. Hong Kong 'is like a hulk off the mainland of CHINA. It should not lightly be given up.' Sir George Moss then elaborated on three additional courses open to Britain. One was to reserve all British rights and refuse international discussion or official pronouncement until the problem could be seen and weighted in the perspective of post-war conditions. This course appeared to him to be the best line opened under the prevailing circumstances. The other two were the unilateral retrocession of Hong Kong to China in generous appreciation of the part China played in the war, or an indication that the British government might be disposed to consider planning Hong Kong under the aegis of an Allied New Order after the war. By way of conclusion, Sir George Moss expressed his detailed *credo* in a style becoming an Old China Hand. His views, however, represented on the whole the beliefs of younger and more 'progressive' colleagues. A fuller assessment of the policy *vis-à-vis* the Hong Kong question, he stressed, should be made in post-war light. Only then should a realistic forecast be made of the special interests of Britain, her trade with China, its prospects, the value of British investments and the cost of rehabilitation in varying circumstances, together with an assessment of Britain's financial undertakings and commitments in China and Hong Kong. The stakes of the Dominions in China would then also be assessed.

As for the problem of China herself, Sir George asked whether China's promises and records were such that Britain could afford to give up a substantial base in Hong Kong in an exchange for 'shadowy promises'. What if China fell into civil war and decay? In the intervals between civil wars and discord, Moss reminded his colleagues, China had, under strong rulers, expanded her frontiers throughout the centuries. There was in China 'a great tradition of Nationalism and Secret Societies' and in this respect there was no great difference between the Koumintang and the Chinese Communist Party. Both carry on those traditions. Chinese 'Nationalism and Imperialism' in Moss' view, were so well organised and directed through secret channels, that no matter what internal weakness and political divisions might prevail for the moment, Britain had to reckon with 'the Chinese policy of social expansion which aims at long-term recovery of Chinese influence in all regions where once they did enjoy political ascendancy, however tenuous and vague'. Sir George Moss had no doubt that the Chinese also aimed at penetration into new fields and that Tibet, Burma, Siam, Indo-China and Indonesia all came within the scope of the Chinese traditional ambition. On top of the traditional ambitions, the Chinese had already indirectly greatly profited from 'Japanese pan-Asiatic propaganda, the result of which will persist in Asia long after the defeat of Japan'.

Sir George insisted, just as the research group functioning in India under the auspices of Sir Olaf Caroe mentioned above,[8] that 'whatever the future of CHINA, should she develop in unity under Koumintang, should she be torn by civil wars, or should the Koumintang eventually be displaced by the Communists backed by the USSR, we must be prepared for friction with Chinese Nationalism so long as we remain in Power in East Asia'.[9] If Britain decided to hold Hong Kong, the decision must be founded on 'a firm faith in our future and in the strength of our position'. If a short-term policy was adopted there was much to be said in favour of giving up Hong Kong in exchange for whatever advantages could be obtained from China in return. 'But the British Empire certain of its Destiny, must take long views.' In view of the uncertainties of the future, Moss was inclined to think that it would be 'most unwise even to entertain the idea of giving up Hong Kong'. The British flag should be rehoisted there 'without recrimination or friction'.

Hong Kong, just as Malaya, had to be freed before the Allies could proceed to drive the Japanese out of China and Manchuria. This scheme, as already hinted at, had, on the whole, been accepted by many of the decision-makers in London. In due course they were to act accordingly.

At the Research Department of the Foreign Office, G. F. Hudson, minuting on Sir George Moss's memorandum, maintained that the Hong Kong issue could serve as a good opportunity for the Japanese to throw 'an apple of discord' among the Allies in the last stage of the war. They could leave Hong Kong as 'a political time-bomb' behind them, especially if they allowed Wang Ching-wei, the Head of the Japanese puppet regime in Nanking, to declare it restored to China and hoist the Chinese flag there. Chiang Kai-shek, who would find it hard to be outdone in patriotic irredentism by Wang or to pull down the Chinese flag on Hong Kong after it had once flown there, might then try to take over the colony relying on America. 'Would it not be better', asked Hudson, 'to offer at an early date to open conversations with China on matters of common concern to both countries, not especially on Hong Kong, but indicating that Hong Kong would be within the scope of the talks?'[10] The negotiations need not, in Hudson's opinion, move very fast and Britain could do some hard bargaining. Yet the mere fact that the subject of Hong Kong was officially under discussion could 'take the sting out of the behind-the-scenes agitation in China and make it less likely that Chungking would be carried away into a "Fiume" adventure'. If the colony was to be rendered, it had to be made on principle, such as 'recognition of China's services to the cause of the United Nations, and not on grounds of geographical and ethnic claims by China; otherwise it would serve as a precedent for Gibraltar'. L. H. Foulds, at the Far Eastern Department, believed that the secession, when it was made, as it had to be, should not be a 'futile gesture of appeasement to China, but a contribution to arrangements for international security'.[11]

The view that rendition of Hong Kong to the Chinese should be seriously contemplated was a minority view. The risk that the colony would become a Chinese 'Fiume' eventually tilted the scales to the other option. When Churchill was asked in the House of Commons whether Hong Kong was excluded from his earlier declaration that it was not proposed to liquidate the British Empire, it was Attlee, the Deputy Prime Minister, who took it upon himself to answer. He stated categorically that no part of the British Empire or Commonwealth of Nations was excluded from the declaration referred to.[12] He confirmed, moreover, that all encouragement would be given to British firms to prepare plans for re-establishing themselves in Hong Kong and getting on with British export trade in that area. By way of a rhetorical question, Mr Shinwell stressed that members of the Labour Party were as keen to advance the well-being of the British Empire as were members of the Tory Party.

Up until the opening of the Potsdam Conference there had been no indications as to the moment, or the manner, in which Hong Kong would be recaptured. Roosevelt held the view that the colony should be returned by Britain to the Chinese who, on their part, should immediately declare it a free port under Chinese sovereignty.[13] As for a possible military operation against Hong

Kong, a memorandum prepared for the President stated that it was 'undesirable from the political point of view that American forces be employed for the reoccupation of the island or the adjacent Kowloon leased territory'.[14] In London, on the other hand, the recapture of the colony in a sea-borne operation by the Americans or, conceivably, by the British after arrangement with the Americans, seemed most likely.[15] The Colonial Office even based their plans for resuming the administration of Hong Kong on this possibility. So far as China was concerned they only had in mind the possibility that the Japanese might pull out without a fight and that Hong Kong might be occupied by Chinese irregular forces operating in the neighbourhood.

The Colonial Office scheme called for the rapid infiltration of British personnel into Hong Kong at the first sign of a Japanese withdrawal, and for the organisation of an emergency administra- tion pending the arrival of a British Commander with regular occupational forces.[16] The British Army Aid Group (BAAG), a small military unit operating in South East China and assisting British personnel who managed to escape from Hong Kong, was to be given a small party of persons sent into Hong Kong and act as a rallying point there. When practical steps were taken in this direction, however, General Hayes, in charge of all British Military personnel in China, made it clear that the project was not practic- able owing to anticipated opposition of the Americans and of General Wedemeyer in particular. Hayes, General Carton de Wiart, the British Prime Minister's representative in China, and Sir Horace Seymour, the Ambassador to China, maintained that, in order for the project to succeed, it had first to be cleared both with the Chinese (who seemed likely to recapture Hong Kong by regular troops) and the Americans at the highest level. Steps in this direction were indeed made in the course of the last days of July as a result of a meeting held between representatives of the Colonial Office, the War Office, and the Foreign Office.[17] Although it was contemplated that the Prime Minister would approach President Truman directly and would thus hasten the process, no move in this direction was eventually made at the Pots- dam Conference. Ernest Bevin, the new Labour Secretary, decided that the matter should be taken up through the usual channels.[18] It was in this light that a memorandum was prepared for the Prime Minister, and a minute on the arrangement for the administration of Hong Kong in the event of its liberation by regular Chinese forces was attached to it for further consultations.

The first document[19] specified that 'assuming that the Chinese are prepared . . . to hand Hong Kong to HMG it would neverthe-less be embarrassing to have to receive it from them'. The note stated that the question of whether it was practicable for Hong Kong to be recaptured by British (including Dominion) forces, or with the participation in some degree of British forces, was one for the appreciation of the Chiefs of Staff. If neither course was practicable Britain could not but accept the position. In that case it was at all events important that Britain should be able to assume the administration of the British Colony 'as soon as the military situation allows'. The note made it clear that no understanding with the Chinese government existed in respect of their accep-tance of British Civil Affairs policies in any British territory included in their operational sphere. A most embarrassing situa-tion might therefore arise in the event of Hong Kong being liberated by Chinese forces, unless there was a clear agreement with Chiang Kai-shek in advance as to Britain's role in the adminis-tration of Hong Kong.

The second document was coupled with a copy of a memoran-dum prepared in the Far Eastern Department on the political issue between Britain and China regarding Hong Kong.[20] In it, a brief historical background on the colony was given. In the course of the negotiations which preceded the abolition of exterritoriality in China, it was stressed that the Chinese government had made a request for rendition of the New Territories (part of the colony of Hong Kong) leased for 99 years by the Peking Convention of 1898. Though the British government refused to consider the question in connection with exterritoriality, it agreed that it might be discussed with the Chinese after the war. The Chinese, claimed the memorandum, were most likely to face the British with the proposal that the 1898 Agreement should be terminated and that the area should revert to Chinese sovereignty. It was appreciated that the Chinese ultimate object was to recover the whole colony ceded to Great Britain. They were likely to claim, on top of the geographical, economic and demographic arguments, that the colony had been wrested from them under the unequal treaties, and that its rendition would erase the last of China's humiliations suffered under the treaties. Against these Chinese arguments, it was emphasised, Britain could remind the Chinese that in 1842 Hong Kong was a desolate island with no inhabitants except a few fishermen. Its development as one of the greatest seaports was a direct result of British enterprise and good government. Likewise it could be argued that, with the removal of the protection afforded by exterritoriality and a probability of unsettled condi·tions in China for some years after the war, Hong Kong was likely to acquire increasing importance and value as a base from which British merchants and industrialists would be able to operate in China. Last, it was stressed that, having lost Hong Kong to the enemy, it was a point of 'national honour' for Britain to recover it and 'restore it to its normal state of order and prosperity'.

The Japanese surrender came with dramatic suddenness. For the people of Hong Kong 'the reaction was not so much one of surprise as of numbed relief'.[21] On 16 August 1945, the Imperial Rescript on the Japanese unconditional surrender was read by a Japanese officer outside the Hong Kong Hotel, first in Japanese and then in Chinese.[22] In Stanley Camp the internees had no authentic news until Franklin Gimson, Colonial Secretary, asked for an interview with the Japanese Camp Commandant on that day at which he was told of the surrender. Gimson asked to set up a provisional government under himself as the senior Hong Kong government official present. Yet, unlike the dramatic description from James Morris, who insists that when Hong Kong was liberated 'it was only the immediate action of one Briton . . . that kept it British',[23] the developments outside were most crucial. The limited preparations in the colony itself only matched the diplo·matic and military preparations made by the British government. On top of the steps taken at the highest quarters, a planning unit in London had arranged to set up a military administration in the colony under a Military Civil Affairs Unit.[24] Since the surrender came before its personnel could get to Hong Kong, Gimson was instructed to set up an interim administration. He received his instructions via Chungking and the British Army Aid Group a week after he had acted on his own initiative.[25] Soon he estab·lished himself and a key administrative personnel in the French Mission Etrangeres building. However, the Japanese, believing that the surrender should be made to the Chinese, still remained responsible until the surrender had actually been made and the British forces arrived. As in other parts of their occupied terri·tories, they ensured the maintenance of law and order until they formally surrendered.

But the recapturing of the colony by Rear-Admiral C. H. J.

Harcourt was not at all easy to agree on. As indicated above, the Chinese were adamant in not allowing the British to accept the Japanese surrender. The British, on their part, argued that, irrespective of operational theatres, whenever the sovereign power (and they regarded themselves as the legitimate sovereign power in Hong Kong) had significant forces available, it had to assume its authority and accept the Japanese surrender in its own territory.[26] They suggested that a representative of Generalissimo Chiang Kai-shek was welcome to participate when the British received the Japanese surrender. They insisted that they could not accept the interpretation that the term 'within China' in the order of surrender included Hong Kong. 'Moreover', it was stated, 'His Majesty's Government feel confident that, as a soldier himself, His Excellency, the President, will understand that, as the United Kingdom was forced to relinquish possession of Hong Kong to the Japanese, it is a matter of honour for his Majesty's Government to accept the Japanese surrender there.'[27] Indeed, as already indicated, Bevin, like Attlee, felt that 'when your house is swiped and you have contributed to its retaking you have an obligation to your own to reoccupy'.[28]

National honour was time and again mentioned as the reason for returning to the colony. Immediately after the Japanese surrender, Sterndale-Bennett, the head of the Far Eastern Department, to give one more example, mentioned this reason in his conversation with the American ambassador in London.[29] The long-term future of Hong Kong seemed much less significant than the question of the immediate return. Dealing with Washington, it was by far easier and more acceptable to argue for the right to retake the colony by military means as part of the immediate postwar operations than for the right to pursue a century-old civil colonial regime there.

At the same time, no second thoughts existed within the new Labour government as to the desirability of colonial restoration in Hong Kong. On 23 August 1945, Attlee reassured Churchill that arrangements were being made for the Japanese surrender in the colony to be accepted by a British force commander and that plans for re-establishing British administration in the colony were fully prepared.[30]

As wide official agreement on the question of Hong Kong existed in Britain, the most important issue remained, throughout the crucial period, the triangle relations London–Washington–

Chungking. As indicated earlier, the news that Japan would accept a defeat urged the British government to secure American consent to despatch a British naval force to Hong Kong hurriedly, in order that it be a British commander who would accept Japan's surrender and assume full powers of military administration in the colony. The Japanese accepted defeat on 14 August 1945. Rear Admiral Harcourt's naval force did not arrive until 30 August.

On 18 August 1945, Attlee, encouraged by the Chiefs of Staff,[31] urged Truman, in a top-secret message, that Britain could not accept any interpretation of General Order Number One, the first Allies' order to the surrendering Japanese, as meaning that Hong Kong, which was British territory, was included in the expression 'within China'. Without awaiting Truman's reaction, Attlee added that, as had 'already been notified to the Joint Chiefs of Staff and the Chinese Government, a British naval force is now on its way to release Hong Kong from Japanese occupation, to bring aid to prisoners and internees situated in the colony and to restore the British administration'. As regards the possibility that Japanese commanders on the spot might regard Hong Kong as being 'within China', Attlee asked Truman to instruct the Allied Supreme Commander, General MacArthur, 'to order the Japanese High Command to ensure that the Japanese local commanders in the British Colony of Hong Kong shall surrender to the commander of the British naval force on his arrival'.[32] Later the same day, President Truman informed his adviser, Admiral William Leahy, that he had discussed the matter with James Byrnes, the Secretary of State. As a result, the War Department was instructed to remove Hong Kong from the China Theatre for surrender purposes.[33] It was on 18 August, therefore, that the United States, at least formally, accepted the British position on Hong Kong.

However, a day later, on 19 August, the Chinese government reiterated its desire and its right to reoccupy Hong Kong, and to resume its authority there as the legitimate sovereign power. Washington was thus advised that a representative of Chiang Kai-shek should participate in receiving the Japanese surrender.[34] Chiang Kai-shek, encouraged by Wedemeyer, stressed that he could by no means accept the new American stand on Hong Kong. He consequently instructed Dr K. C. Wu, the acting Minister for Foreign Affairs, to protest to the Allies and state that the Chinese government had been striving for the best interests of the Allies. The British authorities, on the other hand, were attempting to 'violate agreements' and showed no intention of returning Hong Kong to the Chinese authorities. The following day Chiang Kai-shek advised Truman that he had heard indirectly of the President's acceptance of the British line on Hong Kong and the subsequent instructions to MacArthur. If, however, this was not the case and no telegram had yet been sent to the British, he would strongly advise against 'any unilateral alteration of the terms of the Potsdam Declaration and the surrender terms already issued by the Supreme Commander for the Allied Powers'.[35] If, on the other hand, the telegram to Attlee had already been sent, Chiang Kai-shek suggested that the Japanese forces in Hong Kong should surrender to Chiang's own representative in a ceremony in which both American and British representatives would be invited to participate. 'After the surrender', insisted Chiang Kai-shek, 'the British will be authorised by me to land troops for the reoccupation of the island of Hong Kong.' The British should not, under any pretext, land any troops on the mainland of China. Chiang made it clear that it was with reluctance that he was making this concession and expressed his hope that the President would support China's position.

Replying to Chiang Kai-shek, Truman informed him that three days earlier he had written to Attlee that from the United States' standpoint there was no objection to the surrender of Hong Kong being accepted by a British officer, provided 'full military coordination is effected beforehand by the British with the Generalissimo on operational matters'. General MacArthur, wrote Truman, would be instructed to arrange for the surrender of Hong Kong to the British Commander whenever the above coordination was effected. Truman stressed that the situation with regard to the Japanese surrender at Hong Kong presented, as far as the United States was concerned, a military matter of an operational character. 'No question arises with regard to British sovereignty in the area and it is my understanding that you do not desire to raise such a question.' Taking the British line of argument, the President explained that it seemed reasonable that, 'where it is practicable to do so, surrender by Japanese forces should be to the authorities of that nation exercising sovereignty in the area'.[36] He thus rejected Chiang Kai-shek's suggestions.

On 23 August, Chiang Kai-shek, in order to extricate himself from the Hong Kong tangle, informed Truman and Sir Horace Seymour, the British Ambassador to China that, as the Supreme

Commander of the China Theatre, he had notified the British that he agreed to delegate his authority to a British Commander to accept the surrender of the Japanese forces in Hong Kong. He likewise stated that he would designate a Chinese and an American officer to participate in the acceptance of surrender in Hong Kong and asked the British to effect the necessary military coordination on operational matters beforehand as had been suggested by Truman.[37]

The Labour government's reaction to this Chinese move is illuminating. It underlines the fact that the new authorities in London produced no basic change in Britain's traditional imperial policy in the Far East.[38] It refused to accept the moderate solution advocated by Chungking, a solution aimed at saving the face of the Chinese. This uncompromising line was taken despite Seymour's insistence that the Chinese formula 'seems to give us what we want'.[39] Even General Ismay, acting as intermediary between the Minister of Defence and the Chiefs of Staff, maintained that the Chinese face-saving compromise, although 'not perhaps entirely satisfactory, was, from the military point of view acceptable'.[40] Yet it was Bevin and subsequently the head of the Far East Department, Sterndale-Bennett, who stuck to an uncompromising line, maintaining that Britain must re-establish the *status quo ante bellum* in Hong Kong.[41] The British government thus adamantly declined to recognise the Generalissimo's authority to delegate power to a British commander to accept the Japanese surrender at Hong Kong. Rather, Britain insisted that Chiang Kai-shek should waive his power as Supreme Allied Commander of the China Theatre so far as Hong Kong was concerned.[42]

Hurley, the American ambassador to China, regarded this British line as 'a threat of force ... ignoring all courtesies'. He consequently recommended that Chiang Kai-shek put the case to the bar of world public opinion.[43] The idea, accepted by the Generalissimo, was to press for the reformulation of Washington's policy *vis-à-vis* Hong Kong, as the existing one had given 'much aid and comfort to the arrogant attitude of the British'. Anyway, while doing everything to avoid conflict with the British colony, he intended to resist with force any British action in other places in the China Theatre.[44]

The adamant British stand on Hong Kong received almost no popular support in the United States. One of the many letters from citizens, by no means exceptional in its style, which was received in the Division of Public Liaison in the Department of State read:

> That Great Britain wants Hong Kong returned to her is the most discouraging piece of news I have read lately. We are going to build a better world on the same old rotten foundations, out of the same old materials, for the same old purpose of enriching European merchants at the expense of weaker Asiatic peoples.

After dwelling on the historical background and insisting that Britain never had any legitimate claim to the ownership of Hong Kong, the writer of the letter added a *postscriptum* note in handwriting: 'The more I think of this thing, the madder I get. Britain lost Hong Kong the same way she got it – by conquest. It has now been reconquered from Japan, but that was done not by Britain but by China and the United States. The fleet the British are sending is to retake it from China by force.'[45]

British policy remained unshakable.[46] The Generalissimo's suggestion that a British officer should accept the Japanese surrender in Hong Kong as his delegate was rejected outright. The British government was merely willing to welcome a Chinese representative, along with an American officer, to participate in the surrender. This would be accepted by a British officer empowered for this purpose under General Order Number One. The Chinese and American officers designated by the Generalissimo could only attend 'as representatives of the Supreme Commander of the China Theatre'. On the assumption that there was a surrender document, they would sign as witnesses and nothing else.[47]

This line was too much even for Carton De Wiart, the Prime Minister's military representative in China, who wrote: 'had we been able to contribute to the capture of Hong Kong I feel we might have had some reason to object, but unfortunately we have done nothing and had the war lasted a few weeks longer the Colony would undoubtedly have been liberated by Chinese forces'.[48]

Chiang Kai-shek could not subscribe to the British line. To go beyond the concession he had already made seemed to him to be neither in accordance with the agreements of the Allied Powers nor compatible with his duties as the Supreme Commander of the China Theatre. Acquiescence in the British pressure and *fait accompli* was incompatible with his self-image as the leader of the post-war new China, a China insistent on strict observance of its national rights. He deplored the British attitude and maintained that it would seriously impair the traditional friendship between Britain and China. De Wiart, who telegraphed this message to London added: 'Never have I seen him so moved as he was today.'[49] Indeed, Chiang regarded the Hong Kong question 'as something of a test case'.[50] The British line, as far as he was concerned, smacked of the old unequal treaties system which he so strongly wished to erase forever.

Having heard, however, of the British nomination of Rear-Admiral Harcourt as the British commander in charge of accepting the Japanese surrender in Hong Kong, Chiang was faced with a most delicate situation which threatened his position both as a national leader and a world figure. He thus informed Truman that from that very moment he delegated his authority as Commander in Chief of the China Theatre to Harcourt. He subsequently requested the President to instruct MacArthur to issue the 'necessary instructions to Admiral Harcourt'.[51] On 29 August 1945, the Foreign Office, unsatisfied with the fact that no concrete agreement had been reached with the Chinese, suggested a compromise formula of its own. Admiral Harcourt, on behalf of the British government, would accept the surrender jointly with a British officer, preferably General Hayes, acting on behalf of Chiang Kai-shek. Any other Allied representatives would sign as witnesses.[52] This solution, however, was still unacceptable to Chiang Kai-shek. He was indignant at what he regarded as British overriding of his rights as Commander in Chief of the China Theatre.[53] Consequently, the Foreign Office came up with another formula: Admiral Harcourt would sign a surrender document not only on behalf of the British government, but equally on behalf of Chiang Kai-shek as China Theatre Commander.[54] On the next day, as a result of consultation between officials of the Colonial Office and the Foreign Office, instructions to this effect were sent to Admiral Harcourt.[55] This was at last acceptable to Chiang Kai-shek.[56] Recently published accounts on this question seem, therefore, not to be entirely complete.[57]

Harcourt's fleet was delayed in Subic Bay, the American base in the Philippines, while the Admiral's precise official position was debated. He was not given definite orders until 30 August, by which date he was in the neighbourhood of Hong Kong. According to Endacott, Harcourt signalled the Japanese that he would send a plane to Kai Tak airport at a stated time, and asked that the Japanese representatives should meet it to discuss the take-over arrangements and the entry of the fleet.[58] The powerful British Naval Force reached Hong Kong at 11 a.m. on 30 August. There was no opposition from Japanese guns and the naval parties landed and took over the Naval Dockyard. Soon Gimson came on board *HMS Swiftsure* and later in the day he and Admiral Harcourt went out to Stanley Camp where 2500 European civilians were interned. 'National flags were raised and a thanks-giving service was held.'[59] On 1 September, Admiral Harcourt proclaimed a military administration, Mr. Gimson being appoint-ed Lieutenant-Governor. Everything was ready for the surrender ceremony which had been fixed for 12 September 1945. But there was a formal problem. Was it appropriate that a small part of Chiang Kai-shek's command be empowered to surrender before he himself received the essential overall surrender of the China Theatre? Consequently, the surrender ceremony took place at Government House on Sunday, 16 September.

There is no need to dwell here on the internal difficulties that faced the colony following the Japanese surrender, for example the shortages of rice and fuel, nor is there a need to elaborate on the construction work which was so badly needed both inland and in the harbour. This has already been narrated.[60] It is, however, important to stress that, at this stage, British decision-makers involved in shaping Britain's China policy, were greatly relieved by the successful diplomatic, political and military campaign to return to Hong Kong. General Sir Alan Brooke was impressed that 'the Chinese in Hong Kong do not appear to resent our return and that it should not take long to restore normal life here'.[61] Admiral Harcourt, in a letter to A. V. Alexander, the First Lord of the Admiralty, observed much later that it had been an interesting job to release the British internees and 'to get this very fine Colony going on its feet again'.[62] It was so, even though longer-term problems were far from resolved.

Britain's control of Hong Kong enabled her officials and her merchants to re-establish pre-war contacts with their Chinese counterparts in China proper, for example in Canton, in Chunking, and in Amoy. It was now endeavoured to build up confidence among the Chinese and use the facilities in Hong Kong 'to aid China, recognising that in doing this we shall benefit ourselves from the trade which is bound to accrue'.[63] Harcourt, as Alexander put it, had a big task in reviving the Colony, and in making 'a very good start' there.[64]

That relations with China proper were part of British hopes in Hong Kong emerged soon from the Civil Affairs policy directives relating to the colony. One of these, entitled 'Relations with Canton', stated that 'the close practical relationship with the Provincial authorities at Canton which existed before its occupation by the Japanese in 1938, should be re-established as soon as possible in agreement with His Majesty's consular representative at Canton'.[65]

British intention as regards China proper could not be kept secret. Chiang Kai-shek was much perturbed by rumours that British ships were proposing to enter Chinese ports with a view to safeguarding British interests. He warned that should this happen he would regard it as a hostile act, and that the Chinese nation would certainly consider it as tantamount to a desire on Britain's part to acquire Chinese territory.[66] He made a clear distinction in this respect between the British and the Americans. 'The United States Fleet and the United States forces are welcome at any port in China', he communicated to President Truman. 'The British Fleet and the British forces and other imperialist forces are not welcome in China. I respectfully request that if and when the American fleet enters any Chinese port it will not be accompanied by any British ships or contingent.'[67] Indeed, the Chinese fear of 'the imperialist governments' – France, Britain and the Netherlands – dominated the scene in the period immediately following the Japanese surrender. The Chinese government was greatly worried by what it regarded as an imperialist endeavour to create a situation, especially in Shanghai and Peking, that would give them an excuse for landing their forces in China.[68] Chiang Kai-shek was anxious about the pretext the British had given him that they wished to land troops to protect the people of the cities from the communists. According to Patrick Hurley, the Generalissimo maintained, moreover, that the imperialists were actually co-operating with the communists while both the United States and the Soviet Union were co-operating with his national government.

By November 1945 first steps to facilitate the transition from military to civil administration in Malaya, Borneo and Hong Kong were contemplated. The target date for a civil administration in Hong Kong was set for 1 February 1946.[69] Now that Labour was in power, two contradictory tendencies *vis-à-vis* colonial policies dwelt within the government in London. On the one hand there was the desire to preserve the old colonial heritage and the interests that these accrue, and on the other there existed the hope of approaching the great enlightened ideas of community welfare, freedom and democracy. Shortly before being appointed Parliamentary Under-Secretary to the Colonial Office, Arthur Creech Jones, the Labour leader, expressed this dichotomy. In an introduction to a paper prepared for the Fabian Colonial Bureau, he stressed the contributing factor in the defeat of Nazism which the existence throughout the world of strategic bases played in support of the common cause of the United Nations. 'The war has demonstrated the importance of such bases in any scheme of collective security, and the impossibility of their thoughtless abandonment.' On the other hand, he admitted, there was the fundamental question of the rights and position of the people who inhabit patches of earth that geography had converted into strategic bases. There must be, he asserted, a serious effort to reconcile the two factors.[70]

Old China Hands, however, continued to represent those who lagged behind events, who grasped neither the new post-war reality, nor the rights and position of the people in colonial lands. H. G. W. Woodhead, a well-known British journalist in China and the editor of the *China Year Book* , perhaps expressed the views of this group best. By April 1947 he was still thinking of Hong Kong in terms of playing 'a decisive role in China's post-war rehabilitation', and of affording 'security and protection to foreign firms of all nationalities anxious to trade with China, but nevertheless apprehensive of subjecting themselves to the irritating restrictions of China's company legislation'.[71]

The American official stand, however, remained almost unchanged. Hong Kong's return to China, through agreement between that country and Britain, seemed to be 'in the interest of peace and stability in the Far East, particularly in view of treatment of China as one of the world powers'.[72] At the same time, it was realised that, if that change was made, China, in taking over administration and control of Hong Kong, should make provision for 'the assumption and discharge of the official obligations and liabilities attached to it, and for the maintenance of its free port facilities'. The disadvantages that a retrocession of Hong Kong to China might cause were not overlooked. Such a development might lead to 'minor losses to US investors and traders because of the likelihood that a Chinese administration would be less efficient, impose higher taxes, and treat shipping between Hong Kong and other China coast ports as coastal shipping reserved to Chinese vessels'. It was likewise realised in Washington that after liberation from the Japanese, Hong Kong was made the head-quarters of the British Far Eastern Fleet and that, despite the limited value of the colony for defence purposes, Britain intended to strengthen it even further as 'an outpost of empire'. London was disposed to facilitate British recovery and stabilisation with reference to shipping and trade at the expense of non-British interests. Similarly, it was realised, the Chinese were to be given a feeling of 'not being on an equal footing at Hong Kong with members of the white race in general and with the British in particular'.[73] Thus, on the eve of the communist victory in China, mutual suspicions between Washington and London by no means disappeared. In this sense Britain's successful return to Hong Kong changed very little.

7 British Perception III

In the process of imperial restoration in the territories occupied during the war by Japan, no principle difference could be discerned between the colonial policy adopted by the new Labour government and that carried out earlier on by the Churchill governments. As early as 20 August 1945 Bevin promised the House of Commons that the government would assure all British subjects who had been liberated in the Far East of its 'watchful care for their interests, for the re-creation of their industries and the restoration of their normal life throughout all those territories'.[1] A similar line was taken by another prominent Labour leader, Sir Stafford Cripps, the President of the Board of Trade. Cripps spoke specifically of measures to restore British trade in China, of opening general consulates there, and of returning representatives of British firms to their commercial bases. He expressed his desire that negotiations with the Chinese for a commercial treaty would be opened at an early date.[2] Being aware of Britain's alarming situation in the field of economics, where, in his words, she had suffered 'a very severe blitz', he had stressed earlier on the peacetime problems that would face the nation, especially unemployment.[3] If the British were to maintain their standard of living, he believed they would have to export 50 per cent by volume or perhaps 125 per cent by value more than they had before the war. Full employment upon the production of the right commodities was therefore a crucial target.[4] As for China, Cripps maintained that Anglo–Chinese trade before the war was on a comparatively small scale. British trade to China was scarcely 2 per cent of British exports. Now, he believed, 'a new era has opened'. Restraints and restrictions had been cast off and once the after-effects of war and revolution had been overcome 'a great and wide field of mutual trade will be opened up'. Cripps hoped that the 'new era' would be free from what he termed British 'hangover of the Chinese Imperial regime and the extra-territorial methods of a past age'.

But could there be a new era with no 'hangovers'? The good old dream of the Chinese market had not, after all, faded. Britain, passing through the transition period of painfully regaining the flexibility of her export trade, was making efforts at re-establishing it. Now, however, giving away products on the basis of long-term credits was out of the question. 'We must get imports for what we export to the greatest possible extent' claimed Cripps. Britain was going to restore her old-time presence in China, encourage imports from there and give herself a basis for export to this huge land. Alongside bringing in necessary products such as foodstuffs, 'entrepot trade' was emphasised. According to Cripps, Britain had to be 'the Western base for the distribution of Chinese commodities and, of course, there is no reason at all why we should not import any and every kind of commodity and manufactured article for re-export'. British shipping and services, stressed Cripps, were available to carry as much as Britain could export to China or China could export to Britain. While the lack of any stable relationship between the Chinese currency and sterling was mentioned as the remaining obstacle in the mutual trade, a tone of optimism prevailed in his expressions. Cripps maintained, for example, that all traces of inequality or exploitation had been finally cleared away by the exterritoriality treaty of 1943. The door was open, he inferred, for a new start in Anglo–Chinese relations.[5]

Almost a year after the war ended it was still voiced in the House of Commons, however, that not as much had been done to re-establish the pre-war relations with the Chinese as, for example, had been done by the Americans. 'The United States to some extent have stolen the limelight by sending there that great war figure, General Marshall, who I am sure is playing a very important part in China', stated Major Digby.[6] Was Britain doomed to fall into the position of playing a kind of second string in China? R. A. Butler was likewise worried. Was Britain's position in China being watched properly? Were British consuls re-established in their positions there? Had they re-established their contacts?[7] Air Commander Harvey suggested that a parliamentary mission be sent to China in view of what he regarded as difficulties of British traders there and in view of the pressure that the Americans were putting on the Chinese 'to keep them out'.[8] These voices were echoes of earlier statements by Fletcher, Wardlaw-Milne and others in Parliament.[9]

Similar to the British efforts with respect to Hong Kong and China proper attempts were made to strengthen Britain's position in the China–India border and the Assam Himalaya and pre-empt any moves on China's part directed towards expanding her influence there. Armed posts were placed and plans for the construction of a strategic motor road were examined. A sense of urgency was created by the publication of official Chinese maps embodying territorial rights down to the pre-1914 'Outer Line', and by the realisation that, with Allied victory in the Far East, China would for the first time in many years be free of Japanese attack.[10] In some British quarters it was feared that China was likely to behave aggressively and in an expansionist and irreden-tist way, and perhaps even return to the old Imperial tactics.

As far as Tibet was concerned, here too there were some apprehensions. The province had been, to some extent, under British protection since Francis Younghusband's mission to Lhasa in 1904 and the resultant Anglo–Tibetan treaty. This situation remained even after the 1907 Anglo–Russion convention in which the two parties agreed to have no political relations with Tibet except through China.[11] During the Second World War and immediately after it, the Chinese central government attempted to bring Tibet under its effective control. Under the pretext of wartime necessities it moved military forces to the area and tried to open the routes to transportation. The argument used was that the Tibetans, instigated by Japanese agents and aided by Japanese arms and planes, were planning offensive action against Chinese border provinces.[12] There were clear indications that Chiang Kai-shek was trying to exploit war events in order to re-exert his government's political hold in the area.[13]

After the fall of Burma to the Japanese, for example, investiga-tions had been made into the feasibility of sending back caravans from India along the old tea-route to China across the highlands of Tibet. The Tibetan government agreed with the government of India to allow the transport of non-military supplies through their territory. The Chinese, however, regarded the good offices of the government of India in a matter concerning Tibet as derogatory to their position as suzerain. They tried to deal directly with Tibet, and thus produced a deadlock in the negotiations, since the Tibetan government looked to India for support against Chinese encroachment.[14]

The British government, suspicious of Chinese intentions, was unwilling to accept any changes in what it regarded as a sensitive area. As early as 1943, Eden reminded T. V. Soong that ever since the 1911 revolution Tibet regarded herself as 'in practice com-pletely autonomous' and had opposed Chinese attempts to reassert their control.[15] The British had made attempts to bring about an accord between China and Tibet 'on the basis that Tibet should be autonomous under the nominal suzerainty of China', but the 1914 Chinese–Tibetan–British Convention on these lines had not been ratified by the Chinese government. While admitting Tibet's autonomy, the Chinese government claimed sovereignty over areas that the Tibetan government claimed belonged exclusively to their autonomous jurisdiction. Following the Chinese failure to sign the Convention, the British govern-ment in 1921 stated their intention of dealing with Tibet in the future as an autonomous state under the suzerainty of China. Since then, the British government had always been prepared to recognise Chinese suzerainty over Tibet, but only on the under-standing that Tibet was regarded as autonomous.[16]

In the course of a visit to Lhasa in 1944 Sir Basil Gould, British political officer at Sikkim, gave the Tibetans assurances of Britain's readiness to give them diplomatic support in their intention to retain their autonomy, though the extent of that autonomy was never determined.[17] On 18 August 1945, Chiang Kai-shek on his part declared that if the Tibetans expressed a wish for self-government, China would accord them 'a very high degree of autonomy'. He stated, moreover, that if in the future the Tibetans fulfilled economic requirements for independence, the Chinese government, as in the case of Outer Mongolia, would help them attain that status. As a pre-condition, however, they would have to give proof that Tibet could consolidate its independent position and protect its continuity so as not to become another Korea.[18]

While in the Far Eastern Department historical background on Tibet was gathered and prepared, Bevin surprisingly intervened on 20 February 1946. He expressed his objection to the then proposed diplomatic representations in support of Tibetan autonomy, a move that could be read as an imperialistic interven-tion in China's internal affairs. He argued for aloofness, lest 'we should become involved, and a matter which has hitherto remained dormant should become a live issue, liable to attract the attention of powers like Russia and America, with possible awkward repercussions for ourselves'.[19] Consequently it was agreed that Britain should not take action but leave the Tibetans to handle the autonomy issue themselves with China if they so wished. The basic policy, however, remained as before: Tibet should have a certain degree of freedom and the government of India should, if not aid Tibet against a major enemy, at least continue to meet as far as possible 'reasonable Tibetan requests for the supply of arms and munition'.[20] The domination of Tibet by a potentially hostile major power, the British armed services held, could constitute 'a direct threat to the security of India'. Neither Russia nor China could be allowed to violate Tibetan autonomy, as this might enable them to build roads and airfields to their own advantage and 'vitally affect India's strategic position'.[21] Should it prove impossible to preserve Tibetan autonomy by diplomatic methods alone, or should Russia or China attack Tibet, it was considered necessary for the government of India to provide direct military aid to Tibet. In the light of these observations, it is not at all surprising that Britain made all possible efforts to compete with China, over medical aid to Tibet, for example.[22] The Tibetans, afraid of Chinese cultural penetration as well as of the communists, Chinese and Russians, were inclined to prolong the existing co-operation with Britain.[23] Until Indian independence, British interests were almost entirely concerned to preserve Tibet as a neutral area on the borders of India. Tibetan trade, being insignificant, played no role in the British considerations.[24] Indian independence saw a substantial reduction of British interests in the area.[25]

Another issue that affected Anglo–Chinese relations during the period under discussion were China's traditional aspirations in South East Asia and her unique contact with the Chinese dwelling there – the Overseas Chinese. Since the beginning of the twentieth century these Chinese had been engulfed by mainland Chinese nationalism which, in opposition to itself, stimulated the growth of local nationalism.[26] The rise to power of the Koumintang was signalised by the expression of an aggressive nationalism whose virtual claim was 'where there are Chinese, there is China'. Attempts of the Koumintang to form an *imperium in imperio* in each of the South East Asia countries not only provoked the colonial governments to repressive action, but also aroused the abiding resentment of the indigenous people among whom the Chinese were living.

Under the Japanese occupation the Overseas Chinese were very

much on the defensive. After the Japanese surrender, concurrent
with Britain's efforts made at re-establishing their colonial position
in South East Asia, the Koumintang attempted to reimpose their
control over the whole of China and simultaneously to regain
popularity among the Overseas Chinese. In London, Leo H. Lamb
warned his colleagues of these intensified attempts.[27] He foresaw
'the exploitation of the political and economic potentialities' of
these Overseas Chinese in the future by China, and the
emergence of various demands, for example the raising again of
the issue of the disputed Burma–China border. Indeed, in the
immediate post-war era it became increasingly clear that the
Overseas Chinese could no longer look up to the Metropolitan
Power in the hope of getting their protection. Moreover, by that
time they were already split between the supporters of the
Koumintang and those who had pro-communist leanings. For
Britain this new situation meant endangering her already
weakened position in South East Asia.

While official British circles were well aware of the Koumintang's threat to Britain's position in both China proper and the
surrounding colonial regions, they were only a little appreciative
of the Chinese communist party's potential power and influence.
This myopia was perhaps part of a wider insensibility to the forces
of change in Asia. No British official representative (as distinct
from individuals like Michael Lindsay and Claire and William
Band) lived in the Soviet areas. Information on the communists,
was as a result, always partial, indirect and biased. It flowed from
China in a disorderly manner and remained most of the time part
of a marginal academic debate.

The 1942 Parliamentary mission to China mentioned the
communists in its report to the Prime Minister in general terms,
devoting less than one page out of the forty-five pages of the
report to their activities.[28] They noted that Chou En-lai, the
communist representative in Chungking, impressed them as 'a
man of honesty and candour', but added that they could not say
what his colleagues might have been like. 'The professed aims of
the Communists are identical with those of the Koumintang,'
claimed the report, 'while they are free from the reactionary social
elements by which that party is strongly influenced at present.' It
was assumed that the communists would not attain power without
a long and bloody civil war. However, it was also brought into
consideration that at the end of the war the Generalissimo might

perhaps offer to allow them to continue their administration of the provinces they occupied and play their part in the building of the new China.

Sir Archibald Clark-Kerr, the British ambassador in Chungking until 1942, described the communist regime as 'mild Radicalism'.[29] His successor, Sir Horace Seymour, regarded the communists as agrarian reformers whose policy had 'proved superior to that of the Koumintang in the economic security and social well-being it has brought to the masses of the population'.[30] The communists, while harbouring no intention of abandoning Marxism–Leninism as their guiding principle, aimed, he thought, at adapting it to the Chinese conditions. In the Research Department, G. F. Hudson, an Oxford specialist on China, observed that Mao Tse-tung regarded Chinese communism 'as part of a world proletarian revolution'.[31] Its aim was to establish in China the same economic and political system which existed in the USSR. Owing to the backwardness of the country there would have to be a transitional period in which the communists would be ready to co-operate with the Koumin-tang, provided they were given a share in the government, until such time as they were ready to push out the Koumintang and suppress them. 'To urge on Chiang Kai-shek the necessity for a reconciliation with the Reds', observed G.P. Young, at the Far Eastern Deparament, 'would, I think, be wholly profitless.'[32]

On 21 October 1944, Sterndale-Bennett, the head of the Far Eastern Department, asked Sir Horace Seymour's advice as to whether it was desirable to establish direct contacts with the Chinese communists.[33] He admitted that until then his depart-ment had been inclined to think that in view of the weakness of the Chinese central government it would be dangerous to get in touch with the communists and to put pressure on Chiang Kai-shek to reach a settlement with them. However, it now seemed that, in the interest of building up a strong, united, democratic China, perhaps Britain could add to the American pressure and say that if the central government wanted to be treated as a Govern-ment of China and as one of the Big Four, they must come to an understanding with the communists. If the Chinese communists and the Koumintang did not reach a settlement, he thought, the communists might drift into the Russian orbit. Russia might enter the war against Japan and later demand special security arrange-ments in Manchuria. This in turn might cause her subsequent penetration to north China to such a degree as to prevent the unification of China. In his reply Seymour dwelt on the crisis China was going through, and expressed the opinion that it would be a long time before a strong, united, democratic China emerged.[34] The communists, he thought, aware of the strength of their position, were not likely to surrender any point that they regarded as vital to their continued existence. The communist administration could not be called a democracy, but seemed nevertheless to have popular support. It was doubtful whether their system would work in more densely populated and richer parts of China. He, Seymour, did not think that Britain could do anything to promote an agreement between the two rivals. In any case, without American intervention Britain could not intervene. Indeed, he confirmed, British contacts with the communists had until then been confined to contacts with communist representa- tives in Chungking. He did not see, however, how Britain could open a consular post in a communist area against the wishes of the Chinese government. The idea of altering the policy hitherto taken had consequently been dropped.

On the whole, those in London who paid any attention to the issue adopted 'a flexible approach'. The British government was not going to tie herself 'to the Koumintang Party, or to the existing set-up of the Chinese Government'.[35] It refrained from interfering by extending aid or assisting the communists financially. The idea was to deal with whatever government happened formally to hold power in China. Any interference in internal Chinese affairs, it was felt would invite Chinese interference in Indian affairs. China, under whatever regime – communist or Koumintang –given the existing nationalistic and exclusive tendencies, symbolised a danger to British interests. In the course of time, argued Evan Luard, 'the initial predisposition in favour of the legal and recognised government of the country was quickly counter- balanced by an increasing disillusion with the ineffectiveness of the National Government'.[36] As the civil war in China progressed, and the communists controlled a larger part of the country, there emerged more positive feelings on the part of the British govern- ment towards Chinese communists, despite ideological hostilities. This was due mainly to persistently favourable reports on the efficiency, integrity, even the moderation of the communist leaders in China. This feeling, however, had to be balanced against the desire to act, as far as possible, in agreement with

Britain's principal partners and allies, particularly the United States.

Gradually the British government hoped for some sort of understanding between the Nationalists and the communists. It consequently granted its full support to Washington's efforts to bring about some such solution. A clear policy on this issue was laid down in 1945 and reaffirmed in a series of public statements between then and 1949, the main line being that the civil war was 'an internal problem for the Chinese themselves to resolve'.[37] British attitude to the Chinese Communist Party–Koumintang controversy and to the distress in which China found herself was much cooler and pragmatic and 'less inclined towards acute anxiety and other strong emotions' than could be discerned in the United States.[38]

The year 1946 saw a general improvement in Sino-British relations. British India and Burma policies were basically accepted by the Chinese central government. Hong Kong, though still remained 'a latent cause of friction' between the two countries, caused no deterioration in their mutual relations.[39] Even the initiatives of 'the hot-heads of the Koumintang', a term coined by Sir Ralph Stevenson, the ambassador to China, did not manage to change their basic situation. Economic questions had become the main issue standing between the two countries. Of these the most important was the return of British properties to their owners. 'The limpet-like hold of Chinese military and other authorities on properties seized and reoccupation', reported Stevenson, was still having to be subjected to leverage. The Chinese were also causing difficulties for British firms on the question of opening of the Yangtze ports. They likewise attempted to defeat all British efforts to develop trade and to override what the British Embassy in China regarded as 'the obvious economic advantage to China of such development'. Difficulties were also created for British interests as regards the taking-over of the various International Settlements and foreign concessions. Strenuous negotiations during 1946 put paid to the Chinese intentions to proceed to a unilateral assessment of the rights and obligations that China inherited; and the principle of joint assessment by *ad hoc* bodies in the places concerned had been accepted. As in other parts of the Far East, the British ambassador realised that 'nationalism was rampant in China and, although general xenophobia was happily absent, incidents with American troops and the virulent anti-

Americanism of communist propaganda were clear danger signals'.

The war had undoubtedly changed Britain's historical trading position in China and the special treaty privileges she had enjoyed for years. American influence greatly increased. China was gradually being built up as a big United States war base against Japan. Up to the end of the war, it was estimated that Washington supplied war materials to China under Lend–Lease to the value of some $600 million.[40] China's dependence on the United States could also be seen in the cultural, diplomatic and financial fields. The immediate post-war period saw no change in this respect.

The new situation had some advantages for Britain. She could now 'sit back' and watch the Americans bear the brunt of anti-foreign agitation aimed at them. She could now dissociate herself from American policy where it suited her decision-makers, but could at the same time profit from any benefit that might accrue from it. By contrast with the Americans, maintained G. V. Kitson, at the Far Eastern Department, 'the British merchant, with his long experience of the China market, his greater tact in dealing with the Chinese, and his ability to fulfil the new orders he has been able to accept, has won the Chinese confidence and with it the promise of a valuable basis for future trading relations when we are in a better position to supply the Chinese market'. This statement, though not baseless, was a little too optimistic a view of the British position in China. It was saturated, it seems, with self-satisfaction and was fed to a great extent by the old hope for a resuscitated Chinese market. Kitson and his colleagues in the Far Eastern Department tended to believe that British initiatives such as visits by the United Kingdom Trade Mission and Lady Cripps', Aid to China Project, as well as other 'personal contacts on the part of prominent persons 'from the United Kingdom, had done much to convince the Chinese of Britain's 'genuine interest in China and her future'. They did not sufficiently appreciate the accumulative negative psychological deposit in regard to Britain left in the Chinese leadership during the war. This had been illustrated time and again by statements made privately by prominent Chinese officials and had been publicly expressed in Chiang Kai-shek's *China's Destiny*.

British policy-makers tended, rather, to put a stress on immediate *material* difficulties that supposedly had 'an adverse effect on the position of British properties in Shanghai and else-

where'. Thus Kitson was preoccupied by the fact that British
interests in China were suffering from inflation and a 'severe
economic strain', from 'interruption of communications and
general dissipation of resources brought about by the civil war',
from the rising labour costs in China which virtually strangled the
country's export trade, and, as he assessed it, from an import trade
that could not be financed much longer by reserves of dollars or
sterling.[41] As he understood it, the immediate trading outlook was
'unhealthy'. A continutation of the existing economic strain might
well produce 'an administrative collapse, leading to chaos and
possibly an eventual assumption of power by the Communists'.
Naturally Kitson concluded that Britain must still continue largely
to 'tag behind' the American's China policy, particularly in so far
as that policy was directed toward resisting Soviet influence in the
Far East. 'This influence, if directed against our imperial possessions in the Far East ... through the medium of a Communist
regime in China, is capable of developing into a serious factor
for the future.'[42]

British myopia as regards communism in China prevailed
throughout the period under discussion. It was only in the course
of 1948 that a line more sensitive to the internal upheavals in
China and their possible consequences was eventually adopted.
On 9 December 1948 a Cabinet paper seriously dwelt on the likelihood of a communist domination of China and on the implication
such a development might have on British interests in the Far
East. It included a memorandum submitted by Bevin on recent
developments in the Chinese civil war.[43] Now, indeed, it had
become no longer possible to ignore the communists. They were
already in control of north China.

The paper was based on the assumption, so common in the
emerging cold-war era, that the Chinese communists, if ever
successful in surmounting the economic difficulties, would adopt
the policies of what was described as 'orthodox Communism'. The
political effects of this state of affairs on neighbouring countries
seemed to be that communist activities there would be facilitated.
The economic effects in these areas were likely to be 'an increase
in labour troubles and disturbances in the production of vital
commodities'. These likely effects were of great significance in
Britain's attempts at re-establishing her position in South East
Asia.

As far as China proper was concerned, it was assumed that

there would be 'an immediate period of dislocation when foreign commerce generally will be at a low ebb', and that there would follow a period in which the economic difficulties of the com-munists 'may dispose them to be tolerant towards foreign trading interests'. Likewise it was assumed that the existing 'nationalist tendency towards foreign investments and capital installations' would be enhanced and that 'the intention to work rapidly towards the exclusion of the foreigner will be strengthened'. Finally it was stated that there would be a tendency 'to subject foreign trade, both import and export, to close government control'. This control would not altogether suit the types of trade British merchants aimed at doing in and with China.[44]

Despite these assumptions it was hoped that 'British interests in China might be able to carry on at least for a time and we should encourage this'. The paper, therefore, recommended that Commonwealth countries, the United States, France, the Nether-lands, Burma and Siam should be consulted 'as to the best means of containing the Communist threat to all our interests', that all necessary steps should be taken to strengthen 'our own position in Colonial territories in the area' and that it should be considered whether 'the economic weakness of Communist-dominated China might not offer an opportunity to secure reasonable treatment for our interests'. Thus, at such a late date, in the Foreign Office at least, commercial hopes *vis-à-vis* China were still uselessly linger-ing. Chronologically they survived the shattering of such hopes in other departments, notably the Treasury and the Board of Trade. This development will be discussed next.

8   British Perception IV

On 17 October 1945, Attlee, the new Prime Minister, summed up Britain's obligations in South East Asia as 'disarming the Japanese forces, releasing Allied prisoners of war and internees and helping to restore normal conditions',[1] that is to restitute British, French and Dutch regimes. Originally, in the temporary absence of civilian governments, South East Asia Command (SEAC) had been considered to carry out the responsibilities in the colonies.[2] Authority was to pass through the Chiefs-of-Staff in London to Admiral Mountbatten in Singapore, and in the region itself the supreme commander, his military commanders and the chief civil-affairs officers were to co-ordinate and carry out Britain's policies. Developments, however, took a surprising turn, and Japan's sudden collapse put SEAC in a dilemma. Having neither a plan nor sufficient resources for an immediate and simultaneous occupation of all the Japanese controlled territories, SEAC's troops reached Saigon and Batavia (later Djakarta) after quite some time. They were unprepared for serious political and military complications in the shape of powerful and well-armed nationalist movements in their extended new area of responsibility. Much against their will and contrary to their expectations, therefore, they found themselves in real and escalating danger.[3] While later developments will not be dwelt on here,[4] it is nevertheless of significance to recall that the danger of being dragged into an all-out war against the nationalists in Vietnam and the Dutch East Indies until the return of the French and Dutch, was avoided. The Japanese forces were disarmed, prisoners-of-war and internees were released and colonial regimes were restituted.

Urging its two colonial colleagues to seek negotiated settlement to their problems, the British government was itself preparing its own territories for some sort of self-government. In so doing, it adhered not so much to Labour rhetorics on the colonial question as to efforts not to alienate the Americans and to quieten down international critical views on colonialism.[5] In keeping the colonial peoples tied to the metropolitan power the Labour government differed very little from its predecessor. Indeed, first-hand knowledge of the practical problems of conducting a foreign policy in the world led Bevin to take a line not too distant from the one adopted by the Conservatives, often against members of his own party.[6] His eminent position in the government ensured that the Foreign Office's point of view was seriously considered by the cabinet. He managed to weather storms created by intellectuals, pacifists and various leftist circles against his policies.[7] He certainly did not belong to the insignificant minority that favoured a withdrawal into 'Little England'.[8] 'We still have our historic part to play', he insisted, 'the very fact that we have fought so hard for liberty, and paid such a price, warrants our retaining that position. . . . I am not aware of any suggestions seriously advanced, that by a sudden stroke of fate, as it were, we have overnight ceased to be a Great Power.' And he added: 'it has never occurred to His Majesty's Government, nor I believe to the British people, to apply for a receiving order in bankruptcy'.[9]

Indeed, as D. C. Watt had already observed when discussing the views of two of the ablest senior members of the Labour cabinet, Ernest Bevin and Sir Stafford Cripps, in the context of the emerging cold war in Asia:

> they were nationalists and patriots for an empire they were determined to remake into a multiracial community of civilized self-governing states. To abandon that empire was the last thing they were prepared to concede. On its continuous functioning depended, they believed, the well-being of all its inhabitants, but especially the well-being of the British working classes. In practice their policy in the Far East and in Southeast Asia differed hardly at all from that of their Conservative successors. Where differences are discernible, they can be ascribed mainly to differences of personality and political method.[10]

Later on, Labour ideology, external pressure and internal atmosphere did, however, encourage the Labour government to carry on and to guide the colonial peoples to self-government, and even towards a gradual transfer of the Empire into a multiracial Commonwealth of independent nations. From the very beginning the economic consideration was present with Bevin, who frequently admitted to it. [11] His conception of self-interest was compatible with his recognition that it was necessary to scale down Britain's overseas commitments in order to bring them into line with the country's reduced material resources.[12] He aimed at creating peaceful and stable conditions in the interests of British trade and investments. The idea was to utilise Britain's colonial heritage in Asia, and in other places on the globe, for the economy's good. Britain's relations with her previous colonial and informal imperial possessions cannot, therefore, be described as merely an additional 'promotion' of normal bilateral relations, but rather as an imperial hangover.

On 21 February 1946 Bevin stated in the House of Commons that, 'If we claim to be an Empire, and to be responsible, then the talk cannot only be about these islands; it must be about the people in the British Empire, who are subjects of the King.'[13] Britain, moreover, had to 'nurse' not only dependent territories, emerging into independence, but also China, who had to be helped administratively and provided with experts. When Labour leaders talked about new China they often used terms similar to those used in airing their ideas about the post-war Empire: Britain should not enrich herself at the expense of her overseas possessions, but rather pursue a positive policy of raising the standard of life of the people there. Endeavours should be made to bring to all the peoples within the Empire the economic advantages science made possible. Industrial ability, too, should not remain a monopoly of the white races.[14] Talking specifically about China, Attlee expressed his hope for closer relations with the people of that country, adding: 'we look forward to years of joint endeavour with them in building up the fabric of civilisation and in raising the standard of life of the common people throughout the whole world'.[15]

In the 1930s, preparing colonies for self-government was considered to be an imperial responsibility. The speed of constitutional advancement, however, did not suggest that the final objective of Dominion Status would be reached in the following decade. Nationalist leaders, suspicious of British intentions, certainly did not entertain such hopes.[16] The war with Japan brought about a dramatic change in the situation in Asia. The international climate in 1945 favoured the growth of nationalism. Labour leaders such as Attlee, Sir Stafford Cripps and Lord

Pethick-Lawrence inclined towards settling problems concerning the Empire and, above all, the Indian problem. Britain's post-war economic situation, too, merited a new approach to dependent areas.

In August 1945 there came a warning from the Treasury that the country faced 'a financial Dunkirk', and that without substantial American aid, it would be 'virtually bankrupt'.[17] This was by no means an exaggeration. Four to five million houses had been either destroyed or damaged by enemy action. External liabilities which totalled £476 million in August 1939, had swollen to £3,555 million by June 1945. Their very existence constituted a distinct weakness in the British diplomatic situation.[18] The sale of foreign assets to pay for the war amounted to £1118 million, leaving net investment income from abroad at half the 1938 level. The rise in the price of imports meant that the net spending power of this income was one-fifth.[19] Between 1936 and 1938 there had been an excess of imports over exports in the average United Kingdom balance-of-payment figures of £338 million. But this had been nearly balanced by income from shipping, overseas investments, commissions, insurance, and other sources. This balance was now impossible.[20] Over and above having borrowed heavily abroad, having liquidated foreign investments and having reduced her export trade to about one-third of its pre-war level (often to the advantage of American competitors), Britain's industry had been heavily adapted to, and disrupted by, the war.[21] Britain's total merchant-shipping tonnage had been reduced by 28 per cent and the terms of trade had turned severely against her. No sooner had Attlee's government settled down to digest these statistics than the United States, on 21 August 1945, gave another blow to Britain's economy by cancelling the Lend–Lease and the outstanding contracts, just seven days after the Japanese accepted the Allied terms of capitulation, and even before they formally signed the terms of the surrender. The hope that Britain's financial difficulties would be eased for the transition period to the peacetime era by continued American aid was shattered. Britain was clearly in need of foreign aid, unless she was willing to devalue the pound, cut imports, or massively reduce foreign spending, mainly on defence. The first of these options, as Eatwell has observed, would have imported inflation and probably not increased exports greatly because of production difficulties; the second would have meant massive cuts in living standards; and the third could not produce rapid advantages because of problems in running down commitments.[22]

The British government chose to try to negotiate a free loan from the United States. Without such dollar assistance there was a distinct possibility of widespread unemployment at home and even scarcity of the basic necessities.[23] Yet Washington was far from coming forward. Was it trying to make life difficult for the new Labour government in London? Was there a wider political significance to the financial difficulties piled up? Or was it simply an expression of American dissatisfaction with the British Empire, now extending its hand to receive a subsidy in order to survive?

Eventually the British delegates, who had expected either a grant-in-aid or an interest-free loan, were offered a credit of $3750 million (£930 million) plus $672 million (£167 million) to pay for goods in transit at the modest annual rate of 2 per cent, or rather 1.62 per cent when account was taken of the fact that repayments would not commence until December 1951. The loan was repay-able over fifty years. By the Loan Agreement which was signed in Washington on 6 December 1945 Britain accepted three condi-tions. She undertook to make sterling freely convertible into other currency not later than twelve months after the Agreement came into force; that meant the end of the Sterling Area dollar pool which limited the freedom of Sterling Area countries to spend dollars earned by their exports. She also agreed not to apply quantitative restrictions discriminatingly against dollar goods. Third, Britain had to enter into negotiations with countries hold-ing British sterling liabilities with a view either to scaling them down or refunding them; from the American point of view this could have the effect of diverting to the dollar market the import demands of countries holding sterling balances which they might otherwise liquidate by purchases in Britain.[24]

An additional loan of $1250 million was made by the Canadian government on a basis similar to the American loan. In the financial negotiations between the United States and Britain, Washington urged London to eliminate all forms of discrimina-tory treatment in international commerce and to reduce tariffs and other trade barriers. The American officials insisted that this request was compatible with the Mutual Aid Agreement signed by the two sides on 23 February 1942. After all, there were few expressions to which the American Congress was as sensitive as

'Imperial Preference'. Britain's counter-suggestions and protests were without avail. The Loan Agreement had a cold reception in Britain. Many felt that its dictated conditions were much too harsh. Churchill, now the Leader of the Opposition, hoped that in practice the agreement would defeat itself, a hope that was soon fulfilled. The experiment in convertibility had to be terminated on 21 August 1947, only a month after sterling had been freed, the reason for this being the rush of foreign holders of sterling proceeds from sales to Britain to convert their balances into scarce dollars in order to buy more readily available American goods.[25]

The relationship between Britain's internal policy and external events, made so obvious during the war, remained so in the course of the immediate post-war era. In 1946, shortages, queues and rationing by no means improved; in fact they got worse. Unlike the situation in the 1930s, now there were no longer exports to the New World in the form of raw materials from British overseas possessions such as Malaya; nor were there the conditions that enabled Britain to buy a given volume of imports at favourable terms of trade. No longer did the earning in the United States of the primary-producing colonies of Britain's neighbours in Europe provide London with a supply of dollars through her own sales to Europe.

This was, in most general terms, the economic situation when discussions on China were held in the Far Eastern Department of the Foreign Office, in the Board of Trade, and in the other official and non-official quarters. This was naturally also the background against which decisions were made. Throughout the deliberations one factor remained constant with obvious degrees of intensity – the great old dream of China and its market. E. M. Gull, the secretary of the China Association in London, when discussing the prospects of British trade with China in the post-war period, had insisted as early as April 1943 that the short-term ('ten years or so') outlook was 'quite definitely a good one'.[26] This guarded optimism had not disappeared after the war. Three and a half years after Gull expressed his opinion, in October 1946 – one of the most difficult hours for Britain's economy – Lord McGowan of Imperial Chemical Industries Limited (ICI) spoke at the Anglo–Chinese Chamber of Commerce in similar terms.[27] He expressed an anxiety 'to restore the mutual exchange of commodities and trade' without which China could not develop and improve the living conditions of her people, and promised that, as the opportunity offered, ICI would continue her pre-war activities in China. At the same time he made it clear that 'investment presupposes security of tenure, and sound government'. Political and economic stability was, therefore, a basis for sound commercial and industrial activity. Lord McGowan mentioned Chinese financial decrees, especially those relating to foreign exchange, as likely obstacles in the way of foreign investment. He dwelt on Chinese taxation as a cause for 'considerable anxiety to the trading community'. Lord McGowan thought that Chinese industry had been badly handicapped by a shortage of raw materials, but even more so by the incessant demands of labour for more favourable terms of employment. In real wages, he believed, the Chinese industrial worker was very much better off than he had been before the war, but this progress had been made at the expense of the Chinese economy in general. Although the Chinese were good craftsmen, the workers were much less efficient than their British or American counterparts. Thus, in terms of labour cost, a given piece of work was much more expensive in China than in the highly paid centres of the rest of the world. Consequently China was no longer a cheap producer and many industries were closing down on account of this limitation. Prospects for a revival of light industries could be excellent as soon as some stability was reached between labour costs, raw-material costs and supply, and market prices. Discussing other aspects of the Chinese economy, such as agriculture, communications, import and export storage, Lord McGowan expressed his hope that the restoration to China of Manchuria and Formosa would assist her programme of development. While not feeling there was an occasion for undue optimism, there was equally, he thought, no occasion for despair. 'Great Britain, with her longstanding friendship for China, will do her best to lift that country out of the chaos which prevails today.' ICI would play its part in this policy, 'as a restored economy in China will help the entire world'.[28]

The Times wrote on 9 May 1946 that the inauguration of the Anglo–Chinese Chamber of Commerce would assist considerably in establishing a better understanding between the two countries. The paper stressed, however, that the people of China were rightly not content to be regarded merely as a vast potential market; nor did that view accord with their conception of fitting relations between great nations. The new regulations and laws restricting imports, imposing import duties, business and income

taxes and introducing some monopolistic activities of the govern-
ment-controlled Chinese purchasing organisations abroad[29] were
undoubtedly an expression of China's attempts to assert herself
nationally.

The China Association, still expecting the materialisation of the
old dream on China, attempted to fight the new Chinese laws. Its
officials continued exerting pressure on the various departments
in London to this effect. They religiously followed the new
Chinese legislation on economic, financial and commercial
matters as it was being moulded. They translated the relevant
material into English and distributed every piece of information
they could get hold of to the company-members and to officials
who in their view could help them in their struggle.[30] The hope
for the resumption of trade with China still prevailed despite a
number of handicaps, notably the limitation of supplies and
currency problems that remained. In the Association's annual
report of 1946 it was clearly stated that 'the community of
interests which exists between China and Great Britain, the need
which each has for the products of the other, and the long tradition of friendship and commercial intercourse between the two
Empires, will unquestionably lead to an active revival of business
whenever conditions permit'.[31] In this context the tea trade was
often mentioned along with a hope of British re-export of Chinese
tea. Silk, bristle, hides, wood-oil, tin, wolfram, human hair, horse
hair, gall nuts, feathers, camel's wool, cashmere and various other
Chinese items of exports were also mentioned as greatly required
in Britain.[32] The Association officials lamented that no effective
steps had been taken by the government when the war had drawn
to its close, such as sending a team of men to China with
knowledge of the country in order to safeguard British interests
and properties.[33] The companies operating in China were fortunate enough, it was stressed, to have their respective internees on
the spot. They were sufficiently fit to be able to take action on
their release from the camps and manage to supervise the reoccupation of properties.[34]

The fact that no official steps had been taken along lines that
the China Association had advocated indicated the very limited
influence this organisation had on the policy-makers in London.
This impression is strengthened by reading minutes relating to
meetings Association members held with officials in London. At
the same time, however, ideas so dear to the Association mem-

bers were not at all absent from the minds of officials at various departments dealing with future Anglo–Chinese relations. It is perhaps in this light that sending a commercial mission to China in late 1946 should be examined. As early as 30 November 1944, a Board of Trade minute dwelt on the desirability of such a step.[35] It emphasised that the mission should be entirely exploratory and in no way a selling expedition. Studying China's new legislation affecting economic activity of foreigners (for example, the company law, the insurance law, the land tenure law) was mentioned as one target of investigation. Coupled with this, other matters were stressed – the general financial position in China, the customs, government monopolies, imports and exports, natural resources, industrial development, communications, etc. The minute underlined that sending the mission should be done with a view to showing both Americans and Chinese that Britain was 'interested and active in Chinese trade'. The government could thus educate British merchants and make them feel that it was not neglecting the Chinese market.

Almost a year later, on 8 August 1945, D. H. Lyal, also of the Board of Trade, stated that the mission – by then agreed upon in principle – should make contacts with the Chinese government, government departments, organisations and other prominent bodies and persons.[36] Likewise, it was to examine the general economic conditions in China and discuss the general plans for development, including industry and communications. Again it was stressed that the mission was to create the impression of the live interest British industry maintained in that huge country, despite its preoccupations and limited ability to collaborate financially, technically, or through the supply of equipment. The members of the mission were to discuss and take note of particular projects for subsequent follow-up.

The terms of reference, eventually framed on 12 September 1946, dwelt on the need to consider the best methods of developing trade between China and the United Kingdom so as to provide a firm basis for future expansion.[37] Fostering Chinese interest in the United Kingdom as a source of supply for both capital and consumer goods and convincing Chinese officials and industrialists of British industry to satisfy many of China's needs was also duly emphasised.

The mission, headed by Sir Leslie Boyce and including representatives of British industry, the trade unions and the Board of

Trade, toured China between October and December of 1946. In London, the time seemed opportune for the mission's feelers since China was regarded as being in 'a conciliatory mood'. At the same time it was clearly realised that China's simultaneous desire for self-reliance on the one hand, and her need for progress on the other, would inevitably give rise to 'a contradictory attitude of repulsion and attraction' in her dealings with the outside world.[38]

As indicated earlier, the Chinese had by that time formed new political and economic concepts. Looking for investments, they envisaged trade with Britain on terms favourable to them: reduction on the British side of import duties on raw materials on the one hand, while accepting China's protectionist policy on the other. As for foreign trade in China, they took measures to limit its prospects. Such Chinese expectations caused apprehension at the Department of Overseas Trade. British finances were in grave difficulties after the war, and no funds were available for overseas investments, or only very limited amounts. It was thus decided in London to explain to the Chinese that the role of the commercial mission was exploratory in nature, and that its members had no loans and credits in 'their pockets'.[39] On the issue of tariffs, too, the British side was evasive and non-commital.

Making little attempt to allow for Chinese susceptibilities strengthened the already prevailing impression that both official and non-official British quarters regarded China as a 'profitable field for commercial enterprise'[40] – a market – and that only negligible interest in the people and its culture ever existed on the British side. The tension between the two parties thus continued manifesting itself mostly in the economic sphere.

The Chinese-government's growing involvement in the national economy began before the war. One important result of the Sino–Japanese conflict in China was the destruction, dispersal and decline of foreign interests and an ever-growing increase of government ownership. This was after all the great paradox of Japan's exclusionist policy in the parts of China it occupied. It swept away European and American imperial interests in China and almost purified the country of foreign domination. Once Japan herself collapsed she left China with a relatively small proportion of industry owned by foreigners. The wartime tendency of increasing the proportion of trade going through government corporations could now gain momentum. When private foreign merchants tried to re-establish themselves they found their sphere very restricted, as the official trade corporations enjoyed priority in the allocation of foreign exchange and import licenses. As far as the Western companies were concerned, therefore, China had, during the war years, returned to what one scholar called, perhaps too harshly, 'the xenophonic autarky of the Manchu period'.[41] This development occurred under the Koumintang, not under the Chinese Communist Party. Indeed, the pattern crystallising was to characterise in years to come relations between developing nations and economically developed powers regardless of the affiliation of the former to the communist creed. The wide national rather than the narrow ideological interest apparently played an overriding role.

In 1946 China's national product may have been as much as 20 per cent less in real terms than in 1936. This was hardly surprising in view of the toll of wartime destruction and the severe famines of 1945–6. In the industrial sector there had been severe depreciation, while in the country there had occurred a dislocation of the farm economy. China suffered from inflationary exchange rates at which puppet currencies were transferred into *fapi*. The constant threat of civil war made the government keep the military on a war footing, thus the most significant of expenditures was only little affected by the end of the war. The expulsion of the Japanese managers and technicians from China and the removal of equipment by the Soviet Union from Manchuria greatly hampered the national production.[42] By 1947 Chinese external reserves had fallen to the equivalent of four months' imports, and the capacity of her ports and transport facilities from the coast further limited the size of her import programme. No wonder, therefore, that Chinese policy was directed towards discouraging unessential imports and encouraging exports (which called for a *low* external value of the *fapi*). Likewise, there were attempts at encouraging remittances of overseas Chinese (which called for a *high* external value of the *fapi*). In order to achieve this contradiction several combinations of economic measures were tried, to no avail.[43]

Parallel to Chinese economic self-assertiveness, the spread of Western education, modern banking and business methods amongst the Chinese caused a natural tendency for their buyers to form direct contacts with supplies abroad. Some of the more important Chinese concerns maintained their own offices in New York or London; thus they found British commercial mediation superfluous. To an increasing extent, the Chinese were attempting

to secure agencies previously held by European and British merchant firms established in China. In these circumstances,
Anglo–American economic competition in China continued. The
Americans claimed that what Wedemeyer termed British 'intelligence agencies' were very active throughout China and sought
information as to how China intended to use the $30 million loan
granted to her by the United States.[44] This was by no means a
wrong observation. Indeed, the British closely watched the
increasing American economic activity and influence in China
which, as they perceived it, expanded at the expense of their
traditional influence. For example, the Maritime Customs returns
of the foreign trade of China showed that for the first seven
months of 1946, 53.63 per cent of the total imports came from the
United States and only 4.64 per cent from Britain. For the full year
1937, by comparison, the figures were 19.75 per cent and 11.68
per cent respectively.[45] Indeed, British trade had been seriously
hampered by a shortage of supplies. Through the part played by
the American forces in the Pacific War the United States undoubtedly managed to capture the imagination and the admira-
tion of those Chinese responsible for the anti-Japanese struggle.
The presence of American troops, the circulation of American
dollars, and the fact that the United States was able to ship food-
stuffs, cigarettes, etc. which were in short supply in England,
enabled American importers to take advantage of trading
opportunities almost as soon as the Pacific War came to a close.
However, Britain's traditional position in China still possessed
weighty influence on the British position. British Hong Kong,
having assumed some of the former functions of Shanghai, was
the nearest place to the main centres of population and trade in
China, where there was a system of law and administration on
Western lines with political, economic and financial stability.

On the whole, however, the situation seemed gloomy. The
Economic and Industrial Planning Staff at the Foreign Office
reported in January 1947 that the total value in 1941 of the direct
British business investment in China represented by physical
properties was estimated at approximately £124 million (in
pre-war values).[46] This figure excluded the value of coastal and
inland waterway shipping. Of this sum, £110 million represented
the value of immovable property and consisted almost entirely of
land and buildings, and £14 million represented movable property
such as stocks, machinery and equipment, as well as personal

belongings. The annual remittance to the United Kingdom out of the yield from this investment was approximately £4 million. A considerable balance of income was spent or re-invested in China, some of which represented plant, equipment and other materials purchased in the United Kingdom. Losses estimated to have been sustained by the physical assets as a result of the war totalled £13.7 million, of which possibly £9.4 million represented the value of materials that might have to be replaced by purchases from the United Kingdom. Of the total movable property 75 per cent was believed to have been destroyed or moved.

Another 'stock-taking' memorandum on the Far East prepared by Denning was also discouraging. It made it clear that the British position there had been dominated since V-J Day by three main features:[47] first, the fact that Britain had been defeated by Japan, lost considerable territory, and that the Far East in general considered Britain to have played a comparatively minor role in defeating Japan; second, the predominant part played by the United States in the war against Japan and the leadership she managed to assume in Far Eastern affairs; third, the tide of nationalism that pervaded the whole area and that had received great impetus as a result of the war. 'Our actions today', wrote Denning, 'are regarded critically and it is necessary for us to prove the rightness of our case.' As for China, Denning's memorandum stressed that the fact that the United States had virtually replaced Britain in the role that the latter occupied before the war should not be regarded 'too tragically'. The position Britain had held before,

> though it brought many benefits also imposed certain responsi-
> bilities and burdens upon us. Of these we are now relieved and
> the political and economic anxieties fall mainly to the United
> States as the dominant Western Power in China.

Denning reminded his colleagues that China was in 'a very bad way economically and financially, and the prospects of conducting successful trade are for the time being gloomy'. He thought that meanwhile Britain's task was to keep 'a commercial foothold in China until better days come'. Here there perhaps existed a grain of readiness to give up, at least for the time being, British immediate hopes in China. The only serious threat to Britain in the area, maintained Denning, would be if the Soviet Union were to replace the United States as the dominant foreign power in

China. In such an event Britain might expect not only to lose most of her trade, but also to be faced with a threat which would develop towards the regions further south where there were very large Chinese communities.

It was against this background of reassessment of Britain's position in the Far East that a Parliamentary mission headed by Lord Ammon left for China on 29 September 1947. Following the commercial mission of a year earlier, the Parliamentary mission was to focus a measure of attention on China and afford its members first-hand information about the country with which it was hoping to establish renewed contacts.[48] Indeed, while serious doubts were being expressed concerning the profitability of commercial relations with China, traditional expectations were still running quite high. By the time the mission had left Britain, however, an important and somewhat surprising development took place. It cast a shadow on the mission and *a priori* made its members' impressions and conclusions almost irrelevant.

The turning-point was directly related to the 1946 commercial mission and to second thoughts as regards relations with China emerging after the preparation of its report. The new line, now cherished by the Board of Trade, was perhaps best expressed in a memorandum prepared by H. O. Hooper on 7 August 1947.[49] Hooper stated that any effective plan compatible with the commercial mission's recommendations could be acted upon only in the context of 'a stable and peaceful China'. He believed that the recommendations were 'so numerous and so practical that there is a real danger of their swamping this caveat in the public mind'. In his opinion British trade with China had paradoxically already been going 'almost too well, and in spite of the obstacles, exporters seemed to be showing a greater energy in selling to China than to more desirable hard currency markets'. In the light of Britain's balance-of-payments position, Hooper insisted, 'we may have actively to discourage them from doing this. It may conceivably prove impossible to publish this report without unwittingly giving a greater impetus to immediate exports to China than we desire.' A month later he insisted that the report should be regarded as 'a forecast of opportunities that may be enjoyed in the future rather than a statement of opportunities which can be exploited now'.[50] Without this, he warned, British exporters would get the general impression that the British government was anxious to stimulate an energetic export trade with China. 'We cannot afford to encourage exports to China until our hard currency position is better', he stressed.

Thus, while until that moment Board of Trade officials, so significant for the formulation of Britain's commercial policy in China, distinguished between British trade *in* China on the one hand, and trade *with* China on the other,[51] intending to preserve at least the latter (new conditions permitting the former no longer), now even this seemed out of the question. Too much trade with China was regarded as over- if not counter-productive. This feeling prevailed so decidedly for the first time since the opening of China to foreign trade following the Opium Wars. Contrary to a background of intensive efforts to re-establish the former position in China, it was decided to make a *volte face* and accept, in fact, the view of the ardent sceptics among the decision-makers, notably the Treasury officials who constantly underlined the disadvantages of revitalising Britain's special position in China.

After the Hooper memorandum, the documentary material suggests, sporadic expressions of hope to re-establish Britain's pre-war position in China and plans aimed at its materialisation were no longer significant. The century-old dream was rapidly and constantly fading. Indeed, it was not at all easy to grasp the speedy rate of change occurring since the war had started. By the time one set of changes had been digested, a new one was already present. Britain's hope of restoring her economic position in China and simultaneously of reaping political and strategic benefits could not materialise. The new global reality and the 'philosophy of reconstruction' in China made the re-emergence of anachronistic ideas, albeit under the friendly mentor's mantle, almost impossible. Chinese economists and politicians wanted to see the continuation of Chinese-foreign relations with no political or military strings attached. The foreigner was expected to assist in the launching of an independent Chinese economy on the road to modernisation and to withdraw when requested, to help and not to be helped. This burden was too heavy for post-war Britain to carry.

Conclusion

In the previous chapters an attempt has been made to look into developments that had affected Britain's potent traditional position in China in the course of the Pacific War and immediately after it. This has been done despite the realisation that it is far from possible to distinguish between the objective historical process marking British imperial decline since the dawn of the century, the eventful years of the 1930s and the vicissitudes of the 1940s. The guiding line, however, has been the assumption that the Pacific War had accelerated an already existing process. Reactions in various British circles – official and non-official – to these developments were analysed and evaluated. The main question asked was whether, having been practically expelled from China, efforts had been made on Britain's part to return and regain a foothold there once the war was over, utilising the colonial heritage in South East and East Asia and the informal colonial status previously enjoyed in China. In other words, can terms such as 'imperial momentum' and 'imperial hangover' be used in referring to plans made and actions taken *vis-à-vis* China. In employing such terms, reference has not necessarily been made to the internal malaise of Britain as an ex-metropolitan society, nor to its natural urge to return to territories its soldiers had been expelled from earlier (at times simply in order to withdraw properly later with some honour), but, rather, to developments related to the metropolitan's relationship with a subject of its imperial activity – in our case, to China as a part of Britain's informal empire – at a time when the process of decline appeared so obvious.

Discussions on China as a part of Britain's informal empire are not rare. Britten Dean, for example, has pointed out that 'with the discrediting in certain quarters of formal empire building by the classic strategy of territorial conquest and annexation, Great Britain sought during the heyday of free trade (1830s to 1870) to gain preferential treatment for her nationals by the application of various combinations of tactics'.[1] He underlined in this context gunboat diplomacy, political coercion, internal interference, economic constraints and unfair competitive advantage. In China, Britain exercised significant influence on local government through the unequal treaty system – the principal result of the clash between British anti-imperialism and free trade on the one hand, and Chinese exclusivism on the other. This system, once established by the Opium Wars, was 'largely self-perpetuating'. It manifested itself in the political-diplomatic field as well as in the monetary, economic, military, and the legal spheres. Since all this was done 'without the necessity of establishing formal control through a colonial government it would seem that China had become enmeshed in the web of Britain's *informal* empire'.[2] This was so, despite the fact that the China trade was on the whole unimpressive in size and not very lucrative, and that British merchants failed economically to effectively subordinate China to Britain.[3] It is precisely due to the 'informal empire' question that reference to imperial issues related to South East Asia has been made at various instances. Indeed, on the whole, the documentary material on the 1940s lends itself to some analogies between parts of colonial South East Asia on the one hand, and China on the other. The fact that both had been abruptly put under Japanese rule is significant for our discussion, as it caused inhabitants in the region to react accordingly. All other British colonies (including India) that had not gone through the experience of Japanese occupation in those unique circumstances must in our context be considered as a separate case. There, the issue of Britain's physical return, and of local nationalism revitalised as a result of an occupation by a rising Asian imperial power with all its repercus-sions, simply did not exist.

The British attitude towards China, it has been shown, remained inherently unchanged even after Labour's rise to power in 1945. This was made particularly clear in the case of Hong Kong, where an adamant stand not to yield an inch in face of Chinese nationa-lism was taken by the new government, very much on the lines adopted earlier by the Conservatives. Thus, it had not been in the course of war, nor in the immediate post-war era, that a decision to give up China had been taken. Only in the summer of 1947, when all official quarters had eventually caught up with the view originally adopted by the Treasury officials, had a clear official decision in this respect been reached. In other words, the great dream of the Chinese market took a long time to fade.

It never died. Following Mao Tse-tung's death, for example, and the remarkable changes in China's attitude towards the West, more than thirty years after the events discussed in this study, the dormant great hope regarding the Chinese market re-emerged. An example and an indication of that could be read in a special supplement devoted to China published by *The Times* as recently as 29 September 1978. 'Britain: Closer Links Forged than at any Time in History', read one headline referring to relations with China. Quite a few articles dwelt on the wide-ranging economic prospects awaiting the British industry in China. Under the title 'Oiling Britain's Export Wheels' it was reported that the Secretary of State for Trade regarded Britain's export chances in the energy development sector as good. 'A trebling or even quadrupling of Sino–British trade in the next two or three years', was mentioned. Modernising and expanding China's industry seemed to mean more Western and British machinery exports to China, more Chinese missions shopping in the British Isles, in the aerospace industry for example, more opening for the West's technology in China's communications sector of rail, road, sea and air transport, and even 'mouth-watering prospects for British publishers in a country of some 900 million people, where English is the premier foreign language'.

A feeling of *déjà vu* could immediately engulf the historian of modern China upon reading those optimistic reports. Indeed, the white man, and above all the Briton of the late 1970s and the early 1980s, similarly perhaps to his predecessors of the late 1940s, having lost his prestige and ruling position in Asia and in China in particular, never stopped endeavouring to win a new, if not a higher, prestige there by returning as a friendly mentor.[4]

Strangely enough, when the war ended, the Briton interested in China and in what it could presumably offer, was ready to concede more to the nationalism of colonial people than to Chinese nationalism – the nationalism of a sovereign state. That he found puzzling and difficult to accept. This was apparently due to the fact that in an era of growing self-assertion and increased national feeling all over the globe, the mode of behaviour adopted by an independent state (later to be called developing country), yet one that was part of the informal empire, seemed to be of great significance. If colonies were to become ex-colonies and ideally part of

Britain's sphere of influence, every extreme diversion from her orbit might mean a bad omen for the future and a most undesirable precedent. Another reason for British sensitivity towards the winds of change in China was simply that China was China, with all the historial connotations and expectations attached to this name. During the 1940s the British decision-makers, as well as Old China Hands, allowed only little for Chinese susceptibilities. They radiated, on the whole, an impression that China was mainly, if not solely, a profitable field for commercial enterprise. Thus the brief wartime honeymoon period between Britain and China was precarious and unreal.[5] Equality in its sincere sense was never really entertained. A patronising and condescending attitude towards the Chinese survived all upheavals.

The change of guard between the Conservative and the Labour parties saw almost no alteration in this respect. A clash of views between the two political parties on the question of a desired policy towards dependent and interdependent people existed only when members of the two streams were theorising. Weighing Amery's and Attlee's views, one could discern two entirely different judgements about the values of colonies: a source of national power, profit and prestige *vs* a burden – an almost undesired burden.[6] However, by 1945, the two opposing outlooks, significant as indicators of thoughts and ideals rather than as guidelines of likely courses of political action, seemed to converge. A similar observation could be made as regards Britain's United States policy. While in theory the advocates of a continued colonial reality devised a policy of keeping the Americans out of the colonial empire, and the Labour view stressed the desirability of co-operation with the Americans in colonial development, both were inherently anxious about future American competition in South East Asia and China and, in their turns, acted accordingly.

Enlightened British imperialism seemed, at the war's end, as a need of the hour. At the same time, however, a revival of imperial aims and a consolidation of what had been put in danger also seemed urgent.[7] Thus, Churchill's insistence before the British defeat in the Far East that 'we hold what we have', turned quite soon to an optimistic, even presumptuous slogan cherished by Labour: 'we shall hold what we had'.[8] The views of Labour leaders such as Herbert Morrison, the Home Secretary, who claimed that granting full self-government to many of the dependent territories would be like giving a child of ten 'a latch key, a bank account and a shot-gun',[9] though they did not materialise, did indicate Labour's paternalistic attitude towards colonial peoples. This attitude existed also *vis-à-vis* China. Indeed, as Gupta has already argued, even Socialists believed, with Kipling, that a white man's burden existed and that it had to be borne.[10]

Prominent Americans involved in Asian affairs and, above all, President Roosevelt, were most suspicious of the British, and regarded them, Churchill in particular, as being behind the times. General Joseph Stilwell's mocking at Mountbatten's lordly behaviour was a mere extreme symptom of widely spread American feelings. Expressions made by Hurley and Wedemeyer could be regarded as another example. Official American views on Britain's colonial and China policies were formed accordingly. On the British side, by contrast, many of both Conservatives and Labourites, having been brought up in the post-First World War era, and having absorbed the values of the Empire, formal and informal, regarded it as a fact, part of the world structure. This remained so whether one happened to be critical about an issue related to the empire or not.

Throughout our discussion, China, though formally an independent political entity, has not been treated as an active actor, but rather as a passive subject of British, and to some extent of American, intitatives. This line has been taken even though, in a wide, long-range historical perspective China has undoubtedly been an actor and at times maintained its subtle effect on developments.[11] In our discussion, the focus being from the perspective of British imperial decline, mere references have been made to the transformatory changes within Koumintang China: the internal upheavals and the war-stimulated nationalism manifested in both the economic and the political fields. These changes, at least partly, were an outcome of disillusion with Western, and particularly British, China policies.[12] Along with the deteriorating internal situation in Britain, they played a role in the eventual British decision – taken, after a fashion, by all concerned quarters – to retreat from China. The documentary evidence available suggests that this crucial turning-point had been reached in August 1947 and found its expression in the Hooper memorandum.

Paradoxically perhaps, Koumintang China, just prior to the final communist victory, was found in the midst of a process of becoming less a subject of imperial activity and yet more self-reliant and independent as an actor in the international arena. It was at this point of departure that discussions evaluating the role of the foreigner in China's economic development and on external exploitation in general[13] became anachronistic, part of the historians' debate. It no longer really mattered how colonial economy affected the traditional village or the treaty-port region. Whether 'business imperialism' ('an elusive concept in which emotions substitute for reason, theories for facts, politics for history'[14]) had existed or not was important no more. China seemed to be marching anew on the old road of pride, if not autarky. This was only understandable in view of the fact that she had been reduced to the status of a side-show, and had never had the chance of going through the heartening experience of victory to offset the defeats and losses of the war years. Whether the new course of self-assertiveness was going to be completed under Koumintang or under the Chinese Communist Party seems a marginal question. Both streams after all, having learnt the lesson of events following the foreigner's penetration into China, reached some decidedly nationalist principles. Leaders on both sides of the ideological fence were becoming gradually more persuaded that imperialist exploitation should reach its end forthwith. 'True independence', though diversely defined, if not contradictorily, seemed a proven prescription to improving China's future. Freedom from colonial rule, both sides expected, would of itself bring about a miraculous change for the better. Under such circumstances it is hardly surprising that not only informal imperialism had come to its end, but also that the comforts of 'imperial hangover' could no longer be enjoyed.

Notes

INTRODUCTION

1. A. Shai, *Origins of the War in the East* (London, 1976).

2. Not all the students of that period accept the interpretation that Britain pursued a policy of appeasement towards Japan. See, for example, R. L. Sims's review in the *Bulletin of the School of Oriental and African Studies,* vol. 41, pt. 1, (1978) and S. O. Agbi's review in the *Historical Journal,* (June 1979). Nevertheless, the Chinese certainly regarded the British policy as a policy of appeasement. It was this very feeling that mattered most. Shai. *Origins of the War in the East,* pp. 154–5

3. Ernest Bevin hinted to such a policy in the House of Commons. See Hansard, *Parliamentary Debates*, 5th series (henceforth *Parl. Deb.*) vol. 419, cols 139–2, 21 Feb. 1946.

4. Hugh Seton-Watson, 'Aftermaths of Empire', *Journal of Contemporary History*, vol. 15, no. 1 (January 1980) p.197; and Keith Robbins, 'This Grubby Wreck of old Glories', in the same issue of the *Journal of Contemporary History,* p.81.

5. For a discussion of China as part of Britain's informal empire, see Britten Dean 'British Informal Empire: The Case of China', *Journal of Commonwealth and Comparative Politics,* vol. XIV, no. 1 (March 1976).

6. R. Dernberger, 'The Role of the Foreigner in China's Economic Development', in D. H. Perkins (ed.), *China's Modern Economy in Historical Perspective* (California, 1975); D. C. M. Platt (ed.), *Business Imperialism, 1840–1930* (Oxford, 1977) pp. 1–14; Dean, *'British Informal Empire'.*

7. Though, of course, before the turn of the century it had been argued by some Old China Hands that extraterritoriality was not enough and that China should become another Egypt, if not a second India, before large-scale imperial investment would be feasible. See N. A. Pelcovits, *Old China Hands and the Foreign Office*, (New York, 1948) p. 65. Extraterritoriality, looked at from a totally different angle, marked the foreigners 'inferiority, as they were not worthy to be governed by the great maxims of Chinese reason: O. M. Green, 'The British in China', *World Review* (July 1952).

8. See, for example, M. Brecher, *The New States of Asia – A Political Analysis* (Oxford, 1963) p.ix.

9. 'Our countrymen in China have often been guilty of arrogance and contempt in their dealings with the native population' stated the Parliamentary mission report on 10 February 1942, PRO. Pre. 4 28/5.

10. H. J. Van Mook, *The Stakes of Democracy in South East Asia* (London, 1950) pp. 139–140.

11. J. Pluvier, *South East Asia from Colonialism to Independence* (Oxford 1974) p.

179. Two years after the event, Sir George Sanson, one of Britain's best experts on Japan, believed that the fall of Singapore marked 'a turning point in Far Eastern history', as it showed that the position of Western powers in the Far East was no longer secure and that consequently the whole relationship of Eastern and Western peoples had entered upon 'a new phase': see Sir George Sanson, 'The Story of Singapore', *Foreign Affairs* vol. 22, no. 2 (January 1944).

12. Philip Darby 'British Defence Policy in the Indian Ocean Region between the Indian Independence Act 1947 and the British Defence Review 1966' (D. Phil. thesis, Oxford 1969) p. 30.

13. Ibid, p. 1.

14. Ibid, p. 504.

15. F. R. Van der Mehden, *South-East Asia, 1930–1970. The Legacy of Colonialism and Nationalism* (London, 1974), p.50. For the military dimension of the new, post-war reality, see, for example, Joyce C. Lebra, *Japanese-Trained Armies in Southeast Asia* (Hong Kong, 1977) pp. 169, 179–180, 184.

16. Mehden, for example, stressed that two salient forces aided the growth of nationalism in Asia: commercial agriculture, which made the peasant more independent upon the fluctuation of the world market, and increasing pressure of Chinese and Indian entrepreneurs: Mehden, *South-East Asia, 1930–1970*, p. 30.

17. C. Thorne, *Allies of a King* (London, 1978) p.540. From purely an economic standpoint (as much as it can be divorced from military and political issues), the balance of foreign intervention and assistance since the Opium Wars is not at all easy to determine. It is even more difficult to evaluate. Side by side with the negative repercussions, positive ones also existed. See, for example, Dernberger, 'The Role of the Foreigner' pp. 19–47.

18. See, for example, W. H. Elsbree, *Japan's Role in Southeast Asian Nationalist Movements, 1940–1945* (Cambridge, Mass., 1953) p. 166; C. A. Johnson, *Peasant Nationalism and Communist Power* (Stanford, Calif., 1962).

19. 'Whereas in North and West Africa, in India and Ceylon, the Colonial administration was weakened but managed to survive, in Southeast Asia it was completely destroyed, and this alone had epoch-making consequences.': Rudolf von Albertini, 'The Impact of the Two Wars on the Decline of Colonialism', in Tony Smith (ed.), *The End of the European Empire* (Mass., 1975) p. 13.

20. D. C. Watt, 'Britain and the Cold War in the Far East, 1945–58', in Y. Nagai and A. Iriye (eds), *The Origins of the Cold War in Asia* (Tokyo, 1977) p. 93

21. See, for example, R. Eatwell, *The 1945–1951 Labour Governments* (London, 1979) pp. 33, 47, 48, 74.

22. P. S. Gupta, *Imperialism and British Labour Movement 1914–1964* (London, 1975) p. 280.

23. Ibid.

24. L. Allen, *The End of the War in Asia* (London, 1976) pp. 252–3.

25. PRO War Office 203, vol. 5621; J. C. Sterndale-Bennett to Sir Horace Seymour, Chungking, 24 April 1945.

26. The term is taken from the title of W. Harrington and P. Young's book *The 1945 Revolution* (London, 1978).

CHAPTER 1:   THE WAR BREAKS OUT

1.   S. W. Kirby, *The War Against Japan Vol. 1* (London, 1957) pp. 99–100; Liddell Hart, *History of the Second World War* (London, 1970) p. 221.

2.   Liddell Hart, Ibid.

3.   Chan Lan Kit-Ching, 'The Hong Kong Question During the Pacific War (1941–45), *Journal of Imperial and Commonwealth History,* vol. 2, no. 1, (1973) pp. 56–74.

4.   Liddell Hart, *History of the Second World War,* pp. 224–8.

5.   Ibid., p. 233.

6.   Winston S. Churchill, *The Second World War,* vol. IV (London, 1951) p. 81.

7.   For further details, see, for example, R. Callahan, *Burma 1942–1945* (London, 1978) pp. 33–67.

8.   Liddell Hart, *History of the Second World War,* p. 236.

9.   On the Frontier Fringe, see F. S. V. Donnison, *British Military Administration in the Far East 1943–46* (London, 1956) pp. 11, 14, 34–6.

10.   J. E. Williams, *Britain's Role in Southeast Asia 1945–54* (University College of Swansea, 1973), p. 25.

11.   Churchill, *The Second World War,* vol. IV, pp. 160–1.

12.   Liddell Hart, *History of the Second World War,* pp. 236–8.

13.   W. S. Churchill, *The Second World War,* vol. III (London, 1956) pp. 476–7.

14.   On the boundaries of SEAC, see Thorne, *Allies of a Kind,* pp. 300–1.

15.   J. Terraine, *The Life and Times of Lord Mountbatten* (London, 1968) p. 101.

16.   Shai, *Origins of the war in the Far East,* pp. 208–34.

17.   See, for example, Admiral Harry E. Yarnell, lecture delivered in New York, 17 Feb. 1940. Operational Archives Naval History Division Navy Yard US Navy: Double Zero files (OANHD) Washington DC. Yarnell's personal papers.

18.   Pelcovits, *Old China Hands,* p. 214.

19.   Addressing the US House of Representatives on 18 Feb. 1943, Madame Chiang Kai-shek said, referring to the war in the Pacific: 'Your immediate tasks are to assist in winning victory . . .'. 'Defeating Japan' she added, 'is not secondary in importance . . .'. Hsu Long-hsuen and Chang Ming- Kai (eds.), *History of the Sino-Japanese War (1973–1945),* (Taipei, 1971), p. 43. The Chinese communists wavered for some time. By 1944, however, they too were hoping for American assistance. John Gittings, *The World and China 1922–1972* (London, 1974) pp. 88, 90.

20.   On Chinese requests for assistance and British negative reactions, see L. Woodward, *British Foreign Policy in the Second World War,* vol. IV (London, 1975), pp. 481-3. On British military presence in China, 1941–5, see Thorne, *Allies of a Kind,* pp. 70, 319, 444–5, 557.

21.   M. Schaller, *The US Crusade in China, 1938–1945* (New York, 1979) pp. 47–78.

22.   J. P. Davies, *Dragon by the Tail* (New York, 1972) p. 216.

23.   F. C. Jones, et al., *The Far East 1942–1946* (Oxford, 1955) p. 162.

24.   Schaller, *The US Crusade in China,* pp. 94–6.

25.   Shai, *Origin of the war in the Far East,* pp. 162–5 and India Office Library, Sir Reginald Dorman-Smith's Collection Mss Eur. E 215/28, *Reports on the Burma Campaign.*

26. L. Woodward, *British Foreign Policy*, pp. 484–6.

27. F. C. Jones, et al., *The Far East*, pp. 158–9; Callahan, *Burma 1942–1945*, pp. 38–9; Barbara W. Tuchman, *Sand Against the Wind – Stilwell and the American Experience in China 1911–45* (London, 1970) pp. 236–7.

28. Woodward, *British Foreign Policy*, pp. 487–8.

29. Davies, *Dragon by the Tail*, p. 223.

30. The National Archives of the United States (NAUS), Washington, DC, Department of State: 740.0011 PW/2504; A paper prepared at the Department of State 20 May 1942.

31. Ibid.

32. W. R. Fishel, *The End of Extraterritoriality in China* (Berkeley, Calif., 1952) p. 209.

33. For further details, see Woodward, *British Foreign Policy*, pp. 510–15.

34. At Roosevelt's insistence, the Congress of the United States passed an act which repealed the former Congressional Acts excluding Chinese from emigrating to the United States. The Chinese were henceforth to be placed upon the quota list. They were likewise made eligible for naturalisation. Jones, et al., *The Far East*, p. 163.

35. Foreign Relations of the United States (FRUS), 1943, China, p. 687.

36. Thorne, *Allies of a Kind*, p. 311; and Woodward, *British Foreign Policy*, pp. 513–15.

37. The China Association Papers: *Minutes and Circulars* 9. Jan 1948.

38. Ibid. *General Committee Papers* Kenneth, 27 July 1943.

39. Ibid. See, for example, *Annual Reports*: Chairman's statement (Brig. Gen. C.R. Woodroffe) 9 Feb. 1943.

40. Thorne, *Allies of a Kind*, p. 457.

41. *Parl. Deb.* vol. 393, col. 1121, 10 Nov. 1943.

42. PRO. Pre 4 28/5: Foreign Office to F. D. W. Brown, 10 Downing Street, 19 Feb. 1943.

43. In an initiative with obvious political intention Japan, Italy and Vichy France relinquished also their extraterritorial rights in China, Fishel, *The End of Extraterritoriality*, pp. 213–14.

44. For details of the Cairo Conference, see, for example, FRUS, Conferences at Cairo and Teheran, 1943.

45. Wm. Roger Louis, *Imperialism at Bay* (Oxford, 1977) pp. 279–80.

46. Ibid., p. 281.

47. Thorne, *Allies of a Kind*, p. 312; and the papers of Hugh Dalton (diary) entry for 12 Dec. 1943.

48. Pre. 4 28/9, 22 March, 1943. On 21 March, 1943 Churchill said in a broadcast that 'three victorious powers' would discuss World Organisation. Woodward, *British Foreign Policy*, p. 521.

49. Churchill, *The Second World War*, vol. VI, p. 605.

50. F. Williams, *A Prime Minister Remembers: The War and Post-War Memoirs of the Rt Hon. Earl Attlee,* (London, 1961), p. 60.

51. Churchill, *The Second World War*, vol. IV, p. 119.

52. FO 371, 41607 F2397/127/10; a record of a conversation between Mme Chiang Kai-Shek and B. Gage, 29 Apr. 1944.

53. Hugh Dalton observed, however, that the Prime Minister 'fell for Madame Chiang and feels now that he likes both her and her husband much better

than he did before'. The papers of Hugh Dalton (diary) entry for 21 Dec. 1943.

54. Thorne, *Allies of a Kind*, p. 27.
55. Churchill, *The Second World War*, vol. IV, pp. 289–290.
56. Arthur Bryant, *Triumph in the West* (Connecticut, reprinted 1974) p. 50.
57. Ibid, pp. 55–6.
58. Ibid, p. 53.
59. Louis, *Imperialism at Bay*, p. 285.
60. Thorne, *Allies of a Kind*, p. 527.
61. More on this question, see Akira Iriye, *The Cold War in Asia* (New Jersey, 1974) pp. 47–97.
62. Thorne, *Allies of a Kind*, p. 284.
63. Stalin objected to the idea that China should be one of the 'Big Four' on the grounds that China would be weak after the war, and that European states would probably resent China's having the right to apply machinery against them. OANHD personal papers of Fleet Admiral William D. Leahy, file no. 15. More on the views held by Churchill and Stalin, see Jones et al., *The Far East*, pp. 163–4.
64. FO 371 41607 F3308/127/10, Seymour to Eden, 28 June 1944.
65. Ibid.
66. Ibid.
67. Johnson, *Peasant Nationalism*, pp. 31–32; Elsbree, *Japan's Role*, p. 166; Pluvier, *South East Asia*, pp. 80–81.
68. Pluvier, Ibid., p. 192; J. H. Boyle, *China and Japan At War 1937–1945* (Stanford, 1972); Van Mook, *The Stakes of Democracy*, p. 141.
69. Elsbree, *Japan's Role*, p. 167.
70. Pluvier, *South East Asia*, pp. 80–81.
71. Pluvier, Ibid., pp. 269–281, and Van Mook, *The Stakes of Democracy*, p. 146.
72. Elsbree, *Japan's Role*, p. 10.
73. Ibid., p. 27.
74. In Joyce C. Lebra (ed.), *Japan's Greater East Asia Co-Prosperity Sphere in World War II* (Oxford, 1975).

CHAPTER 2: BRITISH PERCEPTION I

1. Pre. 4 28/5: a Foreign Office (Far Eastern Department) minute, 18 Feb. 1943.
2. For futher details see L. Woodward, *British Foreign Policy in the Second World War*, vol. IV (London, 1975) pp. 503–5.
3. Pre. 4 28/5 a Foreign Office minute 18 Feb: 1943.
4. Ibid.
5. Ibid, The Parliamentary mission report 10 Feb. 1943. More on British military presence in China, 1941–45, see Thorne, *Allies of a Kind* (London, 1978) pp. 70, 319, 444–5, 557.
6. The Parliamentary mission report 10 Feb. 1943; and Woodward, *British Foreign Policy*, p. 498.
7. For a detailed narrative of the loan issue up to August 1942, see Woodward, *British Foreign Policy*, pp. 498–504, 506–9.
8. The Parliamentary mission report, 10 Feb. 1943.
9. BT 11 1995 CRT 1981, 3 Feb. 1945.

10   Ibid, 24 Oct. 1944.

11. By 1933 China indeed absorbed 2.5 per cent of Britain's total exports. Yet this proportion was to decline later in the 1930s. See, for example, E.M. Gull, *British Economic Interests in the Far East* (London, 1943) pp. 179, 244.

12. BT 11 1995 CRT 1981 11 Aug. 1942: DOT memorandum on China.

13. See, for example, A. Shai. *Origins of the War in the East* (London, 1976) p. 61 note 129 and p. 66, note 221.

14. BT 11 1995 CRT 1981 11 Aug. 1942.

15. Ibid., 7 Oct. 1942.

16. *Parl. Deb.*vol. 376, col. 282, 19 Nov. 1941; and Woodward, *British Foreign Policy*, p. 480.

17. Woodward, *British Foreign Policy*, p. 499

18. BT 11 1955 CRT 1981, 29 Oct. 1942.

19. Ibid., 26 Oct. 1942.

20. See Chapter 4, 'British Perception II'

21. FO 371 31714 F7193/4356/10.

22. Ibid., F7821/4356/10: Keynes to Lord McGowan.

23. Liddell Hart, *History of the Second World War*, pp. 362–3.

24. Ibid., p. 365.

25. Ibid., p.363.

26. Hollington K. Tong, *Chinag Kai-Shek* (Taipei, 1953) p. 295.

27. Liddell Hart, *History of the Second World War*, pp. 364–5.

28. Ibid., pp. 368–9, and Callahan, *Burma 1942–1945* (London, 1978) pp. 57–59.

29. J. P. Davies, *Dragon by the Tail* (New York, 1972) p. 225.

30. Ibid., pp. 243–4.

31. Ibid., p. 268. Davies observed that after the fall of Rangoon the British had no intention of making a determined stand in Burma. See NAUS: 740.0011 PW/2869, a report by John Davies, 14 Sept. 1942.

32. Churchill, *The Second World War*, vol. V, p. 494.

33. Ibid., p. 495.

34. Davies, *Dragon by the Tail*, p. 274.

35. NAUS, 740.O11 PW/3525: memorandum entitled 'British Intimation for the Future', prepared by John Davies, 21 Oct. 1943.

36. Ibid.

37. Ibid. Merrell to Hull, 26 Oct. 1943.

38. Ibid.

39. W. R. Louis, *Imperialism at Bay*, p. 570.

40. Thorne, *Allies of a Kind*, pp. 699–700.

41. Ibid.

42. OANHD box 56: Combined Staff Planners, Appreciation and Plan for the Defeat of Japan, Combined Chiefs of Staff 90th meeting, item 6, 8 Aug. 1943.

43. NAUS 740.011 PW/12–3143, 31 Dec. 1943 (italics added).

44. Ibid.

45. NAUS 711.93, Office Memorandum Department of State (Office of International Trade Policy) 23 Aug. 1945.

46. Ibid.

47. Ibid.

48.　NAUS 740.011 PW/2298, 18 March 1942.
49.　Ibid., Wallace Murray to the Secretary of State, 31 July 1942.
50.　NAUS 740.0011 PW/2691 Department of State: Loss of Burma, British Behaviour and Repercussions in China, 26 May 1942.
51.　Ibid.

CHAPTER 3:　THE WAR AND THE CHANGING CHINESE VIEWS

1.　Liddell Hart, *History of the Second World War*, p. 513.
2.　Ibid., p.515.
3.　Ibid.
4.　Ibid., p. 631.
5.　Ibid., p. 638.
6.　Ibid., p. 687.
7.　Thorne, *Allies of a Kind*, pp. 297–300.
8.　WO 203 5621: Denning to FO, 16 Sept. 1944.
9.　Thorne, *Allies of a Kind*, p. 301.
10.　Tong, *Chaing Kai-Shek*, p. 305.
11.　FO 371 41607 F2397/12/10: Gage to FO 23 Apr. 1944.
12.　Arthur Bryant, *The Turn of the Tide 1939–1943* (London, 1957) p. 311.
13.　Pre. 4 25/5.
14.　FO 371 41566 F1916/14/10.
15.　FRUS 1947 vol. VII, the Consul-General at Kunming to the Secretary of State, 13 Oct. 1944.
16.　Federal Archives, Suitland, Maryland, U.S.A, (FASM) South East Asia Command, *War Diary, Records of Headquarters, U.S. Forces, Office of the Commanding General, Files of Major-General Albert C. Wedemeyer,* box 7, a minute of a meeting between Wedemeyer and General Tai Li, in Chungking, 30 Jan. 1945.
17.　WO 203 4832: SAC report 25 Aug. 1945.
18.　Pre. 4 28/5: the Parliamentary mission report, 10 Feb. 1943.
19.J. Terraine, *The Life of Times of Lord Mountbatten*, p. 102.
20.　Pre. 4 28/5: the Parliamentary mission report, 10 Feb. 1943.
21.　FO 371 41689 F4714/4156/10: Seymour to FO, 12 Oct. 1944.
22.　Ibid., F4625/4516/10: SACSEA to FO 6 Oct, 1944.
23.　WO 203 4832, a brief for Supreme Allied Commander's visit to Chungking, 3 March 1945.
24.　Ibid.
25.　See, for example, Woodward, *British Foreign Policy*, pp. 489–97.
26.　Thorne, *Allies of a Kind*, p. 8; Churchill, *The Second World War,* vol. IV, pp. 182–3.
27.　FO 371 31626 F1318/54/10, 6 Feb. 1942.
28.　Thorne, *Allies of a Kind*, p. 61.
29.　Ibid., pp. 237-8. See also Hollington K. Tong, *Chaing Kai-shek*, p. 303.
30.　FO 371 41607 F3308/127/10: Seymour to Eden, 28 June 1944.
31.　Thorne, *Allies of a Kind*, pp. 237–8.
32.　Woodward, *British Foreign Policy*, pp. 522–3.
33.　Thorne, *Allies of a Kind*, pp. 7–8.
34.　Chiang Kai-shek, *China's Destiny*; and *Chinese Economic Theory* with Notes and Commentary by Phillips Jaffe (New York, 1947) p. 20.
35.　FO 371 41607 F3308/127/10: a record of a conversation between Dr K. C.

Wu and Mr B. Gage, 10 June 1944.

36. See, for example, BT 11 1995 CRT 1981: British Embassy, Chungking, to Department of Overseas Trade (DOT) 16 Nov. 1944.

37. FO 371 41601 F233/96/10.

38. See, for example, F.O. 371 46178 F219/57/10: a minute by Sir George Sansom, 1 Jan. 1945.

39. BT 11 1995 CRT 1981: British Embassy, Chungking, to DOT 16 Nov. 1944.

40. W. Y. Lin, *China and Foreign Capital* (Chungking, 1945) pp. 15–19.

41. Ibid., p. 17 (Italics added).

42. R. Dernberger, 'The Role of the Foreigner in China's Economic Development', in D. H. Perkins (ed), *China's Modern Economy in Historical Perspective* (Calif., 1975) pp. 19–47.

43. A. G. Donnithorne, *Economic Developments since 1937 in Eastern and Southeastern Asia and their Effects on the United Kingdom* (London, RIIA Chatham House, 1950) p. 1.

44. Ibid., pp. 3, 8.

45. Ibid., p. 5.

46. Sir William McLean, 'Economic Developments in the Colonies', an address at Chatham House, 21 Nov. 1946.

47. E. Luard, *Britain and China* (London, 1962) p. 57.

48. FO 371 41636 F477/414/10: Seymour to FO, 25 Jan. 1944.

49. FO 371 41607 F3308/127/10: Seymour to Eden, 28 Jan. 1944.

50. V. Purcell, *The Chinese in Southeast Asia* (London, 1965) p. xi.

51. FO 371 41627 F1436/295/10: a minute by G. F. Hudson, 10 Apr. 1944.

52. Ibid., F295/295/10: a Foreign Office minute, 14 Jan. 1944.

53. S. R. Chow, *The Far East in a New Order* (Chungking, 1945) p. 26.

54. Su-ching Chen, *China and Southease Asia* (Chungking, 1945) pp. 47–8.

55. FO 371 46232 F4649/409/10: Seymour to FO, 30 July 1945.

56. Ibid.

CHAPTER 4:   BRITISH PERCEPTION II

1. See Chapter 2, 'British Perception I'.

2. BT 11 1995 CRT 1981: a minute dated 24 Oct. 1944.

3. Thorne, *Allies of a Kind*, p. 307. According to Woodward prices in 1943 were 200 times those of 1937; see L. Woodward, *British Foreign Policy in the Second World War*, vol. IV (London, 1975) p. 519.

4. BT 11 1995 CRT 1981, 9 Apr. 1945.

5. Ibid., 10 Apr. 1945: a minute initialled H.D.

6. Ibid., 3 Feb. 1945 (draft); and CAB. 96/8 F.E.(E)(45) 10 (final), 19 Feb. 1945.

7. See, for example BT 11 2542 CRT 1505 and 1540, and BT 11 3336 CRT 2422.

8. CAB. 96/5 F.E. (44)8.

9. Ibid., F.E. (44)10, 27 Nov. 1944.

10. Ibid. F.E. (44)13, 19 Dec. 1944.

11. CAB. 96/5 F.E. (44)13, 19 Dec. 1944.

12. The Papers of Sir Stafford Cripps, Nuffield College, Oxford, 226/89, notes for a speech in Edinburgh on 5 Feb., 1943 and 286/1185, speech on 2 Feb. 1944.

13. Ibid; and Thorne, *Allies of a Kind*, pp. 195, 319, 445, 557. Also see for

example FO 371 53667 F383/383/10, 1 Jan. 1946.

14. FO 371 53646 F12666/116/10: Foreign Office Brief for UK Trade Mission Members to China, 30 Aug. 1946.

15. CAB 96/8 F.E.(E44)1, 12 Dec. 1944 and F.E.(E44)3, 20 Dec. 1944.

16. Ibid., F.E.(E45)2, 9 Jan. 1945.

17. Ibid., F.E.(E45)10, 19 Feb. 1945.

18. CAB 96/5 F.E. (45) 2nd meeting, 28 Feb. 1945.

19. CAB 96/8 F.E.(E)(45)24, 9 Jan. 1945.

20. See, for example Thorne, *Allies of a Kind*, pp. 558–9.

21. FO 371 46280 F4220/4220/10: O.M. Cleasy, India Office, to J. C. Sterndale-Bennett, Foreign Office, 4 July 1945, and a memorandum attached dated 20 March 1945.

22. FO 371 41670 F2415/1415/10: Gage to Ashley Clarke, 3 May 1944.

23. FO 371 41643 F4569/568/10, 26 Sept. 1944.

24. Thorne, *Allies of a Kind*, p. 318.

25. Based on an interview with Mr John Swire, 14 Dec. 1978.

26. See, for example, BT 11 2542 CRT 1440, 19 March and 3 May 1945.

27. V. Farmer, 'Postwar Opportunity in China': private talk at Chatham House, 9 Aug. 1944.

28. FO 371 41657 F2172/1505/10, 1 May 1944.

29. FO 371 46232 F1331/409/10, 2 March 1945.

30. D. C. Watt, 'Britain and the Cold War in the Far East, 1945–48', in Y. Nagai and A. Iriye (eds), *The Origins of the Cold War in Asia* (Tokyo, 1977) p. 103.

31. Ibid., pp. 94–5

32. See Chapter 2, 'British Perception I'.

33. D. C. Watt, *Britain and the Cold War*, p. 95.

34. Ibid.

35. WO 203 5621: 'Political Factors Affecting British Participation in the War against Japan after the Fall of Singapore' (top secret), a paper prepared prior to Japan's surrender, undated.

36. WO 172 1776, *War of 1939–1945*, Diaries of SACSEA.

37. See, for example FO 371 41607 F3308/127/10: Seymour to Eden, 28 June 1944.

38. Ibid.

39. BT 11 1995 CRT, 11 Aug. 1942.

40. BT 11 2560; Seymour to Eden (copy), 20 Feb. 1945.

41. Ibid.: a minute by L.M. Skevington, 2 July 1945.

42. Ibid.: Seymour to Eden, 20 Feb. 1945.

43. Ibid.: a minute by J. R. C. Helmore, 24 May 1945, and a minute by J. R. Willis, 23 July 1945.

44. Ibid.: a Treasury minute, 9 July 1945.

45. T 236/44.

46. BT 11 2560.

47. WO 203 5621, Denning to FO, 16 Sept. 1944.

48. Ibid., 21 Feb. 1945. See also NAUS 893.00: a memorandum by J. C. Vincent, 11 Jan. 1945.

49. WO 203 5621, Sterndale-Bennet to Seymour, 24 Apr. 1945.

50. Ibid. For more material on the American objective in China, see FASM, the Wedemeyer papers, boxes 1 and 4.

51. R. D. Buhite, *Patrick Hurley and American Foreign Policy* (New York, 1973) p. 239.

52. Ibid., p. 243.

53. Arthur Swindon, *Mountbatten* (London, 1973), p. 70.

54. Ibid., p. 86.

55. Ibid., p. 111.

56. WO 203 5621, Denning to FO, 16 Sept. 1944.

57. W. R. Fishel, *The End of Extraterritoriality in China* (Berkeley, 1952) p. 211 and FO 371 46238: Treaty for the Relinquishment of Extraterritorial Rights in China (1943).

58. FO 371 41601/96/10: Willis to Sterndale-Bennett, 21 Dec. 1944.

59. Ibid.

60. NAUS 740.0011 PW/9–1944: Hull to Stimson, 9 Oct. 1944.

61. Ibid.: a memorandum by John Davies, 19 Sept. 1944.

62. Ibid., Hull to Stimson, 9 Oct. 1944.

63. NAUS 711.93, 12 Jan. 1945.

64. Ibid.: a memorandum dated 27 Apr. 1945.

65. Akira Iriye, *The Cold War in Asia* (New Jersey, 1974) pp. 47–79.

66. Ibid., p. 94; and Herbert Feis, *Churchill, Roosevelt, Stalin,* (New Jersey, paperback edn. 1974), pp. 514–5.

67. Akira Iriye, *The Cold War in Asia*, p. 94.

68. Ibid., p. 95.

69. G. F. Hudson, 'The Sino–Soviet Alliance Treaty of 1945' in Hudson (ed.), *St. Antony's Papers* no. II, Far Eastern Affairs, no. 1 (London, 1957). pp. 22–3.

70. Peter Young, *Atlas of the Second World War* (New York, 1977) p. 168. On 5 Apr. 1945 the Soviet Foreign Minister, V. M. Molotov, made a statement to the Japanese Ambassador, Sato, cancelling the Soviet–Japanese Pact of 13 Apr. 1941.

71. Feis, *Churchill, Roosevelt, Stalin*, pp. 516–7; and Churchill, *The Second World War*, vol. VI, p. 342; and David Carlton, *Anthony Eden: A Biography* (London, 1981) pp. 250–1. More on the British government attitude to the Yalta agreement. See, for example, FO 371, vol. 54073.

72. See FO 371, 54073. This whole volume is devoted to the Yalta Conference and contains not only the text of the agreement but also various minutes and memoranda relating to the Conference and to developments connected with it up to 1946.

73. Akira Iriye, *The Cold War*, p. 96.

74. FO 371 46232 F1331/409/10: A memorandum dated 2 March 1945.

75. Ibid.

CHAPTER 5:   THE WAR ENDS

1. FO 371 46232 F5369/409/10.

2. D. C. Watt, *Britain and the Cold War* p. 93.

3. FO 371 46238 F6134/760/10. (Italics added).

4. FO 371 53641 F151/116/10. See also F827/116/10 and F/1481/116/10.

5. Ibid, F241/116/10: China Association to FO, 1 Jan. 1946, and F1481/116/10: Lamb to Kitson, 2 Jan. 1946.

6. See, for example, F1684/116/10, 24 Jan. 1946 and F1811/116/10, 2 Feb. 1946.

7. FO 371 53573 F33/33/10; Lamb to Kitson, 12 Dec. 1945.

8. Ibid., F243/33/10: Seymour to FO, 4 Jan. 1946.

9. Ibid., F459/33/10: a memorandum by Hutchinson, 4 Jan. 1946.

10. *Manchester Guardian*, 22 Jan. 1946.

11. F.O 71 53601 F105/54/10: Ministry of Transport to G.V. Kitson, 1 Jan. 1946.

12. F.O 71 53611 F1424/69/10: Mrs. D.A. Vivian (BT) to Chinese Purchasing Agency, 23 Jan. 1946.

13. F.O 71 53644 F7241/116/10: an article by Dr Sun Fo in the *China Daily Tribute*, 26 April 1946.

14. Ibid.

15. Liddell Hart, *History of the Second World War*, p. 682.

16. NAUS 740.00119 PW, 28 June 1945.

17. NAUS 740.00119 PW, Oakes (Colombo) to Department of State, 11 Aug. 1945.

18. Ibid.

19. Ibid., 'Future American Participation in South East Asia Command', by George R. Merrell.

20. FASM, The Wedemeyer Papers, box 15.

21. OANHD, box 41, 21 May 1945.

22. FASM, The Wedemeyer Papers, box 15.

23. Williams, *Britain's Rule in Southeast Asia*, pp. 62–5.

24. For more information about British strategic commitment and military administration, see, for example, Williams, *op. cit.*, P. Darby, *'British Defence Policy in the Indian Ocean Region between the Indian Independence Act 1947 and the British Defence Review 1966'* (D. Phil. thesis, Oxford, 1969); and F. S. W. Donnison, *British Military Administration in the Far East 1943–46* (London, 1956).

25. Van Mook, *The Stakes of Democracy in South East Asia*, p. 167.

26. Ibid.

27. Ibid. p. 171.

28. Ibid. pp. 173–4.

29. T. H. Silcock and Ungku Aziz, 'Nationalism in Malaya', in William L. Holland (ed.), *Asian Nationalism and the West* (New York, 1953) pp. 299–300.

30. Ibid.

31. Sir Reginald Dorman-Smith, 'Burma', in *United Empire*, Journal of the Royal Empire Society, vol. XXXVII, no. 6, Nov–Dec. 1946.

32. A. Swindon, *Mountbatten* (London, 1973) p. 127.

33. John Terraine, *The Life and Times of Lord Mountbatten*, p. 120.

34. Ibid., p. 142.

35. Ibid., p. 126.

36. Ibid.

37. A television interview with Mountbatten shown after his death on 27 Aug. 1979.

38. India Office, the papers of Sir Reginald Dorman-Smith, MSS Eur. E.215/9: Return of Civil Government to Burma 1945.

39. Ibid.: Sir Reginald Dorman-Smith to the Secretary of State, Burma Office, 27 Aug. 1945.

40. Ibid.

41. During his visit to Burma, General Sir Alan Brooke wrote in his diary (12 Nov. 1945) 'Would to God that we had a more enterprising youth at home, once more prepared to accept responsibilities throughout the Empire and to seek them out, instead of shackling themselves to picture houses and other comforts of civilization': A. Bryant, *Triumph in the West* (Connecticut, reprinted 1974) pp. 384–5.

42. G. F. Hudson, 'The Sino–Soviet Alliance Treaty of 1945', in G. F. Hudson (ed.), *St Antony's Papers,* no. II Far Eastern Affairs, no. 1.

CHAPTER 6: HONG KONG

1. Foreign Relations of the United States (FRUS), vol. VIII, *China,* p. 492.
2. Ibid., Byrnes to Hurley, 11 Aug. 1945, p. 495.
3. Ibid, Hurley to Byrnes, 12 Aug. 1945, p. 496, and 13 Aug. 1945, p. 497.
4. Ibid, Byrnes to Caffrey, 14 Aug. 1945, pp.499–500.
5. Ibid, Hurley to Byrnes, 16 Aug. 1945, pp.550–1.
6. Ibid, pp. 50–2.
7. FO 371 41657 F2172/1505/10.
8. See, for example, FO 371 46280 F4220/4220/10: an India Office memorandum, 20 March 1945.
9. FO 371 41657 F2172/1505/10.
10. Ibid, a minute by F. G. Hudson, 7 Oct. 1944.
11. Ibid, a minute by L. H. Foulds, 8 May 1944.
12. Ibid, 8 Nov. 1944.
13. NAUS 711.93: a memorandum for the President, 12 Jan. 1945.
14. Ibid.
15. FO 371 46251 F4449/1147/10: a minute by J.C. Sterndale-Bennett, 25 July 1945.
16. Ibid.
17. Ibid, F4739/1147/10, 23 July 1945
18. Chan Lan Kit-Ching, 'The Hong Kong Question During the Pacific War', *Journal of Imperial and Commonwealth History,* vol. 2, no. 1 (1973) p. 72.
19. FO 371 46251 F4854/1147/10 (undated).
20. Ibid, F4855/1147/10, 29 July 1945.
21. G. B. Endacott, *Hong Kong Eclipse,* p. 228.
22. Ibid, p. 229.
23. James Morris, *Farewell The Trumpets: An Imperial Retreat* (London, 1978) p. 465.
24. Chan Lan Kit-Ching, 'The Hong Kong Question', p. 71.
25. Endacott, *Hong Kong Eclipse,* p. 229.
26. NAUS 740.00119 PW: Hurley to Secretary of State, 19 Aug. 1945.
27. Ibid, 20 Aug. 1945.
28. Ibid, 24 Aug. 1945.
29. NAUS, 846g.00, Winant to the State Department, 23 Aug. 1945.
30. Ibid, 25 Aug. 1945.
31. CAB 99/25 COS (45) 536, 200th meeting, item 3 17 Aug. 1945.
32. NAUS 740.00119 PW/8 1845 and CO 129 591/18.
33. FASM, box 8, meeting 77, 20 Aug. 1945.
34. FRUS, vol. VII: Hurley to the Secretary of State, pp. 505–6.
35. Ibid, 21 Aug. 1945, pp. 507–8.

36. Ibid, the Secretary of State to Hurley, 21 Aug. 1945, p. 509.
37. Ibid, Hurley to Byrnes, 23 Aug. 1945; and OANHD, box 12, Wedemeyer to Commander-in-Chief, Army Forces, Pacific Command, Manila; CO 129/591/18: Seymour to FO (Copy), 23 Aug. 1945.
38. See, for example, the view of the United States Ambassador in London on this question, FRUS vol. VII, Winant to Byrnes, 21 Aug. 1945. p. 510.
39. CO 129 591/18: Seymour to FO (copy) 23 Aug. 1945.
40. Ibid: Ismay to Gater, 24 Aug. 1945.
41. Ibid: Gater to Ismay, 25 Aug. 1945.
42. FASM, box 8, meeting 79, 24 Aug. 1945.
43. Ibid.
44. Ibid.
45. NAUS 740.00119, R. H. Strother of Brooklyn, New York, to the Secretary of State, 24 Aug. 1945.
46. CO 129 591/18: F.O. to Chungking, 25 Aug. 1945.
47. FRUS, vol. VII, Hurley to Byrnes, 27 Aug. 1945 (p. 512).
48. CO 129, 591/18: De Wiart to Ismay, 26 Aug. 1945.
49. Ibid: De Wiart to Ismay, 17 Aug. 1945.
50. Ibid: Seymour to FO (copy), 27 Aug. 1945.
51. FRUS, vol. VII, Hurley to Byrnes, 27 Aug. 1945, p. 512.
52. CO 129, 591/18: FO to Seymour (copy) 29 Aug. 1945.
53. Ibid: Seymour to FO (copy), 30 Aug. 1945.
54. Ibid: FO to Seymour (copy), 30 Aug. 1945.
55. Ibid:, FO to Seymour (copy), 31 Aug., 1945.
56. Ibid: Seymour to FO (copy), 1 Sept. 1945.
57. See, for example, Allen, L. Allen, *The End of the War in Asia* (London, 1976) p. 253; and Endacott, *Hong Kong Eclipse*, p. 302.
58. Endacott, *Hong Kong Eclipse*, pp. 231–2.
59. Ibid, p. 232.
60. Ibid: Allen, *The End of the War in Asia*; and Donnison, *British Military Administration.*
61. Bryant, *Triumph in the West*, p. 385.
62. The papers of A. V. Alexander, Churchill College, Cambridge, 5/10/70, 7 Nov. 1945.
63. Ibid.
64. Ibid: Alexander to Harcourt, 25. Nov. 1945.
65. CO 129, 591/81: T. I. K. Lloyd to Sir Mark Young, 13 Apr. 1946.
66. Ibid: De Wiart to Ismay, 26 Aug. 1945.
67. NAUS 740.00119 PW: Hurley to the State Department, 1 Sept. 1945.
68. Ibid.
69. WO 203 4495: Heads of Agreement between the Colonial Office and the War Office, 8 Nov. 1945.
70. The papers of Arthur Creech-Jones, Rhodes House Library, Oxford; Fabian Colonial Bureau, *Strategic Colonies and their Future*, box 26/6, item 1.
71. Woodhead, *Great Britain and the East,* April 1947.
72. NAUS 711.46g: Hong Kong: Policy and Information, 10 June 1947.
73. Ibid.

CHAPTER 7: BRITISH PERCEPTION III

1. *Parl. Deb.,* Vol. 413, col. 293.

2. Ibid, vol. 415, cols. 8–9, 29 Oct. 1945.

3. Sir Stafford Cripps's Papers, Nuffield College, Oxford, 331/288, 'A New Britain in a New World', a speech delivered on 3 Feb. 1945.

4. Ibid.

5. Ibid, 412/181, a speech delivered before the Anglo–Chinese Chamber of Commerce, 26 Feb. 1946.

6. *Parl. Deb.*, vol. 423, cols. 1877–8, 4 June 1946.

7. Ibid, vol. 423, cols. 1854–2, 4 June 1946.

8. Ibid, vol. 430, cols. 1231–2, 25 Nov., 1946.

9. Ibid, vol. 416, cols. 703–5, 22 Nov. 1945, and vol. 406, cols. 227–9, 1 Dec. 1944.

10. H. A. Lamb, *The China–India Border: The Origins of Disputed Boundaries* (London, 1946) p. 165.

11. H. A. Lamb, *Asian Frontiers* (London, 1969) p. 127.

12. NAUS 740.0011 PW/3272: Acheson (Chungking) to the Secretary of State for War (Washington), 25 May 1943.

13. WO 203 4832, Headquarters SACSEA, 25 Aug. 1945, and FO 371 53615 F11187/71/10: British Mission, Lhasa to the political officer Sikkim, 20 June 1946, and F11865/71/10: a minute by G.W. Greighton, 17 Aug. 1946.

14. L. Woodward, *British Foreign Policy in the Second World War,* vol. IV (London, 1975) p. 504.

15. Arthur S. B. Olver, *Outline of British Policy in East and Southeast Asia, 1945–50* (London, 1950) p. 23.

16. FO 371 53613 F585/71/10: FO memorandum (prepared by G.V. Kitson) 2 Feb. 1946. On differences of opinion between the Government of India and the India Office on the one hand and the Foreign Office on the other, concerning Tibet, see FO 371 53756 F2879/253/10: a minute by Sir John Brenan dated 7 June 1943.

17. FO 371 53613 F585/71/10: FO memorandum (prepared by G.V. Kitson) 2 Feb. 1946.

18. Ibid.

19. Ibid, a minute by G. V. Kitson, 20 Feb. 1946.

20. FO 371 53615 F11970/71/10: Secretary to the Government of India in the External Affairs Department to Under-Secretary of State for India, 19 July 1946.

21. Ibid, COS (46)736: aid to Tibet (final paper).

22. Ibid, F12114/71/10: a minute signed S.W.L., 21 Aug. 1946.

23. Ibid, F12444/71/10: British Mission, Lhasa to Sikkum 4 July 1946.

24. See, for example, FO 371 63315 F469/40/10: E.P. Donaldson, India Office, to G. V. Kitson (FO), 10 Jan. 1947; and F3617/40/10: L.H. Lamb (Nanking) to G. V. Kitson (FO), 28 Feb. 1947.

25. Olver, *Outline of British Policy*, p. 22.

26. V. Purcell, *The Chinese in Southeast Asia* (London, 1945) p. xi.

27. FO 371 53656 F223/223/10: a memorandum dated 1 Dec. 1945.

28. Pre. 4 28/5, 19 Feb. 1943.

29. C. Thorne, *Allies of a Kind*, p. 184.

30. Ibid, p. 320.
31. Ibid.
32. Ibid, p. 321.
33. Woodward, *British Foreign Policy*, pp. 528–30.
34. Ibid.
35. Thorne, *Allies of a Kind*, p. 321. See also FO 371 53647 F13726/116/10: minutes of a meeting held on 10 Sept. 1946 to brief members of the United Kingdom trade mission to China.
36. E. Luard, *Britain and China* (London 1962), p. 63.
37. Ibid, p. 64.
38. Thorne, *Allies of a Kind*, p. 320.
39. FO 371 63440 F4491/4491/10: the annual report on China, 1946, from Sir Ralph Stevenson, 1 Apr. 1947.
40. FO 371 63282 F846/28/10: a memorandum by G.V. Kitson, 21 Jan. 1947.
41. Ibid.
42. Ibid.
43. CAB 129/31, CP (48)299.
44. Ibid.

CHAPTER 8:   BRITISH PERCEPTION IV

1. *Parl. Deb.,* vol. 414, col. 1152.
2. Williams, *Britain's Role in South-east Asia*, p. 36.
3. Ibid, p. 39 ff.
4. See, for example, Donnison, *British Military Administration*; and J. Pluvier, *South East Asia Colonialism to Independence* (Oxford, 1974).
5. See also Louis, *Imperialism at Bay*, for example, pp. 549–50 and Thorne, *Allies of a Kind* for example, p. 514.
6. A. Shlaim, P. Jones and K. Sainsbury, *British Foreign Secretaries Since 1945* (London, 1977) p. 28; and M. A. Fitzsimons, 'British Labour in Search of a Socialist Foreign Policy', *The Review of Politics,* vol. 12, no. 2, 1950.
7. Shlaim, *et al, British Foreign Secretaries* p. 30. See also John P. Mackintosh, *The British Cabinet* (London, 1962) pp. 430, 432.
8. Shlaim *et al, British Foreign Secretaries,* p. 38.
9. *Parl. Deb.*, vol. 437, col. 1965, 16 May 1947.
10. D. C. Watt, 'Britain and the Cold War', p. 92.
11. A. Bullock, *The Life and Times of Ernest Bevin* (London, 1960) vol. 1, pp. 631–2.
12. Shlaim, *et al., British Foreign Secretaries*, p. 57.
13. *Parl. Deb.*, vol. 419, cols. 1361–2, 21. Feb. 1946.
14. The papers of Attlee, Churchill College, Cambridge, box 14: a speech delivered at Carmarthen, 3 Sept. 1943, 'Making the interests of the colonial people primary beyond doubt', was claimed by the National Executive Committee as a major goal; and Papers of A. Creech Jones, Rhodes House Library, Oxford, box 16/3: Labour Party, International Department, *Declarations of the Labour Party Concerning International Control of Colonies* (1944). See also National Executive Committee report to the Conference, 1944.
15. The Papers of C. R. Attlee, Churchill College, Cambridge: a speech delivered before a Chinese mission, 1 Jan. 1944.

16. Williams, *Britain's Role in South-east Asia*, p. 86.
17. A. J. P. Taylor, *English History 1914–1945* (Oxford, Pelican Books, 1970) p. 725.
18. F. Northedge, *Descent from Power: British Foreign Policy, 1945–1973* (London, 1974) p. 39.
19. R. Eatwell, *The 1945–1951 Labour Governments* (London, 1979) p. 70.
20. W. N. Medlicott, *Contemporary England 1914–1946* (London, 1967) p. 475.
21. Ibid: and Thorne, *Allies of a Kind*, pp.110, 675.
22. Eatwell, *The 1945–1951 Labour Governments*,, pp. 70–1.
23. Northedge, *Decent from Power*, p. 40.
24. Ibid, pp. 41–2.
25. Ibid. p. 44.
26. E. M. Gull, 'British Trade with China in the Post-War Period', a lecture delivered before the royal Central Asian Society, 21 Apr. 1943.
27. The Royal Institute of International Affairs, Chatham House, Far Eastern Department, no. 11.
28. Ibid.
29. FO 371 53644 F9367/116/10, 9 May 1946.
30. The China Association Papers: and for example, FO 371 53641 F151/116/10: minutes of a meeting held at the Board of Trade, 19 Dec. 1945.
31. China Association Papers, *Annual Report* 15 May 1946.
32. China Association. See, for example, FO 371 53641 F151/116/10.
33. China Association Papers, *Annual Report,* 15 May 1946.
34. Yet, by 1948, a large number of British-owned properties had not been restored to their owners by the Chinese authorities. See China Association Papers, *Annual Report,* 12 Sept. 1948.
35. BT 60 83 C/42889: a minute signed by J.H.K.
36. Ibid.
37. Ibid, 12 Sept. 1946.
38. Ibid: a minute by H. O. Hooper, 12 Sept. 1946.
39. Ibid: J. C. Hutchinson to Dr. T.T. Chang, 23 Sept. 1946.
40. E. Luard, *Britain and China*, pp. 58–9.
41. Donnithorne, *Economic Developments since 1937 in Eastern and South-eastern Asia and Their Effects on the United Kingdom* (London, RIIA, Chatham House, 1950). p.8.
42. F. H. H. King, *A Concise Economic History of Modern China* (Bombay, 1968) pp. 156–8.
43. Ibid, p. 164.
44. FASM, The Wedemeyer Papers, box 16, book IV, HQUSFCT to Washington, 8 Jan. 1946.
45. FO. 371 63302 F1118/37/10: notes prepared by J.C. Hutchinson, 7 Oct. 1946.
46. FO 371 63413 F585/585/10: J.F. Ford to H.O. Hooper, 14 Jan. 1947.
47. Ibid., 63549 F2616/2612/10: 22 Feb. 1947.
48. NAUS, 741.93: Winant to the Secretary of State, 25 Apr., 1947. For the report of the mission, see FO 371 63298 F16175/28/10: Lord Ammon to Bevin, 21 Nov. 1947.
49. BT 60 83 C/42889: a minute by H. O. Hooper, 7 Aug. 1947.

50.   FO 371 63308 F12378/37/10: H. O. Hooper to A.S. Gilbert (copy), 8 Sept. 1947.
51.   O. M. Green 'The British in China', *World Review* (July 1952).

CONCLUSION

1.   Britten Dean, 'British Informal Empire: The Case of China', *Journal of Commonwealth Politics*, vol. XIV, no. 1 (March, 1976) p. 64.
2.   Ibid., p. 68.
3.   Ibid., pp. 69–70 and 75–77. It must be emphasised, however, that Dean argues that the validity of the concept of China as part of British informal empire is most problematic. Even granting that it existed in the minds of Victorian officials (and, we may add, in those of twentieth-century officials), and free-traders themselves, it did not in fact exist. This is so, in his opinion, since 'Empire' once established,

>   implies some sort of *systematic* working out of relations with foreign lands whether formally or otherwise, some systematic process by which British subjects effectively subordinated independent countries by systematic application of non-market constraints. Lacking effective subordination and conspicuous benefits, 'informal empire' fails to be an apt term . . .without system or some classification scheme, 'empire' formal or otherwise, ceases to possess semantic value. . .(p. 76).

4.   Thorne, *Allies of a Kind*, p. 539.
5.   Luard, *Britain and China*, pp. 57–9.
6.   Louis, *Imperialism at Bay*, pp. 33–4; and A. Shalim, *Britain and the Origins of European Unity 1940–1951* (University of Reading 1978) pp. 94–5.
7.   Louis, *Imperialism at Bay*, pp. 100–1, 103.
8.   Ibid., pp. 187–8.
9.   Ibid., p. 14. See also pp. 15–16.
10.   Gupta, *Imperialism and British Labour Movement 1914–1964*, p. 260; and Thorne, *Allies of a Kind* p. 210.
11.   Dean, *British Informal Empire*, p. 76.
12.   Arthur N. Young, *China and the Helping Hand 1937–1945* (Cambridge, Mass., 1963) p. 428.
13.   R. Dernberger, 'The Role of the Foreigner in China's Economic Development', in D. H. Perkins (ed), *China's Modern Economy in Historical Perspective* (Calif., 1975); and Dean, *British Informal Empire*, p.75.
14.   D. C. M. Platt (ed.), *Business Imperialism, 1840–1930* (Oxford, 1977) p. 1.

Bibliography

A. MANUSCRIPT SOURCES

I. Records of the Cabinet and Government Departments.

Great Britain, Public Record Office

> Board of Trade: Files concerning Burma, China, Hong Kong and Malaya (BT 11, BT 60)
>
> Cabinet: Cabinet Conclusions (Cab.65) (Cab. 128); War Cabinet Papers (Cab. 66); Cabinet Papers (Cab. 129); War Cabinet Far Eastern Committee and Far Eastern Sub-Committee (Cab.96); Chiefs of Staff Committee, inter-Allied Conferences (Cab.99)
>
> Colonial Office: Files concerning Malaya (CO 717); British North Borneo (CO 874); Hong Kong (CO 129); Straits Settlements (CO 273)
>
> Foreign Office: General Correspondence, minutes and memoranda, Far East (China, General, Siam) (FO 371); Burma (FO 643)
>
> Prime Minister's Office: Files concerning the Far East (Pre.4)
>
> Treasury: Files relating to China (T.236 and T.238)
>
> War Office: War of 1939–45: Diaries of SACSEA (WO 172); Military Headquarters, Far East (WO 203, WO 205)
>
> Private papers: Great Britain, Public Record Office
>
> Foreign Office: Private Collections of Ministers and Officials (FO 800)

II. *School of Oriental and African Studies Library, London,* The China Association Papers

III. *Royal Institute of International Affairs, London* The Far East Department, Burma I (1943–48); China (political) (1945–47); China (economic) 1937–46); United States Policy in the Far East (Part I) (1940–48)

IV. *Rhodes House Library, Oxford* The papers of Arthur Creech-Jones

V. *Churchill College, Cambridge* The papers of A. V. Alexander, C. R. Attlee, Ernest Bevin

VI. *Nuffield College, Oxford.* The papers of Sir Stafford Cripps.

VII. *India Office Library* The papers of Sir Reginald Dorman-Smith

VIII. *London School of Economics and Political Science.* The papers of Hugh Dalton

IX *The National Archives of the United States, Washington, DC, USA*

> Department of State: Files 740.0011 PW (Pacific War, General); Files 740.00119 PW (Pacific War, Termination of War); Files 711.93 (Sino–American relations); Files 741.93 (Sino–British relations); Files 711.46g, 846g. 00, 893.00 as well as other files on Hong Kong, British Asia and Burma

X. *Operational Archives, Naval History Division, Navy Yard, Washington, DC, USA*
  US Navy: Double Zero files; Personal papers of Fleet Admiral William D. Leahy; China Repository (personal papers of Admiral Harry E. Yarnell, records of US Naval Group China and Vice Admiral Milton E. Miles)
XI. *Federal Archives, Suitland, Maryland, USA*
  South East Asia Command, War Diary: (Records of Headquarters, US Forces, China Theatre of the Office of the Commanding General) Files of Major-General Albert C. Wedemeyer.

B. PRINTED SOURCES

Primary Sources

(a) Published Documents

British United Aid to China, *A Book of Facts and Figures* (London, 1946).
Chinese Ministry of Information (compiled), *China Hand Book 1937–1943.*
Correspondence between the Government of the United Kingdom of Great Britain and the Central People's Government of China on British Trade in China. Presented by the Secretary of State for Foreign Affairs to Parliament by Command of Her Majesty, August 1952 (London, 1952) (Cmd. 8639).
Department of State Washington, *Foreign Relations of the United States*, United States Relations with China (Washington, 1949). 1941 Vol. IV (Washington, 1956) Conferences at Washington and Casablanca (Washington, 1968). 1942, Vol. I (Washington, 1960). 1942, China (Washington, 1956). Conferences at Washington and Quebec, 1943 (Washington, 1970). 1943, China (Washington, 1957). 1943, Vol. III (Washington, 1963). 1943, Vol. IV (Washington, 1964). Conference at Cairo and Teheran, 1943 (Washington, 1961). Conference at Quebec, 1944 (Washington, 1972). 1944, Vol. III (Washington, 1965). 1944, Vol. V. (Washington, 1965). 1944, Vol VI (Washington, 1967). Conferences at Malta and Yalta, 1945 (Washington, 1955). 1945, Vol. I (Washington, 1967). 1945, Vol. VI (Washington, 1969). 1945, Vol. VII (Washington, 1969). 1946, Vo.l VIII (Washington 1970). 1946, Vol. IX (Washington 1970). 1946, Vol. X (Washington 1970). 1947, Vol. VII (Washington, 1972).
Documents Relating to British Involvement with Indo–China Conflict, 1945–1965. Presented to Parliament by the Secretary of State for Foreign Affairs by Command of Her Majesty, December 1965 (London, 1966) (Cmnd. 2834).
Hansard, 5th Series, *House of Commons Debates,* Vol. 374–455 (London, 1941–47.)
Mountbatten of Burma, The Earl of, *Report to the Combined Chiefs of Staff by the Supreme Allied Commander South-East Asia 1943* (London, His Majesty's Stationery Office, 1951).
United States Relations with China, with Special Reference to the Period 1944–1949, based on the Files of the Department of State (Washington, 1949)

(b) Contemporary Newspapers and Periodicals

Christian Science Monitor
Daily Express
The Daily Telegraph

Daily Worker
Evening Standard
Financial News
The Manchester Guardian
The New York Herald Tribune
The New York Times
News Chronicle
The Observer
The Times
Nanyang Siang Pao
North China Daily News
South China Morning Post
Straits Times

(c) Memoirs, Diaries and Contemporary Publications

Acheson, D., *Present at the Creation* (London, 1948).
Air Command – South East Asia, *Weekly Intelligence Summary* (1944–45) issued by c.i.o. HQ ACSEA
Attlee, C. R., *As It Happened* (London, 1954)
Avon, the Earl of, *The Eden Memoirs: Reckoning* (London, 1965).
Bryant, Arthur, *Triumph in the West, 1943–1946* (London, 1959). (Based on the Diaries of Field Marshall the Viscount Alanbrook.)
Byrnes, J. F., *Speaking Frankly* (London, 1948).
Campbell, T. and Herring G. (eds), *The Diaries of Edward R. Stettinius, 1943–1946* (New York, 1975).
Central Office of Information (London), *Sino–British Relations*, SN5938/72 (November 1972).
Chennault, C. L., *Way of a Fighter* (New York, 1949).
Chiang Kai-shek, *All We Are and All We Have*. Speeches and Messages since Pearl Harbor by Generalissimo Chiang Kai-shek, 9 December 1941 – November 17 1942 (New York, 1942).
—, *China's Destiny* (New York, 1947)
—, *Chinese Economic Theory* (New York, 1947).
Churchill, Winston S., *The Second World War*, vols IV–V (London, 1951–3).
Colonial Annual Reports: Hong Kong, 1946 (London, 1948).
Dorman-Smith, Sir Reginald, 'Burma', United Empire, Journal of the Royal Empire Society, vol. XXXVII, no. 6 (Nov. – Dec. 1946).
Farmer, Victor, 'Post War Opportunities in China', Private Talk at Chatham House, Aug. 1944.
Hull, C., *Memoirs*, vol. II (London, 1948).
Ismay, Lord, *Memoirs* (London, 1960).
Leahy, W. D., *I Was There* (London, 1950).
Mao Tse-tung, *Selected Works* (Peking, 1965).
McCowan, Lord, *A Speech* Anglo–Chinese Chamber, 16 October 1946).
McLean, Sir William, 'Economic Developments in the Colonies', an address at Chatham House, 21 Nov. 1946.
Romanus, C., and Sunderland, R., *Stilwell's Command Problems* (Washington, 1956).

—, *Stilwell's Mission to China* (Washington, DC, 1953).

—, *Time Runs Out in CIB.* (Washington, DC, 1959).

Roosevelt, E., *As He Saw It* (New York, 1946).

Royal Institute of International Affairs, *Post-War Economic Policy in China.* Resolution of the Kuomintang, 4 Nov. 1943.

Slim, William 'Some Aspects of the Campaign in Burma 1944–45', *United Empire,* Journal of the Royal Empire Society, vol. XXXVII, no. 2 (March–April, 1946).

Slim, Viscount, *Defeat into Victory* (London, 1956).

Stimson, H. L., and Bundy, M., *On Active Service in Peace and War* (New York, 1948).

Sunderland, R. and Romanus, C.F. (eds), *Stilwell, Joseph Warren, 1883–1946. Stilwell's Personal File – China, Burma, India, 1942–1944* (Wilminston, Del., 1976).

Terraine, John, *The Life and Times of Lord Mountbatten* (London, 1969)

Truman, H. S., *Year of Decisions, 1945* (London, 1955).

Wedemeyer, A. C., *Wedemeyer Reports* (New York, 1958).

Welles, S. A., *Time for Decision* (London, 1944).

Wiart, C. de, *Happy Odyssey* (London, 1950).

Williams, Francis, *A Prime Minister Remembers: The War and Post-War Memoirs of the Rt Hon. Earl Attlee* (based on his private papers and on a series of recorded conversations) (London, 1961).

Winant, J. G., *A Letter from Grosvenor Square* (London, 1947).

Woodward L., *British Foreign Policy in the Second World War,* single volume and vols. I–V (London, 1962–76).

Secondary Sources

Allen, Louis, *The End of the War in Asia* (London, 1976).

Ball, W. M., *Nationalism and Communism in East Asia* (Melbourne, 1952).

Barnett, A. D., (ed.), *The Communist Strategies in Asia: A Comparative Analysis of Governments and Parties* (London, 1963).

Barnett, C., *The Collapse of British Power* (London, 1972).

Baur, P. T., 'Nationalism and Politics in Malaya', *Foreign Affairs,* vol. 25, no. 3 (April 1974).

Belden, J., *Retreat with Stilwell* (New York, 1975).

Berreman, J. V., 'The Japanization of Far Eastern Occupied Areas', *Pacific Affairs,* vol. XVII, no. 2 (June 1944).

Boardman, R. *Britain and the People's Republic of China 1949–1974* (London, 1976).

Boyle, J. H., *China and Japan at War, 1937–1945* (Stanford, 1972).

Brecher, M., *The New States of Asia – A Political Analysis* (Oxford Univ. Press, 1963).

The British Survey, 'British Foreign Policy 1946–56', N.S. 89, August 1956.

Buchan, A. (ed.), *China and the Peace of Asia* (New York, 1966).

Buhite, R. D., *Patrick Hurley and American Foreign Policy* (New York, 1973).

Bullock, A., *The Life and Times of Ernest Bevin,* vols 1 and 2 (London, 1960, 1967).

Caldwell, O. J., *A Secret War: Americans in China, 1944–1945* (Illinois, 1973).

Callahan, R., *Burma, 1942–1945* (London, 1978).

Carlton, D., *Anthony Eden: A Biography* (London, 1981).

Chan Lan Kit-ching, 'The Hong Kong Question During the Pacific War', *Journal of Imperial and Commonwealth History,* vol. 2, no. 1 (1973).

Chen, Su-ching, *China and Southeast Asia* (China Institute of Pacific Relations, Chungking, 1945).

Chow, S. R., *The Far East in a New World Order* (China Institute of Pacific Relations, Chungking, 1945).

Clutterbuck, R., *Riot and Revolution in Singapore and Malaya 1945–63* (London, 1973).

Collis, M. *Last and First in Burma, 1945–8* (London, 1949).

Cole, G. D. H., *Great Britain in the Post-War World* (London, 1942).

Cross, C., *The Fall of the British Empire 1918–1968* (London, 1970).

Darby, P., British Defence Policy in the Indian Region Between the Indian Independence Act 1947 and the British Defence Review 1966 (D. Phil. thesis, Oxford, 1969).

Davies, J. P., *Dragon by the Tail* (New York, 1972).

Dean, B. 'British Informal Empire: The Case of China', *Journal of Commonwealth and Comparative Politics*, vol. XIV, no. 1, (March 1976).

Donnison, F. S. V., *British Military Administration in the Far East 1943–46* (London, HMSO, 1956).

Donnithorne, A. G., *Economic Developments since 1937 in Eastern and Southeastern Asia and their Effects on the United Kingdom* (London, RIIA, Chatham House, 1950).

Dorn, Frank, *Walkout with Stilwell in Burma* (New York, 1971).

Dubinsky, A. M., *The Far East in the Second World War* (Moscow, 1972).

Duncanson, D. J. 'General Gracey and the Viet Minh', in *Royal Central Asian Journal*, vol. LV, part III (October 1968).

Eatwell, R., *The 1945–1951 Labour Governments* (London, 1979).

Eden, A., 'Britain in World Strategy', *Foreign Affairs*, vol. 19, no. 3 (1951).

Eldridge, F., *Wrath in Burma* (New York, 1946).

Elsbree, W. H., *Japan's Role in Southeast Asian Nationalist Movements 1940–45* (Harvard Univ. Press, 1953).

Endacott, G. B., *Hong Kong Eclipse* (Oxford, 1978).

Esherick, J. W., (ed.), *Lost Chance in China: The World War II Despatches of John S. Service* (New York, 1975).

Fabian Society, *Britain and South East Asia* (London, 1966).

Feis, H., *The China Tangle* (Princeton, 1972).

——, *Churchill, Roosevelt, Stalin. The War They Waged and the Peace They Sought* (New Jersey, 1974).

Fellowes-Gordon, I., *The Battle for Naw Seng's Kingdom* (London, 1971).

Fielding, F., *A Socialist Foreign Policy* (London, 1970).

Fishel, W. R., *The End of Extraterritoriality in China* (Berkeley, 1952).

Fitzsimons, M. A. 'British Labour in Search of a Socialist Foreign Policy', *The Review of Politics*, vol. 12, no. 2 (April 1950).

——, Foreign Policy of the British Labour Government, 1945–1951 (Indiana, 1953).

Fontaine, A., *History of the Cold War. From the October Revolution to the Korean War, 1917–1950* (New York, 1970).

Frankel, J., *British Foreign Policy, 1945–1973* (Oxford, 1975).

Frost, R. A., 'Reflections on British Colonial Policy', *Pacific Affairs*, vol. XVIII, no. 4, (Dec. 1945).

Furnivall, J. S., 'The Future of Burma', *Pacific Affairs*, vol. XVIII, no. 2 (June 1945).

Gibbs, N. H., *Grand Strategy: Rearmament Policy* (London, 1976).

Gilbert, M., *Winston S. Churchill, Vol. V. 1922–1939* (London, 1976).

Gilchrist, Sir Andrew, *Bangkok Top Secret: Force 136 at War* (London, 1970).

Gittings, J., *The World and China, 1922–1972* (London, 1974).

Graebner, N. A., *The Cold War. Ideological Conflict of Power Struggle* (Massachusetts, 1963).

Green, O. M., 'The British in China', *World Review* (July 1952).

Grew, J. G., *Turbulent Era*, vol. 2 (London, 1953).

Gull, E. M.,*British Economic Interests in the Far East* (London, 1943).

—, 'British Trade with China in the Post-War Period' (lecture given to the Royal Central Asian Society on 21 April, 1943).

Gupta, P. S., *Imperialism and the British Labour Movement, 1914–1964* (Cambridge Commonwealth Series, 1975).

Harper, N. D., 'Security in the South West Pacific', *Pacific Affairs,* vol, 24, no. 2 (1951).

Harriman, W. A., and Abel, E., *Special Envoy to Churchill and Stalin 1941–1946* (London, 1976).

Harrington, W. and Young, P., *The 1945 Revolution* (London, 1978).

Henser R., 'Chinese Law of Foreign Trade: An Interview', *The China Quarterly*, no. 73 (March 1978).

Holland, W. L., (ed.), *Asian Nationalism and the West* (New York, 1953).

Horowitz, D., *From Yalta to Vietnam* (Harmondsworth, 1967).

Howard, M., *The Continental Commitment* (London, 1972).

Hsu Long-hsuen and Chang Ming-kai, *History of the Sino–Japanese War, 1937–1945* (Taipei, 1971).

Hubbard, G. E., 'The British Loan to China', *Pacific Affairs*, vol. XVI, no. 3 (September 1944).

Hudson, G. F., 'The Sino–Soviet Alliance Treaty of 1945', in G.F. Hudson (ed.), *St Antony's Papers*, No. II, Far Eastern Affairs, no. 1 (London, 1957).

Iriye, A., *Across the Pacific* (New York, 1967).

—, *The Cold War in Asia* (New Jersey, 1974).

—, *Pacific Estrangement* (Cambridge, Mass., 1972).

Johnson, C. A., *Peasant Nationalism and Communist Power* (Stanford, 1962).

Jones, F. C., Borton, Hugh and B.R. Peam, *The Far East 1942–1946*, Survey of International Affairs (Oxford 1955).

Kennedy, P., *The Rise and Fall of British Naval Mastery* (London, 1976).

King, F. H. H., *A Concise Economic History of Modern China* (Bombay, 1968).

Kirby, S. W., *The War Against Japan*, vols 1–V (London, 1957–69).

Kubek, A., *How the Far East Was Lost,* (London, 1971).

Lamb, H. A., *The China–India Border, the Origins of Disputed Boundaries* (London, 1964).

—, *Asian Frontiers* (London, 1968).

Lawrance, A., *China's Foreign Relations Since 1949* (London, 1975).

Lebra, J. C. (ed.), *Japan's Greater East Asia Co-prosperity Sphere in World War II* (Kuala Lumpur, 1975).

—, *Japanese Trained Armies in Asia* (Hong Kong, 1977).

Lewin, R., *Slim. The Standardbearer* (London, 1976).

Li, Dun J. (ed.), *The Road to Communism: China Since 1912* (New York, 1969).

Liang, Chin-tung, *General Stilwell in China, 1942–1944. The Full Story* (New York, 1972).

Lindsay, M., *The Unknown War: North China, 1937–1945* (London, 1975).

Lippmann, W., *US War Aims* (London, 1944).

Lin, W. Y., *China and Foreign Capital* (China Institute of Pacific Relations, Chunking, 1945).

Lloyd, T. O., *Empire to Welfare State. English History 1906–1967* (Oxford, 1976).

Louis, Wm. R., *Imperialism at Bay* (Oxford, 1977).

Luard, E., *Britain and China* (London, 1962).

Lyon, P., *War and Peace in South East Asia* (London, 1969).

Macmillan, H., *The Blast of War, 1939–1945* (London, 1967).

—, *Tides of Fortune, 1945–1955* (London, 1969).

Mansergh, N., *Survey of British Commonwealth Affairs. Problems of External Policy 1931–1939* (London, 1952).

Medlicott, W. N., *Contemporary England 1914–1964* (London, 1967).

Meehan, E. J., *The British Left Wing and Foreign Policy* (New York, 1960).

Mehden, F. R. Van der, *South-East Asia, 1930–1970. The Legacy of Colonialism and Nationalism* (London, 1974).

Miles M., *A Different Kind of War* (New York, 1967).

Mil, L. A., *Southeast Asia* (London, 1964).

Mook, H. Van, *The Stakes of Democracy in South East Asia* (London, 1950).

Morgenthau, H. Jr, *Diary, China,* vols I and II (Washington, DC, 1965).

Morris, J., *Farewell the Trumpets: An Imperial Retreat* (London, 1978).

Nagai, Y. and Iriye, A. (eds), *The Origins of Cold War in Asia* (Tokyo, 1977).

Northedge, F., *British Foreign Policy: The Process of Readjustment, 1945-1961* (New York, 1962).

—, *Descent From Power: British Foreign Policy, 1945–1973* (London, 1974).

Olver, A. S. B., *Outline of British Policy in East and Southeast Asia, 1945–50* (London, RIIA, Chatham House, 1950).

Parker, R. A. C., 'Economics, Rearmament and Foreign Policy: The United Kingdom Before 1939 – A Preliminary Study', *Journal of Contemporary History*, vol. 10, no. 4 (Oct. 1975).

Payne, R., *The Revolt of Asia* (London, 1948).

Peden, G. C., *British Rearmament and the Treasury 1932–1939* (Edinburgh, 1979).

Pelcovits, N. A., *Old China Hands and the Foreign Office* (New York, 1948).

Perham, M., *Colonial Sequence, 1930–1949* (London, 1967).

Perkins, D. W. (ed.), *China's Modern Economy in Historical Perspective* (California, 1975).

Peterson, A., 'Britain and Siam: The Latest Phase', *Pacific Affairs*, vol. XIX, no. 4 (December 1946).

Pettman, R., *China in Burma's Foreign Policy* (Canberra, 1973).

Platt, D. C. M., *Finance, Trade and Policy in British Foreign Policy, 1815–1914* (Oxford, 1968).

—, (ed.), *Business Imperialism, 1840–1930* (Oxford, 1977).

Pluvier, J. M., *A Handbook and Chart of South-East Asian History* (Oxford, 1967).

—, *South East Asia from Colonialism to Independence* (Oxford, 1974).

Porter, B. E., *Britain and the Rise of Communist China* (London, 1967).

Progress Publishers (ed.), (translated by David Fildon), *South East Asia: History, Economy, Policy* (Moscow, 1972).

Purcell, V., *The Chinese in Southeast Asia* (London, 1965).

Quintin, H., 'British Policy: A Conservative Forecast', *Foreign Affairs*, vol. 22, no. 1,

(October 1943).

Rhodes, R. I. (ed.), *Imperialism and Underdevelopment. A Reader* (London, 1970).

Robbins, K., 'This Grubby Wreck of Old Glories –the United Kingdom and the End of British Empire', *Journal of Contemporary History*, vol. 15, no. 1 (January 1980).

Rose, S., *Britain and South-East Asia* (London, 1962).

Roth, A., *Dilemma in Japan* (London, 1946).

Saburo, I., *The Pacific War: World War II and the Japanese 1931–1945* (New York, 1978).

Sansom, Sir George, 'The Story of Singapore', *Foreign Affairs*, vol. 22, no. 2 (January 1944).

Schaller, M., *The US Crusade in China, 1938–1945* (New York, 1979).

Scott, Sir Robert, *Major Theatre of Conflict: British Policy in East Asia* (London, 1968).

Service, J. S., *The Amerasia Papers* (California, 1971).

Seton-Watson, H., 'Aftermaths of Empire', *Journal of Contemporary History*, vol. 15, no. 1 (January 1980).

Sewell, H. S., 'The Campaign in Burma', *Foreign Affairs*, vol. 23, no. 3, (April 1945).

Shai, A., *Origins of the War in the East* (London, 1976).

—. 'Britain, China and the End of Empire', *Journal of Contemporary History*, vol. 15, no. 2, (April 1980).

Shay, P. R., *British Rearmament in the 1930s* (Princeton, 1978).

Shlaim, A., Jones, P. and Sainsbury, K., *British Foreign Secretaries Since 1945* (London, 1977).

Shlaim, A., *Britain and the Origins of European Unity 1940–1951* (University of Reading, 1978).

Simandjuntak, B., *Malayan Federalism, 1945–1963* (London, 1969).

Singhal, D. P., 'Nationalism and Communism in South-East Asia', *Journal of South-east Asian History*, vol. 3, no. 1 (March 1962).

Smith, Roger, M. (ed.), *Southeast Asia: Documents of Political Development and Change* (Cornell University Press, 1974).

Smith, Tony (ed.), *The End of the European Empire. Decolonization After World War II* (Massachusetts, 1975).

Snow, E., *Journey to the Beginning* (London, 1959).

—, *Red Star Over China* (London, 1968).

Steeds, D., 'Reappraising the American Role in Asia', *Royal Institute of International Affairs,* April, 1977.

Stettinius, E. R., *Roosevelt and the Russians* (London, 1950).

Storry, R. G., *A History of Modern Japan* (London, 1962).

—, *Japan and the Decline of the West in Asia, 1894–1943* (London, 1979).

Stratton, R., *The Army–Navy Game* (Massachusetts, 1977).

Suyin, Han, *Birdless Summer. China Autobiography History* (Manchester, 1976).

Swinson, A., *Mountbatten* (London, 1973).

Tang, Tsou, *America's Failure in China, 1941–1950* (Chicago, 1962).

Taylor, A. J. P., *English History, 1914–1945* (Oxford, Pelican Books, 1970).

Thorne, C., *Allies of a Kind. The United States, Britain and the War Against Japan 1941–1945* (London, 1978).

Tong, Hollington, K., *Chiang Kai-shek* (Taipei, 1953).

Toye, H., *Subhash Chandra Bose (The Spring Tiger)* (Bombay, 1974).

Trager, F. N., *Burma: From Kingdom to Independence* (London, 1966).

Tuchman, B., *Stilwell and the American Experience in China, 1911–45* (New York, 1970).

Watt, D. C., 'American Anti-Colonial Policies and the End of European Colonial Empires', in N.A. Den Hollander (ed.), *Contagious Conflict* (Leiden, 1973).

Wesseling, H. E. (ed.), *Expansion and Reaction* (Leiden, 1978).

White, T. H. (ed.), *The Stillwell Papers* (New York, 1972).

—, and Jacoby, A., *Thunder Out of China* (New York, 1975).

Williams, J. E., 'Britains Role in Southeast Asia, 1945–54' (unpublished thesis, University College of Swansea, 1973).

Wint, G., *The British in Asia* (New York, 1954).

Woodhouse, C. M., *British Foreign Policy Since the Second World War* (London, 1961).

Vital, D., *The Making of British Foreign Policy* (London, 1968).

Young, A., *China and the Helping Hand, 1937–1945* (Cambridge, Mass., 1967).

Young P., *Atlas of the Second World War* (New York, 1977).

Younger, K., 'The Dyason Lectures for 1955 on British Foreign Policy, *Australian Outlook* (December 1955).

Zilliacus, K., *Can the Tories Win the Peace? And How They Lost the Last One* (London, 1945).

Index